A HISTORY OF FARM BUILDINGS
IN ENGLAND AND WALES

By the same author
The Farming Kingdom
Farm Work Study

In the Young Farmers Clubs series of booklets
The Story of Farm Buildings
Ditches, Dykes and Deep-Drainage

As 'Hugh Willoughby'
Amid the Alien Corn
(Published in the USA)

A HISTORY OF
FARM BUILDINGS
IN ENGLAND AND WALES

Nigel Harvey

MA, ARICS

DAVID & CHARLES : NEWTON ABBOT

ISBN 0 7153 4957 0

Set in eleven point Baskerville, two points leaded
and printed in Great Britain
by Latimer Trend & Co Ltd Plymouth
for David & Charles (Publishers) Limited
South Devon House   Newton Abbot   Devon

*Dedicated with affection and respect
to the memory of
J. K. W. SLATER
Head of the Farm Buildings Unit
of the Agricultural Research Council
1957–65*

CONTENTS

lems—machinery comes to the farmstead—the end
of an old tradition—the last age of local materials

ILLUSTRATIONS

FIGURES IN TEXT

FOREWORD

by A. N. DUCKHAM, CBE, MA, F I Biol
Emeritus Professor of Agriculture, University of Reading

Farm buildings account for about 60 per cent of the total of over £600 million of long-term capital invested in British agriculture in the last decade. Such buildings provide shelter for our livestock and protection for farmers and workers, for farm machinery, and for stores of grain, feedingstuffs, hay and silage. But while their main function may still be protective, the introduction of grain-drying and handling machinery, of parlour milking, and of feed-conveying systems and the like are giving increasing scope for factory-style production-line methods. The evolution of farm buildings from simple protection against weather, wild animals and thieves to the processing units which are emerging today is the subject of Mr Harvey's book. He traces the development of farm buildings through some 1,500 years. In doing so, he shows us the effects on the farmstead, the cowshed, the piggery and the old barn, both of changing husbandry techniques and of the increasing 'industrialisation' and mechanisation of agriculture.

But interest in farm buildings is not confined to the farmer, the farm worker and the rural landowner. Those concerned with rural amenities, town and country planning, and animal welfare also have points of view which may conflict with the needs of those who live on or by the land.

Mr Harvey's book should prove helpful to both farming and non-farming interests. It is an important and very readable contribution to a rapidly growing, and visible, sector of agricultural investment. History helps us to comprehend the past, understand the present and map the future. This book admirably performs this function. It should be useful not only to farmers, landlords and historians but also to those concerned with rural amenities and with the interactions between food production and the rest of the community.

INTRODUCTION

Farm buildings are among the most conspicuous objects in the agricultural landscape. They are also among the most important and the most interesting. They are important because they are the central storage depots and processing shops of the farms they serve and on their efficiency depends much of the efficiency of the farming system. They are interesting because they record with peculiar clarity many of the technical and economic changes which have come to the farming industry in recent centuries. And it is by understanding the reasons for their present importance that we can best appreciate their value as guides to the farming past.

For it is in the buildings of the farmstead that livestock are housed and fed, dairy cows are milked and manure accumulates for periodical removal. It is here that litter and bulky fodders are stored, concentrate fodder milled and mixed, and seeds and fertilisers, tractors and implements housed. Into the farmstead come animals, machines, crops, fodders and litter from the fields and varied materials from the economic world beyond the farm gate. Out of it go manure and machinery to the fields, milk, crops and livestock to market. The farmstead is the operational centre of the farm, where the farmer spends as much time as in his fields; the demands of the farm on it are considerable, continuous and varied; and each individual building in it was designed to meet a particular selection of these demands.

It is, therefore, convenient to think of farm buildings as tools, each with its own particular jobs to do. But it is more accurate to think of them as means of enabling jobs to be done, for it is the processes they house which determine their form. Only in

terms of the needs they serve are they comprehensible, for they
are planned for and around highly specific jobs and routines
and few considerations other than agricultural efficiency are
allowed to influence their design. These needs may be poorly
interpreted or poorly fulfilled, but the degree of success in
meeting them is the sole criterion by which the farmer judges
his buildings. There cannot be many branches of architecture
in which form follows function as closely and as uncompromis-
ingly as in the design of farm buildings.

In principle, therefore, the farmstead is a group of highly
specific and inter-related industrial buildings designed to meet
a wide and exacting range of industrial demands, and there are
few aspects of the farming system which do not directly or indirectly affect it. Hence, ideally, it should be possible to deduce
from the buildings on a farm the needs they serve, and from
those needs to form a detailed picture of the types of enterprise,
the methods used and the scale of operations of the holding.

In general terms, this is true. A walk around a farmstead
will give the informed observer a fair idea of the size and type of
the farm on which it stands. But in practice, of course, an exact
equilibrium of ends and means is seldom achieved and could
never be maintained. For every farmstead is the product of
history as well as technology, and agricultural needs change
more rapidly than buildings. General remodelling is expensive
and the farmer has normally contented himself with piecemeal
adaptations and improvements which preserve much of the old
pattern of the farmstead and many of the buildings which com-
pose it. In particular, the depression which began in the latter
part of the nineteenth century and lasted until the Second World
War ended the orderly process of farmstead development and
left a lifetime's arrears of modernisation which the present age
is still redeeming. Most farmers have inherited more buildings
than they have erected and, though medieval and Tudor
buildings may be individual rarities, Hanoverian and Victorian work still provides the bulk of the farmer's building stock.

The economic disadvantages of this are obvious. But the
farmer's embarrassment is the historian's opportunity, for in

varying degrees these old buildings preserve the imprint of the farming technologies and systems for which they were originally designed, even as their construction illustrates the state of building development at the time. Further, the manner in which they have been adapted to new purposes and the materials with which they have been maintained and repaired reflect many of the changes that have come to agriculture and the trades that serve it since they were first built. They are, in fact, 'structural documents' and few other industries can show such a continuous and comprehensive series with which to illustrate their past.

Nor are these documents very difficult to read. If you lean on a gate and look across the fields, you will sometimes glimpse behind the combine or the grazing cows the ghosts of the men who created the farming landscape—the farmers of the horse age, the Victorian deep-drainage gangs, the enclosure commissioners with their attendant hedgers and ditchers, the ploughmen following their horned teams up the long acres of the Open Fields, and behind them all the shadowy outlines of the tall trees and the tangled undergrowth and the little groups of men in shapeless suits of hodden-grey who went out with axe and fire and mattock, generation after generation, to win farmland from the primeval wilderness. In so doing, however, you will be relying mainly on your memory of the written word and your constructive imagination, for the land itself will give you little more than hints and suggestions. But if you look at the farmstead with the same eyes, you will not need to summon ghosts from the printed page. You will find the buildings telling their own story, freely and in considerable detail.

Thus the design of the barn reminds us that it was once the workshop of the flailers, who threshed the corn on which England depended for her daily bread. The derelict chimney in the north range recalls the coming of steam power to the farm, the yards the need for housing the increased head of stock which fed on the new crops of the Agricultural Revolution, the cowhouse the new lines of production made possible by the railways and necessary by the overseas competition which overwhelmed so much of the traditional system. The different materials and systems of construction used in the buildings of different ages tell us much about the development of building methods and the growing contribution of outside industries to farming technology, while the conversion of old buildings to new purposes illustrates the ways in which the farmer has striven to adapt his system and equipment to changing needs. And all around you soils and slopes, streams and springs, suggest the reasons why the forgotten founder of the farm, perhaps a Saxon or medieval pioneer, or perhaps a Hanoverian land-owner planning his new enclosed holding, chose this particular spot to build a homestead for himself and his descendants.

These structural evidences can be seen on nearly every farm. But they are growing fewer. Each year, old farm buildings collapse or are demolished and replaced by new ones and, in most cases, the information and understanding they could offer perishes with them; and the rate of destruction is increasing. Agriculturally, of course, such changes are inevitable and desirable, for the farmer can no more work efficiently with obsolete buildings than the manufacturer can work efficiently with obsolete factories. But all this should encourage, not discourage, us. For, surely, the greater the speed of change, the greater the incentive to learn and record as much as we can of the economic epic of the farmer's trade from these varied and fascinating survivals while they are still with us.

The scope for such work is as obvious and considerable as its need. For the buildings of the farm have received curiously little attention from scholars and no general history of their development based on original research has so far appeared. This book, however, does not seek to fill this gap. It merely seeks to summarise the information at present available on library shelves and thus limits itself to collecting and collating part of the evidence with which the gap will eventually be filled. But the author hopes that it tells its story in a way which increases the reader's understanding of our agricultural past and, in particular, enables him to learn more of it for himself from the steadings he sees when he walks or drives in the countryside.

Chapter One

THE PERIOD OF ORIGINS:

TO AD 800

IN THE BEGINNING

Men have farmed the soil of Britain for many, many centuries and from the very beginning have left enduring traces of the pits they dug and the buildings they erected to serve their farming needs. There is, indeed, a growing mass of archaeological evidence on the homesteads of the early peoples from Neolithic to Roman times. But over much of the country the continuous history of farming, and therefore of farm buildings, starts with the Saxons who began their occupation of the lowlands of England in the fifth and sixth centuries AD.

In the five hundred years of their dominance, these newcomers established over most of the south, the east and the midlands a pattern of settlement that endured to Hanoverian times. To a large extent, therefore, the history of farm buildings in England is the history of the development of the farmsteads founded by these early settlers and by their descendants who inherited their system.

But not entirely. In the uplands of the north and west as well as in Wales different systems of farming continued, producing different types of farmstead in a different type of agricultural landscape. This general distinction typifies the multitude of more particular, more local differences in the siting, design and construction of farmsteads, which reflect the responses of farming man to the challenges and opportunities of his place and time. It is these which form one of the themes of our story.

We know very little about the farmsteads of these dark centuries and not one farm building of the period has survived above ground. But by the collation of various evidences, by deduction and conjecture, it is possible to form a general impression of the manner in which our ancestors planned and built their farmsteads in the first age of modern history.

SAXON SETTLEMENT IN THE LOWLANDS

The full story of the Saxon settlement is lost beyond recovery. But it is clear that in physical inheritance, as in language and tradition, the Saxons owed little to their predecessors. It is also clear that they sought the better land, preferring it to the poorer soils where the earlier peoples had tended to congregate, and were prepared to pay for it with the prolonged and piecemeal labour required to clear the hardwood forests that covered so much of the British Isles at that time.[1] It is clear, too, that their primary need was a reliable supply of fresh water, their secondary need shelter from the elements. So they chose sites near springs or streams, taking advantage of whatever protection local topography offered, and there they built their hamlets and reclaimed their fields.[2]

Their general pattern of settlement, traces of which are still preserved in many of our villages—sometimes even in towns where builders have continued the old street plan—was determined largely by the demands of their farming system. For the Saxons were corn growers, whose lives depended on their crops of wheat and oats, barley and rye. The fields for such crops could be reclaimed from the waste by individual effort. The crops themselves could be sown, harvested and threshed by individual men. But the preparation of the seedbed entailed ploughing, which depended on animal power, and no individual settler could muster so considerable a unit as a plough team. Only by combination could the newcomers raise the resources to secure their food supply. So they established themselves in their forest clearings not as individual families but as small communities housed in little groups of steadings huddled together for mutual comfort and support round a central green where stock could graze in safety.

The nature of their main crops dictated a winter sowing, for cereals are slow-growing plants which require planting between October and April if they are to reach maturity before the coming of the next winter. In the autumn, therefore, the communal plough team worked till rain or frost made it impossible to continue, the land ploughed in each day's work being allotted in rotation to each man so that he could cultivate it and sow his corn. In the spring, the work continued in the same way, establishing another area of ploughland divided into similar strips. In theory, these two arable fields were sufficient to secure a continuous if limited rotation of crops. In practice, under such conditions weeds multiply and land tends to lose fertility. So a third field was ploughed and allotted in the same way as the others but not sown, so that the fallow soil could recuperate from two successive crops and the farmers could control, partly by grazing, partly by cultivation, the weeds that grew on it.

Such, in crude, diagrammatic form, were the origins of the Open Field system which, with a variety of local differences in the number of fields and the types of crop they carried, fed most of the people of England for many centuries.[3] For over a thousand years, its strange, bleak landscape was the economic home of the normal Englishman. Today, it survives in only one parish in all England, Laxton in Nottinghamshire, a fragment of an older countryside to which scholars make pilgrimage. But some knowledge of it is essential to any understanding of farmstead history.

In particular, the needs of the Open Field corn crops called into existence the primary building of the farmstead. For the harvested corn required protection from the elements if it was to be safe, and threshing before it could yield the grain on which the farmer's life depended. Hence arose the primitive barn, a shelter in which the precious harvest could be stored and gradually and laboriously threshed by flail on a hard floor in the winter days when little other farm work was possible. But man, of course, does not live by bread alone and the Saxon farmer depended on his livestock for meat and manure, milk, leather and wool as well as power. The strictness and detail with which grazing rights on the village green and other common land were defined from the earliest times for which records are available bears striking witness to the importance of livestock in the Saxon economy.

At this stage, however, the demands of his animals on the farmstead were small. The horse had not yet become a farm animal. Sheep required, at most, a yard where they could be better protected against wolves and thieves and where, incidentally, their manure could beneficially be accumulated. Pigs could support themselves for much of the year on the beechmast, acorns, grubs and carrion which the woodlands around the village provided. Indeed, they were still pastoral rather than agricultural animals, and the horse which the swineherd needed to collect his half-wild flock recalled a time in human history before the coming of the plough. This left only cattle, which grazed in the open in the summer months but required some sort of shelter in the winter. Yet the number of cattle requiring such shelter was small, for the size of the herds that any community could support was rigidly and inescapably limited by the amount of winter fodder available.

For at that time and for centuries to come the farmer knew only one way of conserving the surplus of summer-grown forage to feed his ruminants in the winter months when nothing grew. He made grass into hay; and the supply of hay made by men working by hand in an exceptionally unreliable climate was limited. Yet the amount of hay available controlled the number of cattle which could be kept through the winter. Every autumn, therefore, when the pastures failed, the farmer measured his store of hay and slew and salted down for his larder all those cattle he could not afford to keep until the spring. The number of cattle which survived the winter determined the amount of power and manure available for the ploughlands, and this in turn controlled the future supply of corn on which the life of the community depended. Here, then, was one of the limiting factors to food production which endured till the days of the Agricultural Revolution. The individual thoughts of the Saxon farmers have perished, but it is significant that the emblem of their patron saint, the forgotten Walstan of Bawburgh, was not a plough but a hayrake.

We do not know the form in which the Saxon farmer met his simple needs of protection for his corn crop, a threshing floor and shelter for a limited number of cattle. The protection for his corn crop may have been no more than thatch on a stack, and the threshing floor and cattle shelter a part of the farmer's home. It has been suggested, for instance, that archaeologists searching for the yet unknown dwellings of the more substantial Saxon peasantry should expect to find traces of the dual-purpose buildings now called longhouses, rectangular structures in which the farmer and his family lived at one end, the in-wintered livestock at the other.[4]

This combination of cover for corn crop and threshing floor, which developed into the barn, and shelter for cattle, which developed into the yard, illustrates the basic characteristics as well as the basic structural needs of the mixed-farming system which is so fundamental a theme in our agricultural history. One served the farmer as corngrower, the other served him as stockman. Yet both were interdependent. The processes of the barn provided the yard with straw for litter as well as fodder for the cattle it housed; the processes of the yard provided the fields with manure and so contributed to the contents of the barn.

Here was the beginning of a tradition which lasted almost down to our time. In the centuries to come, we shall see many changes in the buildings of the farm. But from the days of the Heptarchy to the days of Queen Victoria, the alliance of barn and cattleyard dominated the lowland farmstead even as the alliance of corn and horn which created and maintained it continued to dominate the farming system. The barn is now obsolete, but to this day the yard of concrete and asbestos-cement sheeting depends on the barn's successors for its straw and so takes its place in a technical line of descent which stretches back unbroken to the primitive cattle shelters of the early Saxons.

The pioneering Saxons, however, occupied only the lowlands. In the more mountainous and wetter areas of the north and west, the Celtic peoples continued an older and more pastoral system of farming based not on compact villages but on dispersed farmsteads standing sometimes in isolation, sometimes in small groups. Here the climate was harsher, the winters longer, and livestock needed more protection for more months than in the milder lowlands. In such areas, the longhouse already had a history measured in millenia—its ancestry goes back to the Neolithic Age[5]—and the protection it gave and the warmth it conserved secured its continuance by local farmers and its adoption by at least some of the newcomers to the uplands right down to the time of our grandfathers. This type of building was known in the lowlands in early times but failed to survive there and few modern visitors to the countryside are even aware of its existence. Nevertheless, it has served more generations of farmers in this country than any other type of steading and only in our own century has it ceased to provide shelter for the farmer and his stock.

Certain upland farms may also still preserve another structural tradition from times far beyond the written record. For the design and stonework construction of some thirty circular, conical 'pigsties' which survive in Wales[6] and occasional potato cellars in the Yorkshire Dales[7] suggest a connection with the ancient beehive huts of Wales, Scotland and Ireland. (See illustration, p 33.) None of these curious structures can be dated and nothing is known about their history. But it is not impossible that the farmer continued to use this simple and traditional method of construction for housing his stock and crops long after he and his family had sought more comfortable accommodation.

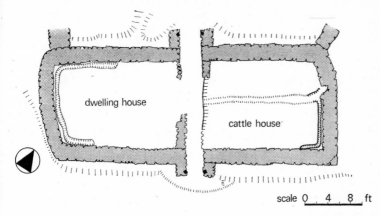

1   Plan of the simplest form of longhouse. This example, which dates from the thirteenth century, was excavated in Devonshire. (Based on *Mediaeval Archaeology*, vol 6–7, 1962–3, p 343)

TRANSHUMANCE

Open Field farmsteads and longhouses alike assumed settled cultivation. But in suitable areas farmers from the earliest times practised transhumance, the seasonal grazing of cattle away from the main homestead on pastures served by a secondary homestead or improvised shelter. In upland areas, the migration of man and cattle to summer grazings higher up the mountainside from which it was impossible to carry hay home was an obvious means of improving the supply of fodder. But place-names show that the system was also known in the lowlands from the beginnings of the Saxon settlement. Somerset, for example, derives its name from the summer dwellers who occupied islands in the marshes during the good grazing months and retired to their villages on high ground when winter came.[8] The pastoral migrations of this early period have left few traces, but it is probable that many of these temporary settlements later became the sites of permanent farmsteads.

BUILDING MATERIALS

Clearly, we know very little about these early farmbuildings.
But one thing is certain. The farmers of the Dark Ages, like their
successors for so many centuries, built their farmsteads from
such material as local nature saw fit to provide. Their homesteads, like their tools and their human or animal power, their
clothes and their food, were the products of a self-sufficient
community which required only salt and iron from outside
sources. Thus from the start farm buildings illustrate the
characteristics of the rural economy of which they form part.

NOTES

1. 'The incoming Saxons had a good eye for country. They always
found the best soils. . . . If we are told there were fifteen farms on a
particular manor in 1066 and there are twenty-five farms there
today, we can usually discover most of the original farms by asking
local farmers which are the best farms in the parish. We may then be
sure that we have discovered most, if not all, of those of Saxon
foundation or older.' (Hoskins, W. G. 'Farmhouses and history',
History Today, vol 10, no 5, May 1960, p 336.) Elsewhere the same
author notes that the first Saxon villages in Leicestershire were
built on the islands of sand and gravel which were drier and warmer
than the surrounding clays. (*The Midland Peasant*, 1957, p 3.)

2. 'We can often discover on going to farms recorded in Dooms-
day Book that there is, usually in the back court, a never-failing
spring of fresh water.' (Hoskins, W. G. 'Farmhouses and history',
History Today, vol 10, no 5, May 1960, p 336.) For detailed local
studies of the effects of water supplies and topography on Saxon
settlement see Grigson G. *An English Farmhouse*, 1948, pp 14–15 and
Havinden, M.A. *Estate villages*, 1966, pp 23, 25. The natural desire
for shelter may be illustrated by the abandonment of an early Saxon
settlement on the bare chalk downs at Puddlehill in Bedfordshire,
apparently in favour of a more protected site at Houghton half a
mile distant. (Personal communication from Mr C. L. Matthews,
site director of the Manshead Archaeological Society of Dunstable.)

3. This is the traditional view of the origins of the system in this

country. Recently, however, it has been suggested that the system
was a gradual development. See Orwin, C. S. *The Open Fields*, ed
Thirsk, J., 1967, pp xiii-xv.

4. C. A. R. Radford suggests lengths of 40 to 60ft and widths of
12 to 15ft for these hypothetical homesteads. ('The Saxon House',
Mediaeval Archaeology, vol 1, 1957, p 36.) For a review of available
information on the rural buildings of the Saxon period see Wilson,
D. M. 'Anglo-Saxon rural economy', *The Agricultural History Review*,
vol 10, pt 2, 1962, pp 71-5

5. Trow-Smith, R. *Life from the Land*, 1967, p 43

6. Peate, I. C. *The Welsh house*, 1944, pp 42-5. One example of
this type of building has been found in Somerset. (Naish, R. B. 'A
traditional Welsh pigsty in Berrow village', *Proceedings of the Somer-
setshire Archaeological and Natural History Society*, vol 107, 1962/3, pp
108-9.)

7. Walton J. *Homesteads of the Yorkshire Dales*, 1947, p 29

8. Quayle, T. 'Our first dairy farmers', *The Milk Producer*, vol 4,
no 2, February 1957, p 7; Hoskins, W. G. *The westward expansion of
Wessex*, 1960, p 6

Chapter Two

THE LONG, SLOW CENTURIES:

AD 800-1500

AGRICULTURAL EXPANSION

After the Saxons came the Normans, after the Normans, the Angevins and the Plantagenets, the Lancastrians and the Yorkists, until the better part of a thousand years separated the farmer from his forgotten ancestors who had served or conquered the Roman Empire. Throughout this long period, the needs of a growing population compelled a steady increase in the area of farmland and the number of farms. Sometimes this agricultural expansion was achieved by communal action, by the foundation of settlements by king, abbot or baron, or by a group of migrant peasants. Sometimes it was the result of the efforts of individual pioneers who added new strips from the surrounding scrubland to their Open Field holdings, or hewed their pattern of hamlets and single farms from the wilderness. Patiently and doggedly, generation by generation, the reclamation continued until by the end of the Middle Ages the greater part of the country was effectively settled. The triumph of the farmer over his wild environment was symbolised by the destruction of one of his ancient enemies. According to tradition, the last wolf in England was killed in the last years of this period. The plough was conquering the primeval waste.

This general colonisation included a slow but constant advance by the Saxons and their Anglo-Norman successors into the Celtic lands of the west and the creation of new, mixed patterns of settlement.[1] But this did not overthrow the ancient distinction between the agricultural economies of hill and plain.

Throughout this period, the Open Field system, with its little groups of farmsteads in the midst of huge arable fields, reigned in the lowlands, the pastoral system with its dispersed homesteads in the uplands.

Neither was there any drastic technical development. Villages, hamlets and scattered farms were larger and more numerous, but those who inhabited them won and worked their land in much the same way as had their ancestors. In particular, they could neither avoid nor overcome the shortage of winter fodder which continued to set such rigid limits to the number of cattle the farm could carry and therefore to the production of food. They fed more people by cultivating more land, but systems and methods of farming changed little.

Thus, Benedict, son of Edric Siward, who established his farm at Cholwich Town on the south-west slopes of Dartmoor in the early thirteenth century settled as an individual, not as a member of a migratory band. But otherwise he behaved much as his forefathers had done in the days of the Saxon Conquest. He chose a site where there was a reliable supply of water—the spring still flows in the farmyard—and shelter in the lee of a ridge from the bitter winds which swept down from the heights above him. He then reclaimed his fields from the surrounding wilderness, using the stones he cleared from them to build his farmstead and the banks of the lane which still leads to it, and farmed his new land with implements and stock little different from those used in the days of the Heptarchy.[2]

PEASANT AND MAGNATE

Nevertheless, Benedict was many generations away from primitive tribalism, and it is significant that he chose to establish his farming home in these unprepossessing uplands, since by his time the growing population had occupied most of the better and more easily-won land. Transhumance continued but the increase of settled cultivation now confined it to areas even lonelier than Dartmoor. It is also significant that we know Benedict's name, which is preserved in the charter that granted him the land. For he lived in the literate, stable, hierarchic community of medieval Christendom, of the feudal system, which over the centuries had made possible concentrations of power and wealth and therefore forms of agricultural exploitation unknown in earlier ages. The temporal and spiritual lords of the land, with their huge estates and their minor bureaucracies of seneschals, clerks and accountants to administer them, now lived in a different economic world from that of the peasantry; and this difference dominated the sources of farmstead history. The medieval magnates left a mass of estate documents which include a certain amount of varied information on the steadings with which they equipped their land. The medieval peasantry left few references to their buildings on the written record.

THE BUILDINGS OF THE PEASANTRY

In recent years, however, archaeological research has begun to recover something of their story. In particular, it seems clear that the longhouse, the common form of housing in the uplands, was also known in the lowlands—it was, for instance, a recognised form of peasant housing in Worcestershire in the late Middle Ages[3]—but in other lowland farmsteads of this period the house and the service buildings stood separate in modern fashion, though the difference between the two types of steading was reduced by the need of the longhouse farmers for outbuildings. They sheltered their cattle under the same roof as their families, but sometimes at least they housed some other livestock in other buildings and threshed and stored their corn in barns. In the wetter areas the corn was sometimes dried on kilns which have been found in excavations of longhouse steadings in Devon and Cornwall.[4] On some farms the longhouse may have been the only building, whereas on others it may have been only the main building of the farmstead.

In the lowlands, it is possible that these dual-purpose homes served the poorer peasantry while their more substantial bretheren lived more comfortably in farmhouses standing apart

_ge 33_   (_right_) A 'Welsh pigsty';
low) Laxton in Nottinghamshire,
e last Open Field village in
gland. As in Saxon times, all the
msteads stand in the village. Part
the West Field can be seen in the
ckground

Page 34 (above) A medieval livestock building forming part of an upland homestead o
Dartmoor. The photograph shows the stall and pen at the north end of the building (se
p 38 and Fig 4); (below) medieval longhouse in Cornwall, probably thirteenth century
The section of the building nearest the camera is the cowhouse. The flat vertical stone
near the walls formed mangers. Holes were bored in them to allow for tethering (se
Fig 2)

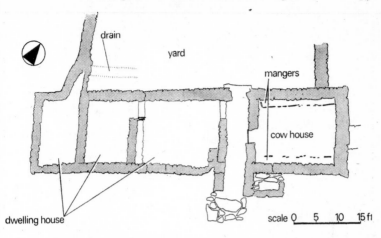

2   Plan of longhouse shown on page 34. (Based on *Cornish Archaeology*, vol 5, 1966, p 44)

from the service buildings. It is also inherently probable that the use of the longhouse decreased as the standard of living improved and an interesting excavation in Wiltshire has traced the development of a twelfth-century longhouse steading into a thirteenth-century steading consisting of one longhouse converted into a farmhouse, another converted into a cattlehouse, and a new barn[5]. (See Fig 3.) But such generalisations are no more than hypotheses based on the findings of a few dozen digs and scanty documentary references. The evidence, particularly the archaeological evidence, on the buildings which served the mass of the population for so many centuries grows year by year. But it will be some time before we have even an outline history of the development of peasant farmsteads in this period.[6]

THE MANORIAL FARMSTEAD

Most surviving evidences concern the buildings of the magnates and are sufficient to show the kinds of problem faced by the substantial farmers of the time and the manner in which they met them.

The main crop was corn. Consequently on large farms the

c

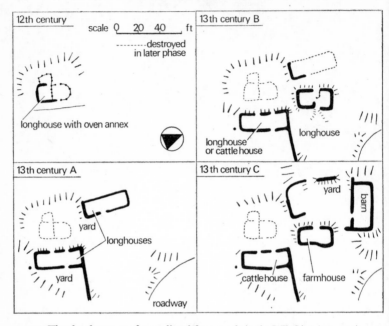

3 The development of a medieval farmstead site in Wiltshire (see p 35).
(Based on *Mediaeval Archaeology*, vol 10, 1966, p 215)

main building was the barn—preferably two barns, one for the wheat which was sold off the farm, one for the spring corn which was fed on it. The standardised pattern of this type of building was determined by the storage and processing needs of the grain harvest. Its two ends housed sheaves or straw, while the central area, where the waggons entered, provided the hard floor on which in the winter months the corn was threshed by flail and winnowed by being tossed with a wooden shovel into the draught of air created by opening the two doors on opposite sides of the threshing floor. The first detailed reference to such a barn comes from the records of an ecclesiastical estate in Essex in the twelfth century and describes a building 49ft 6in long, 35ft 6in wide and 24ft 6in to the ridge with lean-to's at both ends.[7] Barns of such a size must have been the largest secular buildings in the villages they served and they and their successors continued to dominate the landscape almost down to our own age.

It is probable that the various livestock houses and yards stood in the shelter of the barn. Cattle were the most important type of stock here, though by the later Middle Ages the horse had begun his career as an agricultural animal. Presumably fattening and rearing beasts were housed in sheds or yards, but draught animals and dairy cows required some form of tie-up stable for ease of yoking or milking. Pigs were still largely woodland animals and a thirteenth-century treatise warned landowners against keeping pigs on manors where there was no marsh or woodland.[8] Nevertheless, they were beginning to spend more time in the farmyard, for the ancient woodlands, which the Domesday Book commissioners had assessed in terms of the pigs they could support, were now shrinking. In Saxon times, it was common for pigs to graze in the forest for the last four months of the year. By the fourteenth century, a period of six to eight weeks was more usual.[9]

None of the livestock buildings of this period now survives and the only documentary information on them comes from occasional references in manorial records. In the twelfth century, for instance, there is mention of an oxhouse 33ft long and 12ft wide on the estate of the canons of St Paul's Cathedral at Kensworth in Hertfordshire, and in the fourteenth century of a cattleshed on the Templars' farm at Rothley in Leicestershire, which held twenty-four oxen, eleven cows, nine bullocks, four calves and a bull.[10]

Excavation has also provided a case-study of a more pastoral type of steading which was built on Dartmoor by the monks of Buckfastleigh Abbey in the middle of the thirteenth century and apparently abandoned after the Black Death a hundred years later. Sited in a sheltered spot near a spring, this consisted of a two-roomed house joined by a walled yard to a general-purpose livestock building. The walls were of granite boulders taken from the remains of a nearby Bronze Age settlement—the first recorded example of the use of second-hand materials in farm buildings—the roofs were of thatch on timber frames, and the

doors were secured against the moorland winter by iron fasten-
ings, traces of which were found by the archaeologists. A lay
brother probably slept in the house, the herdsman either in the
house or, at calving or lambing time, in the stockbuilding which
contained a hearth. Together they looked after the monastery's
livestock grazing on the bleak uplands and brought them into
shelter when hard weather threatened. (See illustration on
page 34 and Fig 4.)[11]

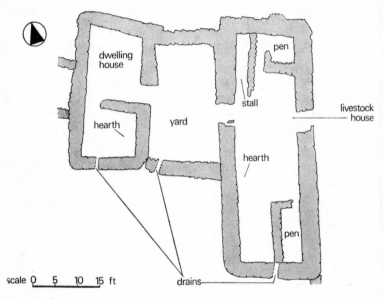

4　Plan of upland steading shown on page 34. (Based on *Mediaeval Archaeology*,
vol 2, 1958, p 146)

A less predictable type of housing served the flocks on which
the farmer of the Middle Ages depended for much of his dairy
produce, as well as for wool and mutton. For in this period the
sheep was the primary dairy animal, since most medieval cows
probably gave little more milk than their calves required.[12] So
on large enterprises the shearing sheds with boarded floors for
storage of fleeces were matched by dairies equipped with
strainers, settling pans, presses and churns for making ewes'

milk into butter and cheese.[13] Further, by the thirteenth century experience had shown the value of protecting the flock
from the worst of winter weather, and Walter of Henley's recommendation that sheep should be housed in bad weather
'between Martinmas and Easter' seems to have been followed
for at least some of these months on the better-managed estates[14].
Some structural evidence of this is provided by the thatched
'bercaries' of stone and timber, with their hayracks and
mangers, on Wiltshire farms, the sheephouse 100ft long and
14ft wide built at Appledore by the monks of Battle Abbey in
1352, another 39ft long, 12ft wide and 22ft high, presumably to
allow for the storage of hay over the stock, and a smaller
lambhouse at Kensworth.[15]

BUILDINGS FOR LOWLAND FARM AND UPLAND RANCH

In most cases, the value of surviving evidences on the farm
buildings of this period is greatly reduced by lack of information on the particular farming system of which they formed
part. By a fortunate chance, however, the records preserve fairly
detailed accounts of two groups of buildings serving substantial
but sharply-contrasted enterprises.

The first was the steading of the 'home farm' of an estate at
Cuxham[16] in South Oxfordshire owned by Merton College. This
was a big farm which in the early fourteenth century grew
nearly 300 acres of corn and carried a dozen plough-oxen and
four plough-horses, a dairy herd and a pig herd. The documentary references confirm the agricultural deductions. The
buildings, which were grouped round a yard, included two
barns, one for wheat, one for oats and barley, a granary, cattlesheds, a stable and a carthouse, a hayhouse and a strawhouse, as
well as a henhouse and dovecotes. There was also a pigsty, for
there were no woodlands on this particular estate. But, it seems,
many of the pigs spent some of their time foraging in the woods
of nearby Ibstone. (See Fig. 5.)

The second was a series of cattlesheds, each 80ft long, built
for a specialised agricultural venture very different from this

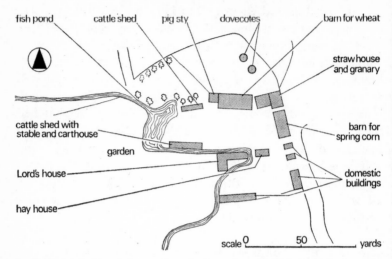

fish pond   cattle shed   pig sty   dovecotes   barn for wheat

straw house and granary

cattle shed with stable and carthouse

barn for spring corn

garden

Lord's house

domestic buildings

hay house

scale 0 ___ 50 ___ yards

5   Conjectural plan of the steading of a large farm in Oxfordshire in the early fourteenth century. (Based on *A Mediaeval Oxfordshire Village. Cuxham, 1240–1400* by D. P. A. Harvey, 1965, p 33) (See p 39)

mixed farm in prosperous and well-settled Oxfordshire. In the same period, the Earl of Lincoln undertook the conversion of a huge area of wild Lancashire moorland into a cattle ranch for the production of cows and working oxen. Here he built sheds for his 'vaccaries', each of seventy-five to eighty beasts, half of them breeding cows with their appropriate bull, the rest heifers or young steers. It was an ambitious project which at one time comprised nearly thirty vaccaries. But the physical and economic difficulties were too great for it and eventually the moors and the buildings on them were abandoned to the wolves which from time to time had taken toll of these premature upland herds.[17]

TITHE BARN AND DOVECOTE

No traces are now left of either of these sets of buildings. Indeed, few traces are left of any of the farm buildings of this period and, predictably, those which remain were the work of the great lords of Church and State. The large barns generally described as 'tithe barns' are among the glories, and the

medieval dovecotes among the delights, of the English, countryside. But they survived because they were exceptional and they
tell us nothing about the normal medieval farmstead.

Indeed, many of the huge and gracious barns of the church-
men were hardly farm buildings at all. Some, presumably, fulfilled the functions of the conventional farm barn in which the
harvest of the surrounding fields was threshed and stored. But
others were primarily the central storage depots of huge agricultural estates, housing the harvests of scattered farms run by
bailiffs and any dues or rents which were paid in corn. The true
descendant of the tithe barn is not the farmer's grainstore but
the merchant's warehouse.[18]

The tithe barn, therefore, illustrated ecclesiastical wealth.
The dovecote illustrated feudal privilege, for from Norman
times onwards the right to keep pigeons was a doubly valuable
monopoly of the lord of the manor. On the one hand, it secured
for him a supply of fresh meat and eggs in the winter months
with which to alleviate the monotonous diet of salted beef produced by the autumn culling, as well as adding rich residues to
his dunghill. On the other, it provided these benefits at the cost
of his neighbours whose crops helped to fatten his birds. It was,
in effect, a means of levying a crude form of taxation in kind.

The massive stone dove-towers of the early Normans which so
substantially symbolised this privilege were later replaced by
lighter, more ornamental buildings. But the general design
altered little, and they remained roofed walls thick enough to
contain rows of nesting holes which could be reached by ladder
or from a wooden frame revolving round a central stanchion.
From these cotes fluttered the hundreds of birds—five to six
hundred was a common size of flock—whose ceaseless depreda-
tions are remembered in the old agricultural proverbs of the
four grains sown in a row,

> One for the pigeon, one for the crow,
> One to rot and one to grow.

The order is significant.[19]

STONE AND CLAY, TIMBER AND THATCH

Nevertheless, partly by example, party by contrast, the tithe barns and dovecotes which survive from this period provide indirect evidence on the farm buildings of their time. For, in general, they have survived because they were built of stone, local stone—it is no accident that so many of the barns are concentrated in the areas of good building stone within a radius of some seventy-five miles of Bristol.[20] They thus reflect the dependence of rural builders on local materials, for in this period, as for centuries later, farmers built their farmsteads with materials won from the local farmlands—timber from the woods, straw from the fields, reeds from the marshland and heather from the upland waste for thatching, clay from village pits and willow and hazel rods for wattle-and-daub walling. They used whatever the neighbourhood provided. But the failure of their buildings to survive shows that few built in such a substantial and intractable material as stone, though many, no doubt, used stone for such limited purposes as wall-footings. Wealthy landlords like the twelfth-century Cistercians of Warden Abbey in Bedfordshire, who brought stone from a quarry thirty miles distant to build their steading at Bradfield, might do so.[21] So might farmers like Benedict, son of Siward, to whom desolate Dartmoor offered little else,[22] or the builder of the Wiltshire longhouse who used sarsen stone from the slopes around his new home.[23] But this was exceptional, and most farmers depended on the more perishable materials which the woods and fields of their parish provided.

Their buildings have now returned to the soil from whence they came, but various references in the written records illustrate this use of local resources. The Earl of Norfolk, for instance, built the walls of his farm buildings with local clay, framed their roofs with local timber and thatched them with local straw—though he chose the longer-lasting reed-thatch for his hall.[24] The Earl of Lincoln used timber and thatch for his upland cattle shelters;[25] the peasants of the Isle of Axholme cut turves for walling as well as for fuel;[26] and the preference of the medieval thatchers of Wigston in Leicestershire for reeds from a certain pool earned the slope on which it stood the name of 'Thatchers Hill'.[27] Similarly, the detailed descriptions of the building of two barns, an oxhouse, a sheephouse and a dairy in the thirteenth and fourteenth centuries list felling timber, gathering withies for wattling, making daub walls, carting straw for thatching and stones for foundations and collecting moss for waterproofing a tiled roof. These tiles were probably local products and only the iron for nails and hinges came from an economy beyond the boundaries of the estate.[28]

Such documentary survivals, however, are few and little is known about the methods of construction used. Presumably the smaller buildings were merely walls or uprights with a thatched roof on a crude timber framing. But it is probable that the barns and larger livestock houses on the farms of the more substantial peasantry used the familiar 'cruck' system of long, heavy timbers cut from naturally curving trees, roughly squared, split in two and set opposite each other in the earth or on a stone base to make the arches which formed the framework of the building.[29] There is, indeed, a suggestion that the common spacing of approximately 16ft between crucks found in various types of building in and after the Middle Ages originated in cattle sheds, since a bay of this width holds two pairs of oxen conveniently.[30] The belief is reasonable and, if true, implies the common use of this method of construction in the medieval farmstead.

Crucks offered a simple and effective method of providing a framework for walls and roofing with such materials as were locally available. But they set rigid limits to the height and width of buildings. The bigger manorial buildings, therefore, continued the aristocratic tradition of the Saxon nobleman's hall, using the more sophisticated and expensive post-and-truss, or 'framed' construction, in which upright posts supported roof members to form aisled structures. This was the type of construction used for many of the tithe barns. It was also, more relevantly, the type of construction used in the manorial

barn mentioned on p 36. Such buildings were probably confined to the large estates and wealthy corn-growing areas of the
south-east.[31] But this is one of the very few generalisations we
can at present make on any class of medieval building. For the
next age is the first to have left sufficient evidence to allow informed conclusions on the various types of buildings used by the
farmer, and on the manner in which he combined them to form
his steading.

NOTES

1. In the West Country, compact villages and their Open Fields
existed side by side with dispersed farms and hamlets. In Devon, it
seems, the Saxon villages were founded first and individual pioneers
later created their farms around them, whereas in Cornwall the
Saxon villages were imposed upon the Celtic pattern of scattered
steadings. (Beresford, M. W. 'Dispersed and group settlement in
mediaeval Cornwall', *Agricultural History Reivew*, vol 12, pt 1, 1964,
p 13.) Similarly, in South Wales Open Field villages in the coastal
lowlands and main valleys, where English influence was strongest,
contrasted with the scattered homesteads of the pastoral uplands.
(Davies, M. 'Rhossili open field and related South Wales field
patterns', *Agricultural History Review*, vol 4, pt 2, 1956, pp 86–7)
2. Hoskins, W. G. and Finberg, H. P. R. *Devonshire Studies*, 1952,
pp 78–81. The history of the Wyanscroft family who, about 1200,
received a grant of 15 acres in the Forest of Arden from an Earl of
Warwick anxious to encourage the colonisation of this area, and by
1250 farmed a compact holding of 45–50 acres equipped with a
cattleshed and sheepfold, provide another instance of this same
general process. (Roberts, B. K. 'Mediaeval colonisation in the
Forest of Arden', *Agricultural History Review*, vol 16, pt 2, 1968, p
107.) So do the account rolls of the Bishop of Winchester in the
1250s, which give details of the equipment of newly reclaimed land
in Wiltshire and Berkshire with buildings, in the first case a barn, an
oxhouse and a sheephouse, in the second a dairy and, presumably,
milking accommodation. (Titow, J. Z. *English rural society, 1200–
1350*, 1969, pp 198–202.)
3. Field, R. K. 'Worcestershire peasant dwellings, household
goods and farm equipment in the later Middle Ages', *Mediaeval
Archaeology*, vol 9, 1965, pp 114–15, 119–21

4. Jope, E. M. and Threlfall, R. I. 'Excavation of a medieval settlement at Beere, North Tawton, Devon', *Mediaeval Archaeology*, vol 2, 1958, pp 112–25; Dudley, D. and Minter, E. M. 'The mediaeval village at Garrow Tor, Bodmin Moor, Cornwall', ibid, vol 6–7, 1962–3, pp 273–94, and 'Houndtor, Devon', ibid, vol 6–7, 1962–3, pp 341–3

5. 'Bratton, Wiltshire', *Mediaeval Archaeology*, vol 10, 1966, pp 214–15

6. For further information on such farmsteads see Walton, J. 'Upland houses', *Antiquity*, vol 30, 1956, pp 142–4 and Hoskins, W. G. 'Farmhouses and history', *History today*, vol 10, no 5, May 1960, p 339. The latter refers to a fifteenth-century building on Dartmoor with two storeys, the ground floor for cattle, the first floor for the farmer and his family, ie a version of the longhouse principle in which the distinction between accommodation for livestock and humans was horizontal, not vertical; Barley, M. W. *English farmhouses and cottages*, 1961, pp 10–13; and the sections in *Mediaeval Archaeology* on excavations in progress on farms and villages.

7. Horn, W. and Born, E. *The barns of the Abbey of Beaulieu and its granges of Great Coxwell and Beaulieu St Leonards*, 1965, pp 11, 13, 17. This barn stood on the estates of the Dean and Chapter of St Paul's which in this period owned thirteen manors, the number of barns on each manor varying between three and five. 'Thirteen of these barns are so well described (in the estate records) that they can be reconstructed on the drawing board.' (Horn, W. 'On the origins of the mediaeval bay system', *Journal of the Society of Architectural Historians*, vol 17, no 2, Summer 1958, pp 11–12.) See also Rigold, S. E. 'The Cherhill barn', *Wiltshire Archaeological and Natural History Magazine*, vol 63, 1968, pp 58–65. This paper describes a large barn originally built in the early fourteenth century, though later modified, which served an estate which was apparently selling off much of its corn crops as well as sending away its corn-tithe.

8. *Seneschausie* in *Walter of Henley's Husbandry*, ed Lamond, E., 1890, pp 113–15

9. Davidson, H. R. *The production and marketing of pigs*, 1966, p 230

10. Trow-Smith, R. *A history of British livestock husbandry to 1700*, 1957, p 113

11. Fox, Lady Aileen 'A monastic homestead on Dean Moor, S. Devon', *Mediaeval Archaeology*, vol 2, 1958, pp 140–57

12. Trow-Smith, R. *Life from the land*, 1967, p 59

13. Trow-Smith, R. *A history of British livestock husbandry to 1700*, 1957, p 114

14. *Walter of Henley's Husbandry*, ed. Lamond, E., 1890, p 31

15. Trow-Smith, R. *A history of British livestock husbandry to 1700*, 1957, pp 113–14

16. Harvey, D. P. A. *A mediaeval Oxfordshire village, Cuxham, 1240–1400*, 1965, pp 32–9. The steading of a similar type of farm in Norfolk with 200 acres of corn as it was in the later years of the thirteenth century is described in Davenport, F. G. *The economic development of a Norfolk manor*, 1906, pp 21, 27, 33–5. This consisted of a barn and a granary, a cattleshed, a hayshed and three stables, a dairy and poultry housing. Pigs are mentioned, but there was no piggery. Presumably they foraged as best they could according to the season either in the yards on farm and household waste or in the local woods.

17. Trow-Smith, R. *A history of British livestock husbandry to 1700*, 1957, pp 107–8

18. See eg Ward, J. D. U. 'Tithe barns of the south-west', *Agriculture*, vol 65, no 4, July 1958, pp 195–8 and Fenn, E. A. H. 'Tithe barns and some conversions', *Wood*, vol 31, no 1, January 1966, pp 37–9. References to individual tithe barns abound in architectural and topographical works and in the general press, though Ward's hope that these barns might be 'surveyed, measured and listed comprehensively and systematically by trained scholars' (p 198) has not yet been fulfilled. But recent research has added greatly to our knowledge of the dating and construction of all types of medieval barn. See Horn, W. and Born, E. *The barns of Beaulieu and its granges of Great Coxwell and Beaulieu St Leonards*, 1965; Hewett, C. A. 'The structural carpentry of mediaeval Essex' and 'The barns of Cressing Temple, Essex, and their significance in the history of English carpentry', in *Mediaeval Archaeology*, vol 6–7, 1962–3, pp 240–71 and *Journal of the Society of Architectural Historians*, vol 26, 1967, pp 48–70 respectively; Horn, W. and Charles, F. W. B. 'The cruck-built barn of Middle Littleton in Worcestershire, England', *Journal of the Society of Architectural Historians*, vol 25, 1966, pp 229–39; and Rigold, S. E. 'The Cherhill barn', *Wiltshire Archaeological and Natural History Magazine*, vol 63, 1968, pp 58–65

19. See Cooke, A. D. *A book of dovecotes*, 1920; Smith, D. *Pigeoncotes and dove houses of Essex*, 1931; Mansfield, W. S. *The farmer's friend*, 1947, pp 25–6. There are many references to dovecotes in general publications but no comprehensive study of these buildings and the part which the domesticated pigeon played in agricultural history has so far appeared.

20. Ward, J. D. U. 'Tithe barns of the south-west', *Agriculture*, vol 65, no 4, July 1958, p 195

21. Trow-Smith, R. *Life from the land*, 1967, p 79

22. It has been suggested that certain granite buildings, apparently of longhouse type, on the fringes of Dartmoor may date from the original colonisation of the Moor in the thirteenth century. (Barley, M. W. *The English farmhouse and cottage*, 1961, p 11.)

23. 'Wiltshire' Fyfield Down, Wroughton Copse', *Mediaeval Archaeology*, vol 5, 1961, p 330

24. Davenport, F. G. *The economic development of a Norfolk manor*, 1906, pp 21, 32. Early in the fourteenth century, however, another wealthy landowner, Merton College, used tiles instead of thatch on new and reconstructed buildings on one of its 'home farms'. (Harvey, D. P. A., *A mediaeval Oxfordshire village, Cuxham, 1240–1400*, 1965, p 37.)

25. Trow-Smith, R. *A history of British livestock husbandry to 1700*, 1957, p 108

26. Barley, M. W. *English farmhouses and cottages*, 1961, p 36

27. Hoskins, W. G. *The Midland peasant*, 1957, p 191

28. Titow, J. Z. *English rural society, 1200–1350*, 1969, pp 198–204

29. For a detailed description of this system see Charles, F. W. B. *Mediaeval cruck building and its derivatives*, 1967

30. Addy, S. O. *The evolution of the English house*, 1933, pp 85–8

31. S. E. Rigold comments on the distinction between 'the broad, aisled timber barns whose extensive distribution extends eastwards (from Wiltshire) to Kent and Essex and north-east to the vicinity of Huntingdon and Thetford' and the single-spanned variation on the cruck theme, often with stone walls, of the western areas. ('The Cherhill barn', *Wiltshire Archaeological and Natural History Magazine*, vol 63, 1968, p 64), see also note 18, above.

Chapter Three

THE END OF AN AGE:

1500-1750

We are accustomed to regard this period as the time in which our own age was formed. When it began, England was a medieval country. The Renaissance, the Reformation and the rise of the national state were still in the future. By the time it ends, we are safely in the familiar world of parliamentary government, transatlantic trade, the stock exchange, newspapers and coffee shops.

Politically and intellectually, this may well be true. Agriculturally, it is false, for the scope and scale of these prodigious changes were not reflected in the farmlands. There was certainly considerable expansion of the cultivated area during this period. There was also, less precedently, considerable technical development in its last century, notably the use of new forage crops and a consequent increase in the livestock population. But there was no dramatic rural revolution. The improved agricultural system which Defoe saw from horseback in the days of George I was a recognisable version of that which the Royal Society strove to survey in the days of Charles II, and which was in turn a recognisable version of that which Tusser described in the days of Elizabeth.

These names, however, remind us that we have now reached the age of the printed word and general literacy, and from Tudor times onwards our sources of information on the history of farming, and therefore of farm buildings, increase with each succeeding period. There was as yet no specialist literature on

48

farm buildings, but the incidental references to them grew proportionately with the increasing mass of general and agricultural
books, of legal records and estate papers. At the end of this
period, for example, we meet the first descriptions of the ancestor of the most familiar of all farm buildings, the cowhouse,
with manger and tie, its stalls 'a yoak wide', its floor hard and
sloping to carry away the liquids.[1] Further, this is the first age
to leave us examples of the normal farm buildings of the time.
Yet we must not exaggerate the importance of such structural
survivals, for their historical value is limited. Few can be dated,
fewer still can be assessed in terms of their original agricultural
context. In a general way, they illustrate the resources and
practices of this period, but for coherent and systematic evidence on farmstead development we must still rely almost entirely on the written record. This provides the text of the story.
The surviving buildings are little more than rather casually-
chosen pictures which add to its interest.[2]

MORE FOOD FOR MORE PEOPLE

Agriculturally, however, this new documentary information
tells an old economic story. But it tells it in more urgent form.
For the population was growing more rapidly than in the
Middle Ages. In 1500, there were probably under three million
people in England and Wales, in 1600 four million, in 1700
some five and a half million. Further, more and more of these
newcomers were living in towns. Both absolutely and proportionately there were more mouths for the farmer to feed. By the
end of the seventeenth century, for instance, London housed
over half a million people and the demands of this huge market
brought butter from Suffolk, cheese from Cheshire, cider from
Devon, and cattle for meat from Wales and Scotland. Yet for
many years the ancient tradition of increasing food production
by adding to agricultural area rather than improving agricultural methods continued to meet the needs of the time. Generation by generation, new farmland was reclaimed from the
ancient forests, from the hills, from marshes, fens and sea coasts.

It was won with increasing difficulty and expense, as by this time the more promising areas were already under cultivation. But until the days of the Stuarts it was sufficient to maintain the necessary increase in the nation's food supply. Only in the later years of this period was there enough technical improvement to make any substantial contribution to the rise in agricultural production.

NEW BUILDINGS, NEW FARMSTEADS

Sometimes the new fields were added to old farms. The corn store which John Lyson of North Coates in Lincolnshire added to his steading in the early seventeenth century[3] and the two new barns and the new beasthouse with which Nicholas Sampson in the manor of Sheffield doubled his accommodation in the same period[4] may reflect such expansion. Sometimes they formed new farms, such as the holdings reclaimed from the forestland around Tonbridge in the later sixteenth and early seventeenth century, which included two keepers' lodges converted to farmsteads,[5] and William Zellacke's lonelier creation of Moorhays Farm near Cruwys Morchard in mid-Devon. In 1653 he secured a ninety-nine years lease of 'all that parcell of waste grounde and lande lyinge in near or by the highwaye adjoining the moore commonly called South Moore' for a yearly rent of six shillings and one capon, provided he built a house upon it. He also built farm buildings and by 1694 the new farm was worth 10s a year and a fine at entry of £150.[6] But such 'parcells of waste grounde' were becoming scarce and many of the new farms were won from land already used for seasonal or extensive grazing rather than from uncultivated wilderness.

Thus, in the 1670s, 2,245 acres of White Coombs uplands in Cheshire were rented to a group of eleven graziers. By 1750, this area was divided into three farms each with its own farmstead.[7] More particularly, the same pressures were now beginning to end the ancient practice of transhumance. In Northumberland, frontier conditions favoured its survival and Camden referred in Tudor times to the summer migration of

Page 51 (left) A cruck barn in Herefordshire; (below) a late medieval aisled barn in Middlesex

Page 52 (*left*) Internal view of a medieval dovecote in Somerset, showing the revolving ladder from which the nests could be reached; (*above*) threshing in a medieval barn. The door is open to allow a through draught to clear away dust and chaff

lowland farmers there to the wild upland grazings where they 'lay out scattering and summering with their cattle in little cottages which they call sheals or shealings'.[8] But in more settled Wales in this period, some of the old summering houses became the centres of permanently-settled farms, and by the end of the seventeenth century the traditional system apparently continued only in a few limited districts.[9]

THE END OF THE LOWLAND LONGHOUSE

All this meant new farm buildings and new farmsteads, but it did not mean any radical break with the past. The old dependence of site on natural water supplies, the old principles of planning, the old methods of construction continued and it is typical of the times that the most striking change was in regional tradition.

For in this period the lowland farmer abandoned the longhouse. After early Tudor times separation of the domestic and industrial buildings of the farm was the rule except in hill areas.[10] The scale of this change is difficult to estimate, for present evidence on the incidence of different types of steading is less than scanty. Its causes, too, are obscure, though presumably the contemporary rise in the standard of living and comfort was partly responsible. But its importance in farmstead development is decisive. In the lowlands, from this time onwards, the house of the farmer stands apart from the buildings of the farm.

The change, of course, was not immediate. Cheshire farmers, for example, continued to house their cattle under the same roofs as themselves well into the seventeenth century.[11] Then, too, there was an inevitable interim period. Thus, in the early seventeenth century, the 'backhouse' of East Anglian farms had become a combination of kitchen, milkroom and buttery, whereas in more conservative Yorkshire in the same period the lower end of the house was a general storeroom which had not yet acquired any regular domestic function. The cattle had left it too recently for the possibility of their return some hard winter to be forgotten.[12] These, however, were passing ana-

D

chronisms. The contrast which Harrison drew in 1577 between the one-roof steadings of 'some of the north parts of our countrie' and the functionally divided buildings elsewhere was prophetic,[13] and the modern historian's surprise at finding in a conventional farming area of Devon the 'unusual arrangement' of dwelling house and farm buildings under one roof dating from this period bears witness to the completeness of the change.[14] By Elizabethan times, it seems, the longhouse was no longer being built in the lowlands.

THE LONGHOUSE IN THE UPLANDS

In the uplands of the north and west, however, it continued as a common type of farmstead. In Wales, for instance, surviving examples show that it was widespread in this period,[15] while a later writer contrasted the 'compact' steadings of the higher Yorkshire Dales, many probably dating from this period,

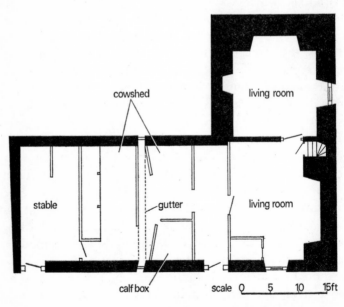

6   Plan of the Welsh longhouse shown on page 87

in which one roof covered barn, livestock buildings and house, with the 'disconnected groups of outbuildings around a central yard' of the lower Dales.[16] Yet even in the hills the new influences were spreading and, as the years passed, the division between the farmhouse and the cowhouse became more pronounced. The creation of partitions or lobbies between the two sections of the building, and the provision of separate doors for men and animals, reflected the farmer's desire for standards of comfort and cleanliness higher than those of his ancestors. In surviving examples on Dartmoor and in Cumberland of longhouses built in the latter half of this period, there is no direct communication between the two parts of the building.[17]

MINOR DEVELOPMENTS IN FARMSTEAD LAYOUT

Technically, however, this period saw no drastic or widespread improvements in methods of husbandry or systems of farming. Economically, patterns of regional specialisation were developing to meet the new commercial opportunities, but the days of the specialist farm were still far in the future. There was, therefore, little change in the demands of the farm on the farmstead and developments were few and simple.

Horses, for instance, were now replacing oxen as work beasts. But this probably meant no more than different animals in the same old stables, though the memory of the oxen is preserved in certain Welsh buildings of this period by the wide doors made necessary by the spread of the great horns of the local breed of ploughteam.[18] Neither did change in systems of pig management cause major change in the homestead. Pigs were still ranched in the woodlands, as the seventeenth-century contrast between the large pig population of well-wooded Hampshire and the small number of pigs kept in poorly-wooded South Wiltshire shows.[19] But the old areas of forest were shrinking fast and pigs were now spending more of their time in sties or yards, where they fattened on the waste products of the fields, the butter or cheese dairy and the farmhouse.[20] In the later sixteenth century, for example, Tusser assumed from his experi-

ence in East Anglia, where woodlands were few, that pigs
would be housed in the farmstead, though not very elaborately
—the winter accommodation he suggested included a brush-
wood shelter and the 'shed ready dight' for tumbrels and carts.

> Where under, the hog may in winter lie warm
> to stand so inclosed, as wind do no harm.[21]

There was little difficulty in incorporating such crude housing
into the traditional type of farmstead.

Typically, the only conspicious innovation in building design
in this period on the general farm, the appearance in the west
and north of two-storeyed buildings created by the addition of
haylofts to traditional types of cattleshed, represented no more
than a new form of answer to the ancient problem of storing and
feeding winter fodder in climatically difficult areas.[22]

Indeed, there were no fundamental changes in this period in
the inherited alliance of barn, beasthouse and yard. In the
arable areas, of course, there was greater emphasis on the corn
barn and granary, in the livestock areas on stock buildings
around some version of 'the great, open courtyard that is typical
of large farms everywhere in western Europe where cattle are
more important than corn'.[23] It remained, however, a matter of
emphasis, and a catalogue of chance descriptions of different
farmsteads in different parts of the country at different times in
the seventeenth century shows this pervading similarity—in
East Anglia, a barn, a carthouse and a stable;[24] in Devon, a
barn, a cowhouse and 'a new stable and a corn-chamber which
I have built';[25] in Leicestershire, a barn, a stable and hovels;[26]
in Herefordshire, 'a large new frame of buildings', including
two barns, a large beasthouse, a swinehouse, a sheepcote and a
pigeonhouse;[27] in upland Yorkshire, a stable, a barn and a
cowshed;[28] and on an estate in lowland Yorkshire, a group
ranging from Richard Wilson's collection of a three-bay corn-
barn, a two-bay haybarn, a four-bay beasthouse, a two-bay
carthouse and a piggery to Simon Heathcot's single hovel for
livestock and 'cornebarn made of poules, very badd'.[29] So barn
and beasthouse continued the medieval tradition, even if on the

exposed hills one building served two purposes, as in the South Pennine barns of this period which contained cow standings as well as threshing floors,[30] and the only novelty is the increasing number of references to cartsheds. These were clearly important and, on the larger farms, substantial. In the same century, the two sheds on Henry Best's Yorkshire farm housed between them seven carts whose repair and maintenance under cover was a standard winter chore—'our folkes were (this year) employed about this business on Powder Treason day'.[31]

Such sets of buildings and the yards they surrounded all alike assumed one form or another of a mixed-farming system producing corn and livestock, the dominant barn, the most substantial building of them all, proclaiming that the primary function of farming was the production of daily bread. It is no accident that the most obvious survivals of this period are barns.

But, of course, these were not the only buildings on the farm. Sheep required pens, though the practice of housing or yarding them in the winter was on the decline and by the end of the period survived in only a few exceptional areas.[32] Pigeons, too, were still a minor but picturesque form of farm livestock—the accounts of Robert Loder, who farmed in Berkshire in the days of Charles I, show that they earned him from £5 to £10 a year in a total farm income of some £400 as well as leaving him valuable manure[33]—and the number of dovecotes in the country was considerable, some 26,000 according to a seventeenth-century estimate.[34] By this time, however, not all of them stood on manorial farms, for the feudal monopoly of pigeon-keeping was abandoned in the early seventeenth century. Indeed, some did not stand on farms at all. They were owned by people without farmland, whose flocks lived on the crops of their agricultural neighbours—a crude but peculiarly profitable form of specialist livestock production.[35]

PROCESSING BUILDINGS

Nevertheless, occasional signs of more general economic change were already visible in the farmstead. All dairy farmers had long been accustomed to processing milk into butter or cheese for sale off the farm—evil communications do more than corrupt good manners, they also render impossible the general transport and sale of such a perishable commodity as liquid milk. These tasks were the responsibility of the farmer's family, whose workshops were rooms in the farmhouse. But now certain farmers began to process certain crops for market. They began to export cider, probably made in the immemorial circular mill in which a horse-driven wheel of stone crushed the fruit in a trough, first from Cornwall to Plymouth, then, more ambitiously, from Devon and Herefordshire to London. They also learnt from Continental neighbours the trade of hop-growing and with it, necessarily, the novel art of hop-drying. At first, in Tudor times, they used maltkilns or improvised drying rooms. But by the middle of the seventeenth century they had adopted the Flemish type of specialised, rectangular oasthouse with a central drying floor of chequer brickwork and were experimenting with improved designs in which the smoke did not pass through the hops. By the middle of the eighteenth century they had developed the more sophisticated cockle kiln, in which flues from enclosed iron stoves circled the inner walls and discharged smoke and fumes through a chimney.[36]

Cidermills and oasthouses alike were confined to limited areas. But both provided early examples of the effects of agricultural change on the equipment and buildings of the farmstead. They also illustrated the growing commercialism of farming. Typically, this same age saw the first reference to grain drying as a means of securing good prices. The story is told by the inventor of the drill, Jethro Tull, one of whose Oxfordshire neighbours used to dry grain on a maltkiln to rid it of 'the superfluous moisture which caused the corruption and made it liable to be eaten by the weevil', and then store it until the market was favourable. The practice was sound, the rewards considerable. 'From a small substance he began with, he left behind him about forty thousand pounds, the greatest part whereof was acquired by his drying method.'[37] But he was a lone pioneer, probably because few could match his personal skill in judging the degree of drying necessary, and the principle he so successfully exploited did not become general practice till the days of the combine-harvester.

THE FIRST TOWN DAIRIES

At the same time, equally prophetic types of intensive production were establishing themselves in London streets. These were the 'town dairies' which made their appearance in the seventeenth century, when the expanding capital began to outgrow its local milk supply. Their origin is obscure. Presumably some developed from farms whose fields were replaced by spreading suburbs, but their connection with traditional farming was purely contractual. For here was 'factory farming' at its most literal, divorced from the farmlands though dependent on them for its animal machines, which it bought newly-calved, milked through their lactation and then fattened for sale, and for the hay and straw which fuelled them. The cowsheds in forgotten courts and alleys which housed the herds of men like Mr Harrard who milked 'three hundred or sometimes four hundred' cows in Hoxton in the 1690s had little in common with the steadings of conventional farms.[38] But they were the ancestors of a line of development with a long and important future before it.

BUILDING MATERIALS AND METHODS OF CONSTRUCTION

The new age brought as little change to the construction as to the design of farm buildings. The ancient tradition of local sufficiency was as yet unchallenged and throughout this period, 'Devon cob and thatch, Dartmoor granite, Dorset plaster and thatch, Cotswold limestone, chalkland flints, Sussex weatherboarding and tiles, midland brick and mud-and-stud, Northamptonshire iron stone, northern slate and millstone grit'[39] continued to proclaim the farmer's dependence on local materials, even as the methods of building he used continued to proclaim his dependence on local skills. For example, in Stuart times, Henry Best's large barn, capable of holding six loaded waggons, was framed in timber, clad in wattle-and-daub and floored in rammed clay, 'which we used to digge and lode for our barne from John Bonwicke's hill',[40] while the walls of another Yorkshire steading were built of stones from a nearby river.[41] More generally, the reference in the accounts of a contemporary landowner to a loan to a tenant who was repairing his house and barn of a horse 'to tread clay and sledge it to the house' and the frugal satisfaction with which he recorded that the barn was thatched with 'sainfoin straw, except a good horseload of rushes' typify the practice and principles of the time.[42]

Neither is there any specific evidence that farm buildings shared in the 'Great Rebuilding' which so improved domestic standards in the countryside in the earlier years of this period.[43] It is probable, however, that they benefitted from the general tendency towards more spacious design and more durable materials. Thus, in the early part of this period the ancient regional distinction between the cruck barns of the West and the more sophisticated and spacious post-and-truss barns of the East continued, but the latter were apparently gaining ground.[44] In Elizabethan times, for example, they were beginning to supersede their rivals in the East Midlands.[45] Again, in the prosperous arable areas of the South East in the same period, the use of brick for barns, the most important and conspicuous buildings on the farm, was increasing as such survivals as the late Tudor barn near St Ives, inevitably called 'Cromwell's barn', bear witness.[46] The general process of change is probably summarised in the conclusions of a classic study of farm buildings in Monmouthshire where the period between 1550–1610 saw the erection of three classes of building—a mass of framed timber buildings, a few cruck timber buildings of the old tradition, and a few stonewalled buildings of the tradition to come.[47]

Presumably, there was a slow and general improvement in the building materials and methods of construction used in the following century and a half as the national standard of living steadily rose. But at no time in these years was the pace of agricultural development sufficient to create any general need for new designs and new methods of construction, and it was typical of the times that the spate of improving agricultural literature which was such a feature of these years made so few references to farmstead problems. Right at the end of this period, for instance, the only specific reference to farm buildings in a 300-page book on the management of farms and estates was the suggestion that they should be roofed with slates or tiles instead of straw, partly to reduce the risk of fire, partly to prevent the loss of the manurial value of the straw.[48] For the writer, like his predecessors and contemporaries, assumed as a matter of course that a combination of commonsense and local tradition would enable any landowner or farmer to equip his land with satisfactory buildings.

In this period, therefore, most farmers built as their ancestors had built before them. In the design and construction of farm buildings, as in other branches of agricultural technology, local resources continued to meet local needs.

NOTES

1. 'A. S., Gent.', 1697, quoted in Fussell, G. E. *The English dairy farmer*, 1966, p 137
2. 'There can be little doubt that the stonebuilt hovels of the uplands and the timbered byres of the lowlands still to be seen on every hand are often relics of the seventeenth century.' (Trow-Smith, R. *A history of British livestock husbandry to 1700*, 1957, p 239.) But only a series of highly detailed local studies could hope to extract any form of chronological history from such buildings. Survivals like the Devonshire barn which bears the date 1604 on a tablet, or the Oxfordshire barn which carries the date 1704 on one of its trusses, are unfortunately very rare (Sheldon, L. 'Devon barns', *Transactions of the Devonshire Association*, vol 64, 1932, p 393; Mackie, J. 'A plea for adaptable buildings' *Farm Buildings Association Journal*, vol 3, December 1959, p 10.) More typical is a Hampshire barn known from later documentary evidence to have been built by a family which left the area in 1696. But 'by the style of the masonry, it could have been built a century or two earlier'. (Cottrill, F. 'Old

farm buildings in Hampshire', *Country Landowner*, vol 17, no 4, August 1966, p 218.) The problem is not confined to this period. The various local studies listed in the Note on Sources make clear the extreme difficulty of dating in any but general terms farm buildings erected before Victorian times.

3. Barley, M. W. *The English farmhouse and cottage*, 1961, p 90

4. Barley, M. W. *The English farmhouse and cottage*, 1961, pp 118–19

5. Chalklin, C. W. 'The rural economy of a Kentish wealden parish, 1650–1750', *Agricultural History Review*, vol 10, pt 1, 1962, p 30

6. Hoskins, W. G. and Finberg, H. P. R. *Devonshire Studies*, 1952, p 329.

7. In 1960 one of these preserved what appeared to be its original cowhouse, a low building with stone divisions between the cows. (Davies, C. S. *The agricultural history of Cheshire, 1750–1850*, 1960, p 8.)

8. Butlin, R. A. 'Northumberland field systems', *Agricultural History Review*, vol 12, pt 2, 1964, p 116

9. Emery, F. 'Farming regions of Wales', *The agrarian history of England and Wales*, vol 4, 1967, pp 117, 149

10. Hurst, J. G. *Agricultural History Review*, vol 9, pt 2, 1961, p 129. A survey in lowland Devonshire of houses built or rebuilt between 1550 and 1640 noted that the earliest examples preserved the general longhouse pattern of rooms and cross-passage but made no provision for stock, for the cows had already retired to the farmstead. (Alcock, N. W. 'Houses in an east Devon parish', *Transactions of the Devonshire Association*, vol 94, 1962, p 226.)

11. Barley, M. W. *The English farmhouse and cottage*, 1961, p 119

12. Barley, M. W. *The English farmhouse and cottage*, 1961, p 120

13. Addy, S. O. *The evolution of the English house*, 1933, p 95

14. Hoskins, W. G. and Finberg, H. P. R. *Devonshire Studies*, 1952, p 144

15. Peate, I. C. *The Welsh house*, 1944, p 59

16. Walton, J. *Homesteads of the Yorkshire Dales*, 1947, p 38. The longhouse type of steading also seems to have been universally employed on the smaller farms of the Cumberland and Westmorland uplands. (Brunskill, R. W. *Design and layout of farmsteads in parts of Cumberland and Westmorland*, RIBA Neale Bursary, 1963, Manchester 1965, Sect 5.) The few examples found in a Shropshire survey were also all on small upland farms, half of them in isolation from other settlements. (Davies, D. C. G. *Historic farmstead and farmhouse types of the Shropshire region*, MA thesis, Manchester University, 1952, pp 89, 91, 105.)

17. Worth's *Dartmoor* ed Spooner, G. M., 1967, pp 407–13; Barley, M. W. *The English farmhouse and cottage*, 1961, pp 236–7. The same division between living quarters for the farmer's family and accommodation for livestock is found in certain two-storey Cumberland steadings of this period. These were built into the hillside and, like the medieval steading mentioned in note 6 to Chapter 2, provided ground floor housing for cattle and a first-floor home for the family. (Walton, J. 'Upland houses', *Antiquity*, vol 30, 1956, pp 144–5.)

18. Raglan, Lord and Fox, Sir Cyril *Monmouthshire houses*, pt 2, 1953, p 81

19. Trow-Smith, R. *A history of British livestock husbandry to 1700*, 1957, pp 185–6

20. Seebohm, M. F. *The evolution of the English farm*, 1952, pp 207, 237

21. Tusser, T. *His points of good husbandry*, ed Hartley, D., 1931, pp 76, 141

22. Alcock, N. W. 'Devonshire linhays; a vernacular tradition', *Transactions of the Devonshire Association*, vol 95, 1963, pp 117–30; Barley, M. W. 'Rural housing in England', *The agrarian history of England and Wales*, vol 4, 1967, p 750

23. Hoskins, W. G. and Finberg, H. P. R. *Devonshire Studies*, 1952, p 144

24. Barley, M. W. *The English farmhouse and cottage*, 1961, p 202

25. Barley, M. W. *The English farmhouse and cottage*, 1961, p 274

26. Hoskins, W. G. *The Midland peasant*, 1957, p 148

27. Thirsk, J. 'The farming regions of England', *The agrarian history of England and Wales*, vol 4, 1967, p 106

28. 'Reynard made a meadow', *Farmers Weekly*, vol 69, no 24, 13 December 1968, p 81

29. Addy, S. O. *The evolution of the English house*, 1933, pp 236–9

30. Walton, J. 'South Pennine barn buildings', *Architectural Review*, vol 90, October 1941, pp 122–4

31. Best, H. *Rural economy in Yorkshire in 1641*, ed Surtees Society, 1857, p 137

32. Trow, Smith, R. *A history of British livestock husbandry to 1700*, 1957, p 245; Garnier, R. M. *History of the English landed interest (Modern period)*, 1893, p 271. Stone houses, dating apparently from the early eighteenth century, which were used for inwintering ewe lambs still survive in the Lake District. (Whitaker, J. M. 'Factory farming', *The Times*, 23 July 1969, p 9.)

33. *Robert Loder's farm accounts, 1610–1620*, ed Fussell, G. E., 1936, table IV

34. Briggs, M. S. *The English farmhouse*, 1953, p 56

35. Garnier, R. M. *History of the English landed interest*, (*earliest times to the 18th century*), 1892, p 338

36. Burgess, A. H. *Hops*, 1964, pp 3, 5, 6

37. Tull, J. *Horsehoeing Husbandry*, ed Cobbett, 1824, pp 215–16

38. Trow-Smith, R. *A history of British livestock husbandry to 1700*, 1957, p 197

39. Mingay, G. F. *English landed society in the eighteenth century*, 1963, pp 233–4

40. Best, H. *Rural economy in Yorkshire in 1641*, ed Surtees Society, 1857, pp 47, 107. Similarly, the Stryt Lydan barn in the Welsh Folk Museum, which dates partly from about 1550, partly from about 1600, was built of timber framing, roofed with wheat thatch and clad with panels of riven oak wattling.

41. 'Reynard made a meadow', *Farmers Weekly*, vol 69, no 24, 13 December 1968, p 81

42. Barley, M. W. *The English farmhouse and cottage*, 1961, p 209

43. An interesting by-product of this development was the relegation of old houses to agricultural purposes. Thus, in the seventeenth century the Martindales, a yeoman family of Lancashire, built a new stone house and used their old wooden home as a barn. (Campbell, M. *The English Yeoman*, 1942, pp 228–9.) Certain semi-agricultural buildings mentioned in a Wiltshire estate survey of 1631–2 were possibly medieval houses partly converted to cowhouses or stables. (Hoskins, W. G. *The Midland peasant*, 1957, pp 287–8.) A generation later a Lincolnshire landowner dismantled a house 'as carefully as may be to prevent the breaking of any wood or tenures' to re-erect it as a barn (Barley, M. W. *The English farmhouse and cottage*, 1961, p 209.)

It has been suggested that re-used timbers in farm buildings believed to come from dismantled ships, a traditional belief about a number of barns of this and later periods, more probably came from demolished houses (Walton, J. 'The timberwork of English farm buildings', *Country Life*, vol 91, no 2370, 19 June 1942, p 1181.) A more recent writer dismisses this belief as a myth, perhaps recalling the time when rivers and streams were used for floating timber down from the upland forests. (Charles, F. W. B. *Mediaeval cruck building and its derivatives*, 1967, p vii.) *Prima facie*, the use on farms near harbours or rivers of timbers from old ships seems not improbable in an age of shrinking forests and growing demands for wood. The only documented case of a farm building built of ship's timbers, however, is the famous seventeenth-century barn near the Quaker Meeting House at Old Jordans in Buckinghamshire. (Personal communications from the Librarians of the Forestry Commission, the Forest Products Research Laboratory, the Timber Research and Development Association, and the National Maritime Museum.) This barn is certainly built of ships' timbers, though it is unlikely that, as has been claimed, they are the timbers of the *Mayflower*. (Harris, R. *The finding of the Mayflower*, 1920; Horrocks, J. W, 'The Mayflower', *Mariner's Mirror*, vol 8, 1922, pp 2–9, 81–8, 140–7, 236–43, 354–62.)

More generally, it is inherently probable that the agricultural expansion of this age encouraged farmers to make what use they could of any building materials which happened to be locally available. In particular, it is likely that some of the stones from the abandoned monasteries, like those from the traditional quarry of Hadrian's Wall, were re-used in Tudor, Stuart or Hanoverian farmsteads. The only documented case of the re-use of monastic materials, however, concerns moulded timber roof trusses in a manorial barn in Dorset which is believed to have been built about 1545. These, it has been suggested, came from nearby Milton Abbey at the Dissolution. (Oswald, A. 'The Story of Three Dorset Houses', *Country Life*, vol 132, no 3412, 26 July 1962, p 202.)

44. Barley, M. W. 'Rural housing in England', *The agrarian history of England and Wales*, 1967, vol 4, p 723

45. Hoskins, W. G. *The Midland peasant*, 1957, p 284

46. Barley, M. W. 'Rural housing in England', *The agrarian history of England and Wales*, vol 4, 1967, p 723; Briggs, M. S. *The English farmhouse*, 1953, pp 85–6

47. Raglan, Lord and Fox, Sir Cyril. *Monmouthshire houses*, pt 2, 1953, p 100. For another local account of the same general process, see Davies, D. C. G. *Historic farmstead and farmhouse types in the Shropshire region*, MA thesis, Manchester University, 1952, pp 65–6

48. Laurence, E. *The duty and office of a land steward*, 1731, p 176

Chapter Four

THE AGRICULTURAL
REVOLUTION:
THE AGRARIAN PHASE, 1750-1820

RECLAMATION AND ENCLOSURE

The Agricultural Revolution was a vast and incoherent movement which sprawled across most of our countryside and more
than a century of our history. It changed alike crops and stock,
the systems and equipment of farming, and much of the physical
landscape itself; and in many areas it created the form and
pattern of the farmsteads we see around us today. It did not, of
course, begin neatly in the middle of the eighteenth century.
Indeed, many of the improvements traditionally ascribed to the
reign of George III were apparent in the previous hundred
years.[1] But the later Hanoverians developed and expanded it
with a new urgency and more drastic consequences, for the
times were demanding.

On the one hand, population was rising rapidly. In the
1750s there were rather over six million people in England and
Wales; by 1801, the date of the first census, nearly nine million;
and by 1821 twelve million. Further, a growing proportion of
these new consumers were concentrated in towns of a size and
number unknown in earlier ages. By the turn of the century, for
instance, London alone offered a market of nearly a million
people. There was no precedent for increases of this scale at this
speed.

On the other, the most obvious traditional way of increasing
the supply of food was now failing, for the reclamation of new

farmland from forest, marsh or hill was nearing its practicable end. The men of the time continued the work of their ancestors energetically, winning, it has been estimated, two to three million acres, more than a twentieth of the entire land surface of the country, from the surviving waste. But by the end of this period little virgin land worth cultivating remained. In 1816, the Duke of Portland began a huge irrigation scheme in the Nottinghamshire sands; in 1820, John Knight started his epic attack on Exmoor Forest; and the extreme physical difficulties they overcame showed clearly that they were winning the last exploitable reserves of the ancient Waste.

The alternative to more farming was better farming, and in the pastoral uplands this took the form of more intensive grazing systems. In Wales in this period, for instance, the expansion of the hill sheep flocks at the expense of summer-grazed cattle meant the end of the ancient practice of transhumance. The Welsh upland farmer ceased to be half a nomad, and sheepfolds designed to segregate the sheep of farmers whose flocks grazed mountain pastures in common replaced the old 'summer dwellings'.[2] But in the arable lowlands, the most obvious way of increasing production was the more general use of certain new fodder crops, most of which had already established themselves in the fields of progressive farmers. These were of two types, on the one hand various grasses and clovers, on the other, the turnip, the swede and the mangold, collectively called 'roots' from their habit of growth. Together, these made possible wholly new systems of husbandry.

In particular, the rootcrops could be planted by the drill, which was gradually replacing hand-sowing, in neat, long rows between which men and horses could hoe and cultivate while plants grew. Thus was ended the necessity for the wasteful bare fallow, since weeds could now be controlled on land that carried a crop. So the first consequence of the new crops was the development of improved rotations, such as the famous 'Norfolk four-course shift' of two corn crops separated by a crop of roots and a crop of grasses and clovers—a far more productive system than the ancient Open Field cycle of two corn crops and a bare fallow. The second consequence of the new crops was a great increase in the amount as well as the proportion of stock-feed grown, and therefore a corresponding increase in the live-stock that the farm could carry. The ancient limiting factor of dependence on hay alone for winter fodder was at last ended.

The third, less obvious consequence, was the new scope afforded to the stockbreeder. Previously, the prevailing low level of nutrition had concealed the inherent genetical capacity of farm animals, but now improved feeding enabled the farmer 'to assess the true, unrestricted potentialities of his stock . . . and perpetuate those desirable traits which had previously lain hidden under the cloak of mediocrity'.[3] It was no accident that Bakewell the breeder was one of the major figures of this period.

The main scope for these new crops and techniques lay in the lowlands, in the Open Field areas which provided most Englishmen with their daily bread. It was certainly possible to incorporate many of these innovations into this ancient system, or to reform it by local agreement in a way which allowed their introduction. Indeed, it is now clear that the old order was considerably more adaptable and progressive in both methods and organisation than was formerly believed. But, in practice, improvement was slow, though the needs of the time were pressing and the opportunities tempting. So the change came in the more drastic form of land redistribution which we call the Enclosure Movement.

The purpose of this movement was the dissolution of the inherited farming system and its replacement by one allowing greater and easier exploitation of the new possibilities. Its principal instruments were, legally, Acts of Parliament authorising the re-allocation of land and, physically, the hedges which divided new farm from new farm, and new field from new field. Its outcome was the farming pattern we know today.

In the early years of this period, when the movement was beginning in earnest, the typical farm in lowland England consisted of arable strips scattered in the Open Fields and grazing rights on the stubbles and on common land. Law, custom and physical necessity bound the farmer in inescapable partnership

Page 69 (right) A Tudor granary presented by the Marquis of Bath to Lackham School of Agriculture, where it was re-erected. The staddle-stones on which it stands provide protection from vermin; (below) a seventeenth-century cowhouse in Derbyshire, partly modernised

Page 70 (*above*) A seventeenth-century brick barn in Hampshire, showing the ventilation slits; (*below*) a livestock shelter of unknown date in the Cotswolds. The pillars are said to have come from a nearby Roman villa

with his fellow villagers. Sixty years later, when the movement was nearing its end, the typical farm consisted of a compact holding of hedged fields farmed as the individual owner or occupier thought best.

LANDLORDS, TENANTS AND FARM BUILDINGS

The leaders of this rural revolution were the landed gentry and the rising class of professional men who served them as advisors and managers. They were also the propagandists who, in their efforts to hasten and extend the benefits of the new methods of farming, produced the mass of pamphlets, manuals, accounts of agricultural travels and experiences and varied publications by farming societies which form the first considerable body of specialised agricultural literature in our history. Typically, the Board of Agriculture, which was founded at their instance in 1793 and dissolved in 1822, was primarily a State-financed information-bureau and its main memorial is a magnificent and comprehensive series of county reports in which its officials gave 'general views' on agricultural practice and development in their particular area. The tradition thus established continued and from the later eighteenth century onwards the agricultural industry tells its own history in its own contemporary publications.

One of the constant themes of the new literature in this period was the planning and construction of farm buildings. For this there was an obvious general reason. The new farms created by reclamation or enclosure needed new farmsteads, the old farmsteads needed extension and improvement to enable them to meet the demands which agricultural change thrust on them. Consequently, building and rebuilding was a major pre-occupation of the contemporary farming industry. Indeed, this is the first agricultural age which has left us any substantial and readily identifiable structural legacy. But there was also a particular reason for the increasing interest of landowners and their agents in the buildings of the farm. By this time the landlord-and-tenant system dominated the countryside and the varied

E

arrangements of earlier times had hardened into the familiar division of functions whereby the landlord, in return for a cash rent, provided the land and its fixed equipment which the tenant-farmer stocked and worked. The erection and maintenance of farm buildings was now the prerogative of the landlord, and therefore among the main responsibilities of his agent.

In Hanoverian times, farmers seldom owned the land they cultivated. Many landlords kept a 'home farm' in hand, but few farmed on any scale and nearly all this land was leased to tenants. The terms of agreement between the two partners in agriculture varied in detail from area to area, from estate to estate. But they all assumed the distinction between the provider and the user of farm buildings. In practice, tenants who enjoyed little security in law but a good deal in practice sometimes erected buildings at their own cost, trusting that the landlord would not give them notice until they had recovered the value of their investment. Bakewell, for instance, was prepared to build at his own expense new stalls and sheds and convert an old barn for livestock to house his increasing herd.[4] But such convenient arrangements did not alter the accepted principle. The advantages of a system which divided the heavy burden of raising agricultural capital were obvious. So, less agreeably, were its disadvantages, for it failed to ensure any necessary connection between the needs of the farm, as identified by the man who worked it, and the ability or willingness of the landowner to meet them.

In general, of course, expenditure on farm buildings depended on the fortunes of agriculture. But expenditure on any particular farmstead depended on the policy, resources and personality of a particular landlord. And a landlord might be rich or poor, wise or foolish; he might employ a shrewd agriculturist or an attorney ignorant of farming matters to manage his estate. At one end of the scale were such wealthy and progressive agricultural magnates as the Duke of Bedford, or Coke of Holkham, at the other backwoods squires and wastrels. Between such extremes were a mass of men of varying means and different outlooks. All these differences were reflected in the buildings of the farms for which they were responsible.

NEW FARMS, NEW FARMSTEADS

Some of the land reclaimed from the uncultivated waste was added to existing holdings, but most of it was divided into new farms and equipped with new farmsteads, thus continuing the system of individual farms which had long been familiar in the remoter and hillier districts. In the Open Field areas, however, the significant change was not in the number of farmsteads. It was in their siting. For here the new needs created a radically new pattern of settlement.

Traditionally, the lowland farmsteads clustered in the villages from which the farmers went out to their daily work on their scattered strips. But the compact farms created by the enclosures required farmsteads standing on their own land. Distances for men and stock and haulage were shorter, movement simpler, control and inspection easier. The advantages were manifest. Indeed, they were among the reasons for the enclosures, and those responsible for the new order naturally sought the maximum advantage from it. And so, as the years of George III's reign passed and more and more parishes were enclosed, new farmsteads appeared among the newly-hedged fields which replaced the old patchwork of arable strips and common grazings.

The benefits of this replanning of the countryside was a common theme of the Board of Agriculture's surveyors who toured the country between 1793 and 1815 to compile the series of *County Reports* which give us, amongst other things, the first systematic information on the farm buildings of England and Wales. They constantly contrasted the traditional village steadings separated from their distant fields with the new steadings, such as those built by Jonathan Ackom of Wiseton in Nottinghamshire,[5] and the Rev Mr Lloyd of Aston, in Shropshire, 'in a centrical part of the farm'.[6] The point is well illustrated by the criteria for siting a farmstead given by the Board's surveyor for

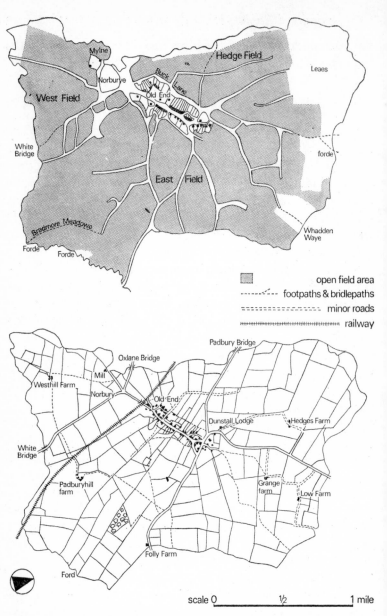

open field area
footpaths & bridlepaths
minor roads
railway

7 The effects of Hanoverian enclosure: (*above*) the Open Field parish of Padbury in Buckinghamshire, from a map of 1591; (*below*) the parish today, showing the outlying farmsteads built after the enclosure of 1796. (Based on Beresford, M. W. and Joseph, J. K. S., *Mediaeval England. An aerial survey 1958*, pp 30, 33, 256–7)

Carmarthen and Pembroke in 1794 and applauded by his successor in 1814.[7] Water inevitably came first, for it was still easier
to take the farmstead to the water than water to the farmstead
—it is significant that his colleague in Wiltshire noted that the
lack of water in his county helped to maintain the old system of
farmsteads 'crowded into villages'.[8] Shelter, a general need of
all farmsteads and a particular need of farmsteads sited in the
treeless expanse of the Open Fields, came next. But the third,
'centricity', is less familiar, for the enclosures offered the first
general opportunity since the original settlement of re-siting
farm buildings in positions convenient for the working of the
farm. This choice of a central position reflected the essential
continuity of the farming system, which the enclosures rearranged rather than altered. There were still many reasons
why the farmstead should be convenient to its fields, few why it
should be near a road. The farmer was concerned greatly with
'dispatch in conveying home the crops and carrying the manure
to the fields',[9] little with the periodical sale off the farm of his
staple products, corn and meat, for a few hundred yards of
farm track made little difference to the lumbering waggons or
plodding oxen on their way to market. The days when he
would sell milk off his farm every day and receive in exchange
so many necessities of his trade from the road which linked him
to factory and port were still far ahead.

The change was not, of course, either immediate or complete.
Some new farms could be worked from the old homesteads.
Some landlords followed the advice of the official surveyor of
Northamptonshire and built new farmsteads in the fields they
served only when the old ones in the village were no longer
worth repairing.[10] Some persisted in building new farmsteads
in the villages, thus perpetuating the inconveniences of the old
system.[11] Nevertheless, by the end of this period a new pattern
had established itself in most lowland areas. In the open
countryside, the new buildings slowly mellowed into the landscape until they looked as if they had been there all the time.[12]
In the villages, many of the farmhouses became cottages, inhabited not by farmers but by hired men working for wages,

whilst the old barns, byres and yards were converted into out-houses or allowed to fall into decay. Some still survive, the last structural relics of a system of farming which lasted over a thousand years and has now gone down into history.[13]

The new farming system increased the demands of the farmer on the farmstead. As crop-grower, he needed the maximum quantity of good-quality manure to maintain and improve the fertility of his expanding and exacting arable acreage, and he looked to the farmstead to conserve and compost with a mini-mum of waste the animal and vegetable residues which col-lected there. As stockbreeder, he needed more housing for more beasts. The new fodder crops allowed farms to carry more cattle and sheep, while the livestock improvers were developing new breeds which required better accommodation than their rougher ancestors. In addition, the conversion of forest to farm-land and game preserve was now compelling the last of the woodland pigs to seek the permanent hospitality of the farm-stead, particularly the dairy farmstead, where they fattened happily on the waste products of the farmhouse manufacture of butter and cheese. In Hanoverian England as in modern Den-mark 'the pig hung on the cow's tail'.[14] These demands were new in intensity but familiar in principle and they wrought no revolutionary change in farmstead design. Steadings remained essentially permutations and combinations of buildings selected from the familiar stock of barns and granaries, stables or ox-houses for work beasts, cowhouses, piggeries, cartlodges and henhouses which Young in 1770 regarded as 'absolutely neces-sary to the common practice of business',[15] all arranged accord-ing to local circumstances and traditions. But they were selected more carefully and arranged more systematically, and various writers of the time compared the casual chaos of the old farm-steads, apparently built 'at random, without order, or method, whose buildings had accumulated over the generations', with the more planned and purposeful layouts of the new order.[16]

The main criteria of farmstead planning in this period were convenience of arrangement for routine chores, notably the feeding, littering and mucking-out of livestock, and the effectiveness with which manure could be accumulated. But in the days of rural unemployment and the Speenhamland system, labour was plentiful and cheap, whereas demands for the means of fertility were insatiable. Consequently the importance of the farmstead as a muck-factory, as a 'reservoir' of manure,[17] took precedence and forms a pervading theme in the practice and literature of these years.

Thus in 1814 the official surveyor of Lancashire criticised the farmsteads of his county for inconvenience 'for collecting manure, feeding stock or preserving corn'.[18] The order is significant. By the same token, his colleague in Monmouthshire noted in 1812 that 'the increased quality of dung produced by good farmstead management is the sheet-anchor of the cultivator',[19] while William Marshall regarded 'the loss of the vegetative strength of animal manures' as an index of 'the improper form' of farmstead design.[20] Typically, the installation of gutters and downpipes was approved because it decreased dilution by rainwater of manure in the yards,[21] the replacement of thatch by other materials partly because it ended the diversion to roofs of straw required for the midden.[22] It was this preoccupation with manure, and therefore with yards, that determined the basic pattern of the Hanoverian farmstead. For into the yards went straw, into the stockbuildings around them went hay, straw and roots. Out of the yards and buildings came manure to join the straw litter which the cattle confined in the yards were trampling into more manure. The yards were as central to the farming system as they were to the farmstead which surrounded them.

Essentially, this type of farmstead consisted of three parts. The first was the barn in which corn from the stackyard was threshed and from which straw was distributed. The second was the collection of livestock buildings, including buildings for workbeasts, in which straw and hay were processed into manure. The third was the yard, formed by the barn and the livestock

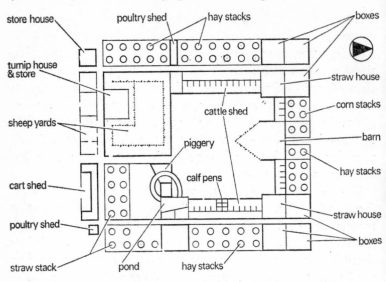

8   The first advisory drawing of a model farmstead, published in 1770. It contains various unusual or impracticable features but illustrates the general layout
so typical of the time (see p 111)

buildings, where stock exercised and manure accumulated.
This functional relationship was described with classic brevity
in a publication of the Board of Agriculture. 'The fodder consumed on the farm goes progressively forward from the barnyard through the cattle to the dunghill, without the unnecessary
labour generally occasioned by carrying it backwards and for-
wards,' while the hay stacked behind the cattle buildings ,'followed the same progressive course to the dunghill.'[23] And then,
in due course, the dung was carted to the fields to grow the corn
which returned to the barn and so continued the cycle of farmstead operations.

So the farmsteads of this period took the form of a series of
buildings round open yards, sometimes in a square, but more
usually on three sides of a square, some with one yard forming a
U-pattern, some with two yards forming an E-pattern. The
farmhouse, commonly to the south of the main steading, completed this agricultural factory. On dairy farms it housed the
substantial, stone-floored dairies where, with laborious tradi-

tional skills, the farmer's wife, daughters and maidservants processed milk into butter or cheese.[24] On all well-planned farms it was sited to allow the farmer a good view of the buildings, for 'servants and stock cannot be too much under the eye of the master'.[25] An improved system of farming was demanding a higher standard of management and supervision.

The yards faced south to catch the sun and avoid some at least of the rain-bringing south-west winds. They were sheltered on the north by the most substantial building on the farm, the barn—on larger farms by two or three barns, ideally one for each type of grain—and by the north-facing sheds for carts and implements whose timber required protection from sun and rain alike. Into these barns from the rickyard to the north of them came corn for threshing and winnowing on the central floor, out of them came grain, which was generally stored either in a small separate building on staddles to protect it from climbing vermin, or in a room over the cartshed. From here, too, came straw for littering the various livestock buildings and, above all, the yards. From this north range and at right-angles to it ran the wings which formed the yards and contained a medley of buildings, some of them for storage, but most of them for livestock, and preferably arranged in accordance with this need for straw. Fattening cattle, which required most straw, stood nearest to the barn, then young cattle, and finally cows, working oxen and horses, the latter commonly in stables facing east to catch light of the early morning sun. Pigs, housed in the familiar pen-and-run sties which had now become standard practice, lived near the farmhouse because they depended on dairy and household by-products, as did poultry because they were the concern of the farmer's wife. Convenient to the cattle-yards, sometimes in a barn, sometimes in stacks, stood the hay-store. In its combination of arable buildings and livestock buildings the Hanoverian farmstead proclaimed the nature of the mixed farming system it served.

On the larger farms this simple pattern was complicated by the variety of enterprises and functions it was required to include. Sheep housing, for instance, was now seldom practised, but

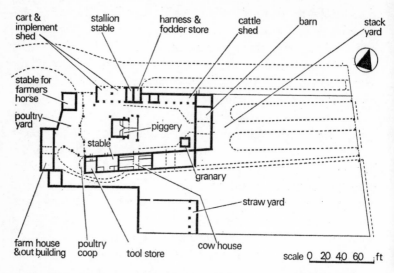

9 The first contemporary plan of a new farmstead, published in 1783. This steading was built in 1775 to serve a 500-acre farm at Croydon (see p 111)

yards and sheds for the flock were still found on some farms—for instance, Ellman of Glynde, the creator of the modern Southdown, used to house his ewes in bad weather.[26] Then there was a miscellany of minor buildings, many of them semi-domestic, such as the henhouse, the nag stable for the farmer's riding-horse, housing for his gig, a cider press in apple-growing areas, and sometimes a workshop, a forge or a slaughterhouse. Thus, the steading of a 600-acre Norfolk farm of the period contained no less than fifty-five buildings, apart from the farm-house.[27] This was, of course, exceptional and a number of them served the household rather than the farm. But the figure illustrates in an extreme form the multiplicity of the demands made on the farmstead by the farming system of the Agricultural Revolution. In only one respect did the new order reduce the number of minor buildings the farmer might require. The new fodder crops, which had ended the need for autumnal culling and with it the diet of salt beef to which pigeon-pie provided so welcome a relief, greatly reduced the importance of the dovecote. Many farms continued to keep pigeons as domestic assets but their economic value was now negligible.[28]

Many of these minor buildings, however, were in the nature of 'optional extras'. They did not affect the general patterns of north range and south-facing yards which throughout those years were universally familiar and universally accepted. There were, of course, an infinity of differences to meet local needs, local circumstances and the different sizes and types of farm. At one end of the scale, the buildings of small dairy farms in Cheshire were catalogued in the 1770s in terms of 'cowhouse for six cattle, stable, three-bay barn with a carthouse'; a 'good old timber barn, stable and cowtyeing for fifteen cattle'; and 'a very low, mean old barn, six feet on the wall with cowtyeing, altogether five bays, and a little stable for two horses'.[29] The buildings of a typical Cumberland farm in the next generation were similarly listed as 'a barn, a byre for housing cattle in winter, and a small stable'.[30] At the other end of the scale, the steadings of the large farms in southern England were described as 'magnificent series of buildings, stables, cowhouses, granaries or barns . . . mixed with smaller habitations for pigs, dogs and poultry',[31] those in the Holderness area, more succinctly, as 'small villages'.[32] Between these extremes stood such steadings as the 'two barns, a good stable, cowhouse, woodhouse, yard and garden and a carthouse or hayhouse' which in the 1750s served a 153-acre farm 'pleasantly situated near Hendon Church,[33] the 'barn, stable, cowhouse, carthouse and hoghouse' of a 250-acre farm in Suffolk in 1774,[34] the 'three barns, two stables, cartshed and cowhouse' of a Sussex farm twenty years later[35] or, more generally, the 'barn with two floors, the stable, oxhouse, cowhouse and carthouse which constituted every necessity of most Dorset farms'.[36] But all these were no more than variations on a central theme. The hypothetical farmsteads shown in the advisory writings of the time, the new farmsteads described by the Board of Agriculture's surveyors in counties as different as Berkshire, Dorset, Lancashire, Northumberland and Yorkshire, all alike were virtually interchangeable.[37]

Never before had farmstead design been so consciously

standardised. The differences in detail were great; but so also was the similarity in principle. There were, of course, exceptions, such as the longhouse-type steadings with dwelling-house, cow-house and barn all under one roof built to serve the small farms created when Macclesfield Common was reclaimed between 1796 and 1804.[38] There were also local developments like the two-storey 'bank barns' built into a hillside and housing live-stock on the ground floor and hay on the first floor with access at both levels which appeared in certain northern counties.[39] But such deviations were rare. Even in Wales, where longhouses were still in common use, the new pattern was taken for granted on the larger farms. 'To give a description of (the new farm-steads)', wrote the Board of Agriculture's surveyor for South Wales in 1814, 'would be useless, as they are on plans and principles known and adopted in every part of the kingdom where improvements have taken place; that is, a main body or corn barn having a tangent wing at each end for stables, cow-tyes, open sheds, etc, the yard opening to the milder points, the south or the south-east.'[40] In due process of time the systematic plan of many Hanoverian farmsteads was obscured by additions and alterations until they came to resemble the disorderly accretions condemned by their designers. Yet the strength of the tradition thus formalised was shown over a century later when an assessment of farm building needs after the Second World War started with the justified assumption that 'the ordinary farm building layout in England is generally three or four sides of a quadrangle with offshoots'.[41] You cannot go far in the modern countryside without seeing something of the standardised creations of our tireless great-grandfathers, the masterful men of the Agrarian Revolution.

OUTLYING BUILDINGS

Nevertheless, there were some conspicuous and interesting exceptions to these general rules. For example, not all new buildings stood in the central farmstead. On the larger farms, notably those in Hampshire and Wiltshire which included reclaimed downland, it was often economic to winter bullocks in outlying fields to save the carriage of manure from distant yards.[42] There must have been a good many reports in this period like the survey of a 1,000-acre farm in Hampshire which, in 1799, recommended the building on a distant part of the farm of 'a cottage for a carter and a shepherd, a good barn and stable and a fold' to serve land 'which at this time lies too far from home to receive a due return in manure for its produce' and make possible further reclamation of the furze-covered Downs.[43] Such arguments produced the small muck-factories of yard and barn, sometimes including a cottage, sometimes dependent on daily visits from the stockman, which still stand in isolation on so many chalk uplands as witnesses to the reclaiming energies of our forefathers in the last age of the moving agricultural frontier.[44]

INTENSIVE LIVESTOCK HOUSING

Then, too, familiar types of farmstead sometimes contained such unfamiliar but prophetic types of building as the various housing systems designed to serve the intensive livestock enterprises which had arisen in certain areas. Among these were the slatted-floor calfpens of the Gloucestershire veal rearers, in which close confinement secured warmth and guarded against dispersal of expensively acquired flesh by excessive playfulness;[45] the pens in Essex which 'fitted a pig as near as may be' so that it could not waste energy by turning round;[46] the long, narrow, well-strawed houses on farms round London in which lambs were fattened for the Christmas market by ewes turned in at night;[47] and the yards where Herefordshire farmers housed their sheep in winter and sometimes in summer as well to make manure, for their arable land[48]—all representing different applications of the same principle. More radically, in these years a new type of raw material made possible the general intensification of a traditional type of livestock enterprise and therefore made necessary changes in traditional methods of livestock housing. The raw material was oilcake, a by-product of the oilseed-crushing industry, which began to be used as stockfeed in the later eighteenth century. This protein-rich concentrate not only fattened cattle more efficiently than the traditional fodders but also greatly increased the value of the residual manure, so that the farmer who purchased it improved the fertility of his fields as well as the performance of his stock. So began the development of systems of stalls or boxes for the intensive winter-fattening of cattle which the new cake made profitable.

Sometimes these were installed in existing buildings. Sometimes, however, new, special-purpose fattening houses were built to exploit the new possibilities. As early as 1771, for instance, Young noted near Retford 'a most complete oxhouse' for twenty-six beasts with mangers served from outside the house, a water supply and a room for storing and breaking the cake, which reached the farm in oblong slabs an inch thick, into manageable pieces.[49] A generation later, enterprising farmers, like Adam of Mount Nod in Surrey, were fattening several hundred head in buildings 'constructed with great regard to convenience'.[50] New materials created new systems of production, new systems of production called into existence new types of building and, on occasion, new types of equipment suitable for more intensive enterprises—the first reference to a weighing-machine on the farm comes from a description of a fattening house in 1805.[51] The process will become increasingly familiar.

There was, however, particular as well as general prophecy in this development. At first, the cake came from English factories. Later, it was imported from America—the removal of the duty on foreign oilcake in the 1790s was one of the few political achievements of the Board of Agriculture.[52] Thus was foreshadowed the coming a century later of an unprecedented agricultural partnership in which the home farmer provided buildings and livestock, and the overseas producer the steady supply of concentrate foodstuffs which passed through the farmstead to emerge as meat, milk and manure.

But this was for the remote future. In George III's time, the livestock on the farmstead depended for all but a very small proportion of their rations on the surrounding fields. Nevertheless, a more specialised system was already well advanced in the towns. Indeed, in this period the true home of intensive livestock husbandry was not in the countryside but in London.

There were two main types of livestock enterprise in the capital, on the one hand the urban dairy herds on which the townsman depended for his milk, on the other the cattle and pigs which fattened on the starchy waste-products of the brewing and distilling industries. Neither system was new. Cows had been kept in city streets ever since urban expansion separated their inhabitants from dairy farms, while distillers were undercutting pig farmers in contracts for supplying the Navy with pork in the first half of the eighteenth century.[53] But both reached new peaks of importance in this period. Indeed, Regency London, with its 8,500 dairy cows and its annual output of more than 50,000 pigs[54] and an unspecified but considerable number of fat cattle, was a major centre of livestock production.

The dairy cows, nearly half of which were concentrated in the Paddington, Tottenham Court Road, Battlebridge and Grays Inn Lane areas, spent their milking life tethered in stalls from which they were let out into yards for water and exercise for three or four hours a day until the time came for slaughter. In general, sanitary conditions among these 'wretched beasts housed in dark sheds or hovels, standing ankle deep in filth' were indescribably bad.[55] So were the standards and methods of cleaning the dairy utensils. So was the quality of their milk by the time it reached the customer, frequently in adulterated form.[56]

Away in Glasgow, it is true, William Harley showed that good housing and good management could produce clean milk in the middle of an industrial city. When he found he could not obtain clean milk for the invalids who frequented his public baths from cows herded 'in narrow lanes and confined corners', he turned cowkeeper and evolved the first modern cowhouse of which record has survived. By 1814 he was milking 300 head in a huge shed of the familiar modern double-range type, complete

with feeding-passages, ventilation system and a dairy with
equipment for the steam sterilisation of utensils. His cowhouse
was one of the sights of the town; but it was a long, long time
before the standards of the 'Harleian system' became normal
practice.[57]

The London fattening houses, run as subsidiaries of substantial manufacturing firms, were far better built and better
managed than the London cowhouses. Even such potential
nuisances as mass-production piggeries with an output of 3,000
head a year won only praise from the Board of Agriculture's
surveyors. The pigs, they reported, were 'kept with all imaginable care . . . no pains were spared to keep them clean and
sweet, which the superior construction of their very extensive
premises enables (the distillers) to do'.[58] Little information about
such 'extensive premises' has survived, though it is clear that
their size was considerable, their design advanced. Thus,
Messrs Hodgson & Co, distillers, of Battersea, erected a range
of ox-houses 600ft long and 32ft wide, each housing two rows of
individually stalled cattle separated by a feeding passage, and
attempted to provide them with slatted floors which allowed the
cattle to lie dry and clean on 'open trellises or gratings' held a
few inches off the ground by blocks, the dung being removed
from below by hoe. The attempt was unsuccessful and injuries
to the beasts' feet compelled the replacement of this system by
brick flooring.[59] But the experiment is interesting as an example
of the contribution which men outside the traditional farming
economy were beginning to make to the development of farm
buildings.[60]

More generally, the intensive systems of the towns probably
contributed to contemporary interest in the possibilities of
making more intensive use of the buildings on conventional
farms. The practice of 'soilage', of cutting and carting green
fodder to permanently-housed cattle which never set foot in a
field, was inherent in urban dairy enterprises. It was now considered for dairy herds on normal farms, and trials inspired by
the Board of Agriculture concluded that it was more profitable
to keep cows in houses and feed them there than to pasture them

page 87 (*above*) An early eighteenth-century Welsh longhouse. The lower building on the right is a later addition. Since this photograph was taken, this building has been re-erected at the Welsh Folk Museum, St Fagan's Castle, Cardiff (see Fig 6); (*below*) the heading of a 203-acre Middlesex farm in 1715 seen from the south. It was built of timber and tiled roofs and consisted of barns and livestock buildings round a yard. This is the first extant contemporary picture of an English farmstead

The Farm house, B Stables, C Barnes.

Page 88 (above) A stable range on a Hampshire farm built in 1838; (below) a Norfolk barn built between 1776 and 1837 by Thomas Coke, whose initials in iron can still be seen

in fields.[61] Despite such encouraging evidence, this system failed to establish itself on any scale in the countryside, though in some areas it was used for horses in summertime.[62] But the discussion foreshadowed the future development of intensive methods of livestock production and the part that buildings played in them, even as a visionary reference of the time to the use of wheeled stockhouses on iron railways to bring the cattle to the fields which provided their soilage foreshadowed the mechanisation which helped to make such systems possible.[63]

EXPERIMENTS, INNOVATIONS AND IMPROVEMENTS

Such railways were never built. Neither, apparently, was the 'improved granary'—which today would be described as an aerated grain silo—proposed by Sir John Sinclair.[64] Nevertheless, the importance of such unrealised dreams was considerable, for they illustrate the search for improvement which was so characteristic of the age. This produced such minor but useful developments as the provision of 'fother rooms' in stockbuildings for the collection of seeds from the hay stored there,[65] a 'chequer-board' floor which allowed calves to lie dry,[66] and the increased use of staddles to protect cornstacks from rats and mice.[67] It also inspired, more ambitiously, the first general attempt to develop new types of building by trial and error on the farm. We hear, for instance, of such innovations as a cattle-shed based on a north German model,[68] a movable barn built for one of the royal farms at Windsor,[69] an 'umbrella for covering haystacks'[70] and experiments with new forms of all-under-one-roof steadings,[71] and circular or polygonal designs.[72] None of these novelties established themselves in general practice, but the spirit which produced them succeeded in adding to the farmstead repertoire the prototypes of two of the most familiar of all modern farm buildings.

The first of these was the thatched timber skeleton which later developed into the metallic Dutch barn. The idea from which these simple structures were developed had reached this country in Elizabethan times, but it was not until the later years

F

of George III that they were widely used by farmers who found a permanent shelter a better proposition than the seasonal thatch-ing of haystacks and cornricks.[73] The second was the cowhouse which, in the later years of this period, changed on the better farms from a crude hovel to a recognisable version of its modern design. The process was gradual and piecemeal but, item by item, the familiar component parts made their appearance; sloping standings, chain-ties and divisions between cows, inter-nal water supplies, feeding passages and dung-channels flowing to grated outlets. In plan and section, though not in construc-tion, the improved cowhouse of 1820 differed little from its successors of our own time.[74]

NEW NEEDS AND PROBLEMS

Such novelties, however, were exceptional, and the main theme of this period was the universal agreement on the general plan which all properly designed farmsteads should follow. Unfortunately, this was accompanied by equally universal agreement on the general failure of existing farmsteads to meet the demands which the farming system made on them. Young's references in 1770[75] to cows without cowhouses, carts and im-plements without shelter and steadings without central yards, were repeated with variations and expansions throughout the series of *County Reports* which the Board of Agriculture issued in the following generation. Stabling for horses was the only type of building seldom mentioned by these critics. Presumably the proud place of the riding-horse in the life of the time and the immediate effect of poor conditions on the performance of animals on which the farm depended for its day-to-day work combined to encourage the provision of proper housing.[76] Apart from this, however, condemnation was general. Agricultural change had brought great benefits. But it also brought great problems, in particular, a problem which from this time on-wards forms a permanent part of the history of farm buildings.

This problem is predictable and was inevitable. Since farm buildings serve farm needs, changes in farm needs necessarily precede changes in farm buildings. Consequently, as it is quicker to apply new systems of growing plants and raising animals than to build or rebuild, there is bound to be a certain interval between the development of a new need and the creation of buildings to meet it. This interval can be controlled, sometimes almost eliminated, by foresight. More commonly, it is prolonged on owner-occupied farms by the farmer's instinctive preference for investment in directly productive cropland and stock rather than in indirectly productive fixed equipment; on tenanted farms by the inevitable delay between realisation of a need and provision of a means of meeting it. But such attitudes merely increase the consequences of a difficulty inherent in any period of agricultural change.

No doubt similar difficulties arose in earlier times, but it was only in this period that they became sufficiently important to enter the written record. For the changes brought by the Agricultural Revolution were unprecedented in speed and scope and they made unprecedented demands on the farmstead. The point was neatly illustrated by the new doors cut in the massive walls of Buckland Abbey barn in 1792 'with a labour nearly equal to that of cutting solid rock'. For the barn dated from the days of 'packhorse husbandry', when corn was brought from the hilly harvest fields on horseback, and the doors sufficient for such primitive transport were not sufficient for the waggons of a later age.[77] More generally, contemporary condemnation of the wastage of manure on ill-planned steadings[78] and the 'pernicious' practice of wintering cattle in fields to the detriment of soil and animals alike because there were insufficient yards to house them,[79] reflected the inability of the agricultural partnership in their capacity as farmstead-builders to keep pace with the needs they were creating in their capacity as producers of crops and stock. The new steadings they built required periodical improvement. The old steadings they inherited required more drastic modernisation. But the difference was one of degree, not of principle.

In the abstract, a continuous process of reconstruction is the only conclusive answer to this problem, but for obvious reasons this is no more than a dream of ultimate efficiency. In practice, the landowners and farmers of Hanoverian times, like their successors, contented themselves with more modest, less radical remedies. They built anew when they could, but it is probable that throughout these years the building of new farmsteads was matched by the adaptation of old farmsteads to new needs, sometimes by the addition of new buildings, sometimes by more comprehensive schemes of replanning and reconstruction.

There is little evidence from which to estimate the extent of this practice, which is essentially a matter of piecemeal change in individual farmsteads and so makes little impression on historical literature.[80] But it is certainly suggestive that the first recorded 'before and after' case-study of such change dates from this period and was used by Charles Waistell, a highly practical agriculturist, to demonstrate the benefits that could be secured by the rational re-arrangement of farm buildings. He described the remodelling, apparently about 1820, of a sprawling old Surrey farmstead to which buildings had been added over the generations 'with no regard whatever to the situation of previously existing conveniences'. An unwanted barn was removed, new livestock accommodation, a waggonshed and a granary were built, and particular enterprises, and therefore particular types of work, were concentrated in particular areas. This reconstruction enabled the farm to carry more stock and the farmer to run his farm with less effort. In general, these benefits were secured not by the development of a new system but by the literal reformation of an existing one. The change did, however, include one technical novelty, a new intensive fattening shed for cake-fed cattle. This example, with its mixture of reorganisation and modernisation, provides a useful introduction to a continuing theme in farmstead development.[81]

MACHINERY COMES TO THE FARMSTEAD

A more spectacular sign of the changing times was the appearance of machinery on the farmstead. This began, innocently enough, with the development in the later eighteenth

century of small, hand-driven machines for cutting hay and
straw into chaff to reduce wastage by cattle at feeding-time, for
grinding corn and beans for livestock, and for winnowing by a
system of sails on radial arms which replaced the wind on which
the farmer had previously relied to separate grain from cav-
ings.[82] Such simple forms of barn machinery could be installed
with little difficulty in existing buildings, for they required no
more than minor alterations in working routines. But they were
followed by a more drastic change, the mechanisation of threshing, which, in due course, brought to the farmstead the unprecedented and revolutionary factor of inorganic power.
From this time onwards, it is buildings rather than men which
rearrange themselves around the new equipment.

The process of technical evolution, however, was gradual.
The earlier eighteenth century had seen various attempts to
mechanise threshing, one of the dreariest and most unhealthy
chores of the farming year, by harnessing manpower, water-
power or literal horse-power to equipment which imitated the
action of the human flailer. But it was not until 1786 that
Andrew Meikle, a Scots millwright, hit upon the sounder principle that is still in use today. He built a drum fitted with pegs
which revolved in a concave cover and rubbed and beat the
grain off the straw as it turned. The grain fell into a container
and the straw was carried away.[83] His invention spread rapidly
and within twenty years mechanical threshing had become
established practice in most areas. By 1800, 'common wrights'
in Yorkshire villages were beginning to make threshing
machines,[84] and in a few years time the official surveyor of
Northamptonshire 'wondered much' at their absence from his
county.[85]

Some of these installations were driven by horses, some by
water—readers of the delightful *Carrington Diary* will remember
Mr Deacon of Tewin Bury who, in the early 1800s, 'turned the
river by his wheat barn through the farme yarde for a thrashing
macheen'.[86] But a few were driven by steam; and here was a
portent indeed. For this was the first time that man-made
mechanical power entered the farmstead and its appearance

marked the first definite break with the older tradition of rural self-sufficiency. The principles which the steam-engine incorporated, the fuel it consumed, and the technical knowledge required for its operation all came from the rising industrial economy that lay beyond the farm gate. It had no ancestors on the farm. But it had many descendants there.[87]

In the early 1800s, however, the future of steam-power on the farm was a matter for speculation, the implications of mechanical threshing presenting more immediate questions. The most obvious was the development of a new type of barn, smaller than its predecessors and differently sited. For the threshing machine required less working height than the swinging flails and could keep pace with a steady flow of sheaves from the rickyard, thus making unnecessary the storage of unthreshed corn in the barn. Further, the chain of operations it involved required for full efficiency a building standing with one end towards the stackyard and the other towards the cattleyard, whereas the older order needed a building which lay lengthways between them. Change in farmstead methods implied change in farmstead structures.

Arthur Young, that percipient agricultural journalist, saw all this clearly. With his accustomed enthusiasm, he proclaimed that the mechanical thresher 'promised speedily to put an end to all barn building'[88]—an over-simplified thought which a more cautious colleague rightly and amusingly modified to the probability that 'the gradual introduction of the threshing machine will render barns of the present size and number less necessary'[89]—and even foresaw the development of wheeled frames on iron rails to carry the stacks of corn to the thresher.[90] His appreciation of the opportunities offered by the new technique and their consequences was equally prophetic, and his suggestion that the prime-mover which drove the threshing machine should be harnessed to food-preparation equipment developed into one of the most penetrating paragraphs in the agricultural literature of the time. 'The position of the threshing mill,' he wrote in 1809, 'decides that of every other building, for it cuts, or ought to cut, all the hay of the farm into chaff, with much of the straw; and the house that immediately receives the chaff must be so placed as to admit a convenient delivery to the stables, stalls and sheepyards. Thus the straw-house, chaff-house, stables, stalls, haystacks and sheepyard must be placed in consequence of the position of the threshing-mill, or waste and expense of labour must follow.'[91] Here was the first conscious statement of the principle that farm buildings are coverings for farm processes and that their relationship is determined by the demands of these processes. Young's understanding of contemporary change enabled him to see more clearly than any other man of his time the line of future farmstead development.

Indeed, he saw too far and too fast. The farmers for whom he wrote were content with the immediate benefits of the new technique, the saving of time and money, the reduced wastage of corn, the end of reliance on unreliable hand-labour, the ability to market their crop earlier, and they found it easier to fit the machine into the buildings than to adapt the buildings to the improved system made possible by the machine. In general, they replaced flail threshing by mechanical threshing and made little systematic attempt to secure the full advantages of the new process. Young was not the only official to comment sadly that most threshing machines stood in the barn where the flailers had worked, not because the barn was the right place for it but because it was there.[92]

The point is worth emphasis. The farmers who adopted mechanical threshing were not stupid men. On the contrary, they were among the most advanced and informed in the industry. But they were too preoccupied with the demands of their crops and stock to do more than meet an immediate problem with an immediate answer. It was simpler and, at least in the short run, obviously cheaper to put the new machine in the old barn than to plan a general rearrangement of the whole farmstead. Even in new sets of buildings it was all too easy to follow the old traditions with mere minor adaptations. For instance, Waistell's model plans, published just after the end of this period, show barns specifically designed and sited for mechanical threshing. But, apparently, few such barns were built, though the new technique produced one of the few distinctive regional types of building—as opposed to regional variations of general types—which appeared in these years. This was the 'gin gang' of the northern counties, a small round, square or polygonal building which stood next to the barn and sheltered the driving gear of the threshing machine and the circumambulatory horse which powered it.[93] But, on the whole, the men of the time fitted the machine to the buildings, not the buildings to the machine. Their agricultural experience had not prepared them to grasp the full implications or to exploit the full possibilities of the new technology.

THE END OF AN OLD TRADITION

Here were the beginnings of radical change. But it is more obvious to later generations than it was to the men of the time and throughout most of this period the old assumptions continued.

Thus in 1770, Arthur Young, in his advice to prospective tenants, contented himself with listing the familiar principles of good farmstead planning and adding hints on the points of detail which made the difference between a good and a bad steading. The barn, for instance, should be floored not with clay but with oak plank, which gave a better and brighter sample of grain; the granary should contain sufficient space for the storage of two harvests lest the farmer be compelled to sell on a poor market; and the yard should be bottomed with stone or gravel and served by a pond.[94]

Similarly, in 1776 Nathaniel Kent wrote a manual of estate management called *Hints to Gentleman of Landed Property*. Out oɪ a total of 282 pages, only thirteen were devoted to farm buildings, and even there he contented himself with a few casual hints on materials and maintenance. Twenty-eight years later, William Marshall wrote his comprehensive treatise, *On the Landed Property of England*, which allotted no more than half a chapter to 'the laying-out of the homestall'. For these writers, like their contemporaries, took it for granted that a general knowledge of farming practice and a particular knowledge of local building lore would enable anyone with commonsense to deal adequately with farm buildings problems and the first specialist publication on the subject to appear in this country, a volume issued by the Board of Agriculture in 1796, accepted these pre-suppositions without question. It made a desultory attempt to provide a general exposition of the type familiar in later textbooks, but was clearly much more concerned with the various unproven ideas for improvement it propounded than with the systematic analysis of progressive existing practice.[95]

Such assumptions were reasonable when Young wrote, less reasonable when Marshall wrote, for men faced with the necessity of reorganising farmsteads to meet the implications of a mechanical threshing required something more than traditional wisdom. New developments demanded new sources of information, new skills, new types of approach, and these were slow in coming.

It was indeed typical of the age that the major improvements in the most complicated farm structure then in use, the oasthouse, owed nothing to the engineer. They were the work partly of a gardener who used his experience of hothouse flues to improve the drying system and his knowledge of building to replace the rectangular by the cheaper circular design, and partly of the forgotten growers and their handymen who, about the turn of the century, developed the pivoted wooden cowls which later became a typical feature of the hop-growing landscape.[96] The old order still reigned. But the days when the knowledge the farm taught would no longer be sufficient to answer all the questions the farm raised were not so very far ahead.

This period certainly saw the problem stated. Wedge's suggestion in the 1790s that the Board of Agriculture should sponsor the publication of farmstead plans 'in which utility, economy and neatness might be equally consulted'[97] illustrated the inadequacy of traditional sources to meet it and there must have been many besides Waistell who in these years tried in vain to obtain 'satisfactory information from books for arranging and executing (agricultural buildings) such as were required'.[98] It produced no general remedy, but the time was coming when the art and science of equipping a farm with efficient buildings would cease to be a normal part of the agricultural trade and become something of a specialist's job. The self-sufficient rural technology of the older order was nearing its end, and the coming of the machine to the farmstead was one of the first clear breaks with this ancient tradition.

Nevertheless, this tradition was still dominant and, typically, the standardisation of the principles of farmstead planning in this period was not parallelled by the standardisation of farmstead construction which still reflected the physical variety of the English countryside. For the builder's dependence on local products continued, and even the tar used in Hampshire came as a by-product from the local manufacture of gunpowder.[99] The continuing assumption that 'the materials of which a building is made must depend on local circumstances'[100] is illustrated by the materials listed in contemporary discussion of the best forms of construction for that crucial section of the barn, the threshing floor: oak embedded in masonry,[101] timber on a layer of flints or cinders,[102] flagstones from the 'argillaceous hills',[103] and a mixture of earth, clay, and dung beaten and rolled till it was 'solid, hard and firm'.[104] The only manufactured material mentioned was brick;[105] and bricks were made of clay from nearby pits and fired in nearby kilns. More generally, the common arrangement whereby the landlord provided building materials, such as timber in the rough, for his tenants' repairs, recognised that he would have little difficulty in finding them within the bounds of his estate.

Nevertheless, the *County Reports* show a marked change in the choice of the particular local materials used. Brick and stone, where available, were beginning to oust the cruder forms of construction and a number of the county surveyors contrasted the older buildings of timber, wattle-and-daub and thatch and the new ones of brick or stone and tiles.[106] There were signs, too, of more drastic changes to come, for new forms of manufactured equipment were beginning to make their appearance in the farmstead; milled lead as a substitute for ridge tiles, iron plates for long-life mangers,[107] lead for drinking troughs,[108] metal eaves, gutters and drainpipes to replace the hollowed fir poles or the more primitive rods sometimes used to carry water away from the eaves.[109] Slates, too, were becoming more common as the new canals carried them to unfamiliar areas.[110] But as yet this was little more than prophecy. The particular hope expressed in 1800 by the official surveyor for the North Riding that the canal being built between York and Stillington would carry building materials[111] did not receive general fulfilment until the next age brought that more revolutionary and more pervading form of transport which symbolised the coming of a new technological age.

NOTES

1. For a review of the evidence now available on these changes, see Jones, E. L. *Agriculture and economic growth*, 1967, pp 1–49, 152–72

2. Trow-Smith, R. *A history of British livestock husbandry, 1700–1900*, 1959, pp 8–9. In 1812, 'summer dwellings' were still used seasonally in Caernarvonshire. (Thomas, D. *Agriculture in Wales during the Napoleonic Wars*, 1963, p 179.) This was an unusual survival. Half a century later, a visitor counted the ruins of eight such dwellings on the Llanllechid mountains in this county. (Peate, I. C. *The Welsh house*, 1944, p 127.)

3. Trow-Smith, R. *A history of British livestock husbandry to 1700*, 1957, p 258

4. Pawson, H. C. *Robert Bakewell*, 1957, p 23

5. Lowe, R. *General view of the agriculture of Nottinghamshire*, 1798, p 8.

6. Plymley, J. *General view of the agriculture of Shropshire*, 1803, p 102

7. Davies, W. *General view of the agriculture of South Wales*, 1814, vol 1, p 129–30

8. Davis, T. *General view of the agriculture of Wiltshire*, 1811, p 9

9. Waistell, C. *Designs for agricultural buildings*, 1827, pp 10–11

10. Pitt, W. *General view of the agriculture of Northampton*, 1809, p 275; Hoskins, W. G. *Leicestershire*, 1957, p 99

11. Wedge, T. *General view of the agriculture of the county palatine of Chester*, 1794, p 12; Pringle, A. *General view of the agriculture of the county of Westmorland*, 1805, p 300

12. Sometimes, however, their names betray their origins. The most conspicuous instances of this are the various Waterloo Farms, while such names as Down, Warren or Newbarn Farm recall the reclamation of chalk and other uplands which was such a feature of this period. (Jones, E. L. 'Eighteenth century changes in Hampshire chalkland farming', *Agricultural History Review*, vol 8, pt 1, 1960, p 15.) Detailed local studies would probably produce other less obvious but equally interesting cases. Thus, Hoskins found in Leicestershire a Quebec, a Belle Isle and a Hanover Farm, as well as the less auspicious New York Farm and Bunkers Hill Farm. (Hoskins, W. G. *Leicestershire*, 1957, p 99.)

13. A survey of a village in Berkshire showed that a third of the cottages were originally the homes of Open Field farmers (Havinden, M. *Estate villages*, 1966, p 23.) Presumably similar surveys of other villages in arable areas would produce comparable figures. A study of the surviving farm buildings of such old steadings would make a valuable addition to agricultural literature. But it should be undertaken soon. Few are left and the number is decreasing every year.

14. In this period the use of woodland and scrub for pigs seems to have come to an end except in the New Forest. (Trow-Smith, R. *A History of British livestock husbandry, 1700–1900*, 1959, p 218.) In Cheshire, in the early nineteenth century, the use of pigsties was regarded as an innovation (Davies, C. S. *The agricultural history of Cheshire, 1750–1850*, 1960, p 137.) Similarly, in Shropshire, a contemporary noted the need for pigsties. (Plymley, J. *General view of the agriculture of Shropshire*, 1803, p 108.) The necessary connection between milkhouse and pigsty was a commonplace of the time. 'From the dairy we are naturally led to the hogsty.' (Priest, St J. *General view of the agriculture of Buckinghamshire*, 1810, p 32.)

15. Young, A. *The Farmer's guide in hiring and stocking farms*, 1770, vol 1, p 49

16. Dickson, R. W. *General view of the agriculture of Lancashire*, 1814, pp 96–7. See also Morgan, G. B. *General view of the agriculture of Cornwall*, 1811, p 242 and Pitt, W. *General view of the agriculture of Staffordshire*, 1796, p 19. Similarly, Waistell, describing a Surrey farmstead before he remodelled it in the later years of this period, concluded that 'almost every building would have been placed in

some other situation than that in which it was found'. Yet he did not choose this farmstead to illustrate the extreme consequences of generations of casual building 'at six or seven different periods'. He had seen many farms in his time and knew that 'few ancient farm-yards were better, while many were worse arranged'. (Waistell, C. *Designs for agricultural buildings*, 1827, pp 103–7.)

17. Billingsley, J. *General view of the agriculture of Somerset*, 1798, p 203

18. Dickson, R. W. *General view of the agriculture of Lancashire*, 1814, p 645

19. Hassall, *General view of the agriculture of Monmouth*, 1812, p 25

20. Marshall, W. *The landed property of England*, 1804, p 159

21. Young, A. *General view of the agriculture of Hertfordshire*, 1804, p 21

22. Pitt, W. *General view of the agriculture of Staffordshire*, 1796, p 21; Hassall, C. *General view of the agriculture of Monmouth*, 1812, p 24; Farey, J. *General view of the agriculture of Derbyshire*, 1815, vol 2, p 12. There was also criticism of the tax on tiles which, by increasing their price, encouraged the use of thatch for roofing. (Young, A. *Annals of agriculture*, 1784, vol 2, pp 314–15; Billingsley, J. *General view of the agriculture of Somerset*, 1798, p 87.) In practice, of course, as Marshall pointed out, the straw used for thatching was eventually replaced and much of the old material found its way into the yards and so back to the fields. (*Rural economy of the southern counties*, 1798, vol 2, p 9.)

23. *Communications to the Board of Agriculture on farm buildings*, 1796, p 56

24. The importance of these farmhouse dairies is shown by the fiscal concessions granted to them. In 1795 an Act of Parliament (36 Geo 3 c 117) exempted their windows from Window Tax pro-vided they were made of wooden lathes or iron bars and 'Dairy' or 'Cheeseroom' was painted on the door 'in large roman black letters, of two inches at least in height, and of proportionate width'. In 1808 and 1817 further Acts (48 Geo 3 c 55 and 57 Geo 3 c 25) extended this concession to wire and glass windows respectively. The exemp-tion automatically ended when the Window Tax was abolished in 1851 (14 and 15 Vict c 36). (Personal communication from Mr T. R. F. Skemp.) Surviving examples of such inscriptions are men-tioned in Crump, W. B. 'The little hill farm', *Proceedings of the Halifax Antiquarian Society* vol 35, 1938, p 139; Wood, C. B. 'Fas-cinating houses', *Farmers Weekly*, vol 39, no 14, 2 October 1953, p 85; and Barley, M. W. *The English farmhouse and cottage*, 1961, p 262

25. Waistell, C. *Designs for agricultural buildings*, 1827, p 17

26. Trow-Smith, R. *A history of British livestock husbandry, 1700–1900*, 1959, p 128

27. Bacon, R. N. *Report on the agriculture of Norfolk*, 1844, pp 395–6

28. Dovecotes were still common, but they were no more than survivals from a past economic age. Board of Agriculture reporters emphasised the harm pigeons did to crops rather than the value of the meat and manure they produced (Boys, J. *General view of the agriculture of Kent*, 1805, p 188; Priest, St J. *General view of the agriculture of Buckinghamshire*, 1810, pp 38–40, 332), and in 1800 a writer proposed a tax on dovecotes to reduce the loss from pigeons, which he estimated ate enough grain to supply 100,000 people. (Robinson, D. H. 'A pigeon for the pot', *The Field*, vol 198, no 5146, 25 August 1951, p 298.)

29. Davies, C. S. *The agricultural history of Cheshire, 1750–1850*, 1960, pp 167–75

30. Bailey, J. and Culley, G. *General view of the agriculture of Cumberland*, 1805, p 208

31. Mitford, M. R. *Our village*, 1904, p 133

32. Head, Sir George, *Home tour through the manufacturing districts of England in 1835*, 1836, p 255; quoted in Harris A. *General landscape of the East Riding of Yorkshire, 1700–1850*, 1961, p 11

33. *Church Farm House*. A guide issued by the Borough of Hendon, 1962, p 3

34. Evans, G. E. *Ask the fellows who cut the hay*, 1956, p 83

35. Challen, W. H. 'Crypt Farm, Cocking', *Sussex Notes and Queries*, vol 16, November 1963, p 49

36. Claridge, J. *General view of the agriculture of Dorset*, 1793, p 31

37. This pervading similarity is interestingly illustrated by the conclusions of architectural students competing in 1952 for the Bannister Fletcher silver medal offered for an area study of pre-Victorian farmsteads. A typical Surrey steading was described by the prize-winner as a barn, a yard, a few open shelters for cattle and a granary; a typical Shropshire steading by another competitor as a barn, usually with a granary above, a yard, cattle shelters, a cart-shed, a few outbuildings and pigsties. (West, G. T. *Farm buildings in south-east Surrey*, 1952. In typescript in RIBA library, pp 10–11; Weller, J. B. *Farm buildings of Shropshire before 1837*, 1952, in typescript, kindly lent by the author, pp 12, 17.)

38. Davies, C. S. *The agricultural history of Cheshire, 1750–1880*, 1960, p 15. By this time the longhouse was forgotten in the lowlands. William Marshall expressed surprise at seeing 'an entire farmery

under one roof' in Yorkshire. (*The rural economy of Yorkshire*, 1788, vol 1, p 127.) Similarly a recent writer quoted a case in Shropshire of a farmstead of this period with granary, cowhouse and farmhouse all under one roof. But even in a county so near the longhouses of Wales, this was 'unusual'. (Weller, J. B. *Farm buildings of Shropshire before 1837*, 1952, in typescript, kindly lent by the author, p 12.)

39. Brunskill, R. W. *Design and layout of farmsteads in parts of Cumberland and Westmorland*, RIBA, Neale Bursary, 1963, Manchester, 1965, sect 6. Such buildings presumably continued in wholly agricultural form the tradition of the earlier, semi-domestic semi-agricultural buildings of the same general type. See footnote 17 to Chapter 3.

40. Davies, W. *General view of the agriculture of South Wales*, 1814, vol 1, p 129

41. Portsmouth, Earl of, 'The fixed equipment of the farm'. *Journal of the Royal Agricultural Society of England*, vol 107, 1946, p 100. A survey in Shropshire a few years later found 139 irregular, formless or abnormally-sited farmsteads. But of the 357 steadings of classifiable patterns, 181 were built on three sides of a square, 41 on four sides of a square. (Davies, D. C. G. *Historic farmstead and farmhouse types of the Shropshire region*, Manchester University MA thesis, 1952, p 88.)

42. Davis, T. *General view of the agriculture of Wiltshire*, 1811, p 10, 12; Jones, E. L. 'Eighteenth-century changes in Hampshire chalkland farming', *Agricultural History Review*, vol 8, pt 1, 1960, p 15

43. Milner, A. B. *The history of Micheldever*, 1924, pp 243–4

44. Pilkington, P. includes description of two of these secondary steadings, one over a mile from its homestead, in *Sussex Downland Farms*, a thesis on a survey of farm buildings in the Alfriston area submitted to the Architectural Association School of Architecture in 1962. Similar outlying steadings for wintering cattle were common in the Dales (Tuke, J. *General view of the agriculture of the North Riding of Yorkshire*, 1800, p 34), and in the Cumberland and Westmoreland uplands. No information on the age of the Yorkshire steadings is given but the latter, locally called 'field houses', were probably built between 1750 and 1850. (Brunskill, R. W. *Design and layout of farmsteads in parts of Cumberland and Westmorland*, RIBA Neale Bursary, 1963, Manchester, 1965, sect 7.)

45. Trow-Smith, R. *A history of British livestock husbandry, 1700–1900*, 1959, p 189

46. Young, A. *General view of the agriculture of Essex*, 1807, vol 2, p 343

47. Middleton, J. *General view of the agriculture of Middlesex*, 1813,

pp 46, 453–7. The breed used was the Dorset Horn, which is re-markable in that the ewes will take the ram practically the whole year round, thus making autumn lambing possible.

48. Trow-Smith, R. *A history of British livestock husbandry, 1700–1900*, 1959, pp 210–11

49. Young, A. *A Farmer's tour through the east of England*, 1771, vol I, pp 404–6

50. Stevenson, W. *General view of the agriculture of Surrey*, 1809, pp 523–4

51. Boys, J. *General view of the agriculture of Kent*, 1805, p 32. A little later Sir John Sinclair described a weighing-machine as 'an expensive article . . . but where it can be afforded of much conse-quence' in securing the proper rationing of fatstock. (*The code of agriculture*, 1821, p 136.)

52. Clarke, Sir Ernest. 'The Board of Agriculture, 1793–1822', *Journal of the Royal Agricultural Society of England*, 3rd ser, vol 9, 1898, p 19

53. Mathias, P. 'Agriculture and the brewing and distilling indus-tries in the eighteenth century'. *Economic History Review*, 2nd ser, vol 5, 1952/3, p 252

54. Middleton, J. *General view of the agriculture of Middlesex*, 1813, pp 417, 579

55. Drummond, J. C. *The Englishman's food*, 1957, p 193

56. Middleton, J. *General view of the agriculture of Middlesex*, 1813, pp 422–4

57. Harley, W. *The Harleian system*, 1829, passim

58. James, W. and Malcolm, J., *General view of the agriculture of Surrey*, 1794, pp 34–7

59. James, W. and Malcolm, J. *General view of the agriculture of Surrey*, 1794, pp 31–2; Stevenson, W. *General view of the agriculture of Surrey*, 1809, pp 522–3. This was not, however, the first reference to the use of slatted floors, which had been described nearly a century earlier as a traditional practice in oxstalls in Kent, where the urine was collected for manuring fruit trees. (Mortimer, J. *The whole art of husbandry*, 1721, pp 282–3.)

60. By the same token, Bakewell copied the dung channels in the floors of his bullock-fattening houses from the better type of London cowhouse. (Trow-Smith, R. *A history of British livestock husbandry, 1700–1900*, pp 55, 193.)

61. Curwen, J. C. *Hints on agricultural subjects*, 1809, pp 161–91; Sinclair, Sir John, *The code of agriculture*, 1821, p 487

62. Young, A. *General view of the agriculture of Hertfordshire*, 1804,

p 198; Young, A. *General view of the agriculture of Essex*, 1807, vol 2, pp 346–9

63. Adams, G. *A treatise upon a new system of agriculture*, 1810, passim.

64. Sinclair, Sir John. *The code of agriculture*, 1821, pp 150–1

65. Lowe, R. *General view of the agriculture of Nottinghamshire*, 1798, p 10

66. Young, A. *General view of the agriculture of Essex*, 1807, vol 1, p 46

67. Young, A. *General view of the agriculture of Essex*, 1807, vol 1, pp 47–8; Young A. *General view of the agriculture of Sussex*, 1808, p 20; Vancouver, C. *General view of the agriculture of Hampshire*, 1810, p 64

68. Mavor, W. *General view of the agriculture of Berkshire*, 1809, pp 68–9

69. Mavor, W. *General view of the agriculture of Berkshire*, 1809, p 69

70. King-Hele, O. G. 'The Lunar Society of Birmingham', *Nature*, vol 212, no 5059, 15 November 1966, p 231

71. Boys, J. *General view of the agriculture of Kent*, 1805, p 32; Morgan, G. *General views of the agriculture of Cornwall*, 1811, p 24

72. Such designs were common in that 'extraordinary flood' of expensive albums on *la ferme ornée* which appeared in the later years of this period. (Briggs, M. S. *The English farmhouse*, 1954, pp 199–203.) But these publications merely suggested picturesque accessories to tasteful homes for the nobility and gentry and form no part of agricultural history. There was, however, a limited agricultural interest in the possibilities of such unorthodox systems and the case for a polygonal farmstead was stated by William Marshall, one of the most practical farming writers of the time. (*The landed property of England*, 1804, pp 161–3.) He knew of no set of buildings constructed on this principle, though there was a semi-circular farmstead in Somerset in 1798 and a few years later an ambitious and intensive semi-circular piggery was built in Sussex. (Billingsley, J. *General view of the agriculture of Somerset*, 1798, p 88; Young, A. *General view of the agriculture of Sussex*, 1808, p 381.) Another Board of Agriculture surveyor, however, dealt harshly with designs 'fantastically planned in sweeps, semi-circles, octagons and pentagons. (Such plans) look pretty on paper but when you come to construct them a good deal of difficulty occurs in roofing and a great deal of room is thrown away which cannot be applied to any beneficial purpose.' (Hassall, C. *General view of the agriculture of Monmouth*, 1812; p 25.)

73. The ancestor of the Dutch barn was the 'hanging roof upon postes' that could be raised or lowered 'with pinnes and winches'

G

which Sir Hugh Plat noticed in Holland in the sixteenth century. He built such a barn on his farm in Hertfordshire and may possibly have founded a local tradition there, since Peter Kalm saw a similar type of building in the same area in 1748. (Fussell, G. E. 'Low Countries influence on English farming, *English Historical Review*, vol 74, 1959, p 621; see also Barley, M. W. 'Rural housing in England', *The agrarian history of England and Wales*, vol 4, 1967, p 744.) A little later, T. Lightoler showed such structures and described them as 'Dutch barns' in his wildly impractical album of farm building designs. (*Gentleman and farmer's friend*, 1774, plates 3, 22, 33.) By the early years of the next century, however, farmers had adopted a more practical type of design in which the cumbersome and relatively fragile adjustable roof was replaced by a fixed roof, and the 'open', 'skeleton' or 'Dutch' barn, similar in principle though not in construction to the most familiar of all buildings on the modern farm, was established practice in many parts of the country. (Marshall, W. *Rural economy of the southern counties*, Kent, 1798, vol 2, p 105; Young, A. *General view of the agriculture of Essex*, 1807, vol 1, p 48; Mavor, W. *General view of the agriculture of Berkshire*, 1809, p 69; Pitt, W. *General view of the agriculture of Staffordshire*, 1809, p 20; Gooch, W., *General view of the agriculture of Cambridgeshire*, 1811, p 30.) An example of one of these early Dutch barns is shown in *Country Life*, vol 117, no 3049, 23 June 1955, p 1683. A form of the original Dutch barn with a roof that could be lowered was re-invented early this century by a Warwickshire farmer, but this was no more than a curiosity. (Haggard, Rider H. *Rural England*, 1902, p 412.)

74. Fussell, G. E. *English dairy farmer*, 1966, p 141; Marshall, W. *Rural economy of the Midland counties*, 1790, p 32; Lowe, R. *General view of the agriculture of Nottinghamshire*, 1798, p 10; Marshall, W. *Rural economy of the West of England*, 1796, vol 2, pp 353–4; Priest, St J. *General view of the agriculture of Buckinghamshire*, 1810, pp 33–4; Waistell, C. *Designs for agricultural buildings*, 1827, pp 39–41

75. Young, A. *The farmer's guide in hiring and stocking farms*, 1770, vol 1, pp 51, 53, 54

76. The stable received curiously little attention in the literature of this period. Presumably contemporaries felt no need to comment on a building as familiar and uncontroversial as the modern garage unless some particular feature, such as the lack of divisions between the horses, caught their attention. (Stevenson, W. *General view of the agriculture of Surrey*, 1809, p 30; Murray, A. *General view of the agriculture of Warwickshire*, 1813, p 80.) For a summary of recommended practice at the end of this period see Waistell, C. *Designs for agricultural buildings*, 1827, pp 43–6

77. Marshall, W. *Rural economy of the West of England,* 1796, vol 2, pp 307–8

78. Mavor, W. *General view of the agriculture of Berkshire,* 1809, p 64; Rudge, T. *General view of the agriculture of Gloucestershire,* 1807, p 300; Batchelor, T. *General view of the agriculture of Bedfordshire,* 1808, p 19; and Dickson, R. *General view of the agriculture of Lancashire,* 1814, p 96

79. Young, A. *The farmer's guide to the hiring and stocking of farms,* 1770, vol 2, p 443. See also Pomeroy, W, *General view of the agriculture of Worcestershire,* 1794, pp 24–5; Billingsley, J. *General view of the agriculture of Somerset,* 1798, p 32; Murray, A. *General view of the agriculture of Warwickshire,* 1813, p 30; and Davies, W., *General view of the agriculture of South Wales,* 1814, vol 1, pp 131, 157

80. It did, however, produce the earliest recorded criticism of a farm building on artistic grounds, Wordsworth's denunciation of the 'huge, unsightly barn, built solely for convenience and violating all the modesty of rustic proportions' which Mr K., the substantial Leicestershire farmer who moved to the Lake District for such distressingly personal reasons, tactlessly built on his farm at Grasmere. (*Reminiscences of the English Lake Poets,* De Quincey, 1834, Everyman ed 1929, p 312.) Such standards of judgement would have been considered irrelevant or, more probably, perverse by his agricultural contemporaries who assessed their farmsteads solely in terms of 'convenience' and seldom considered their appearance a matter even worth mentioning in their professional literature.

81. Waistell, C. *Designs for agricultural buildings,* 1827, pp 103–7. William Marshall quotes an earlier case of farmstead improvement but gives few details and no plans. (*Rural economy of the Midland counties,* 1790, vol 2, pp 52–60.)

82. Fussell, G. E. *The farmer's tools,* 1952, pp 158–9, 180–2, 185

83. For the history of the static threshing machine see Fussell, G. E. *The farmer's tools,* 1952, pp 156–62, and the early sections of the unpublished thesis on *The New Bingfield Project* prepared in 1967 by the students of the Mechanical Engineering Department of Newcastle University.

84. Tuke, J. *General view of the agriculture of the North Riding of Yorkshire,* 1800, p 82

85. Pitt, W. *General view of the agriculture of Northamptonshire,* 1809, p 55

86. Branch-Johnson, W. *The Carrington Diary,* 1956, p 26

87. In 1798, Wilkinson, the ironmaster, used steam for threshing on his Denbighshire farm (Davies, W. *General view of the agriculture of North Wales,* 1810, p 122), and by 1810 a Durham quarry-owner had

harnessed for threshing an engine used for pumping water from his workings. (Bailey, J. *General view of the agriculture of Durham*, 1810, p 81.) A year later, Trevithick installed a steam threshing-machine in Cornwall (Coleman, J. 'Report on exhibition of implements, award of medals etc. at the International Meeting at Kilburn', *Journal of the Royal Agricultural Society of England*, 2nd ser vol 15, 1879, p 752). The industrial influence is obvious. But none of these single-purpose machines were the true ancestors of general farmstead mechanisation. That honour goes to a steam plant installed in 1804 on a Norfolk farm, where it drove a grinding mill and a chaff-cutter as well as a threshing machine. (Young, A. *General view of the agriculture of Norfolk*, 1804, p 73.)

88. Young, A. *General view of the agriculture of Essex*, 1807, vol 1, p 47

89. Mavor, W. *General view of the agriculture of Berkshire*, 1809, pp 66–7

90. Gooch, W. *General view of the agriculture of Cambridgeshire*, 1811, p 31

91. Young, A. *General view of the agriculture of Oxfordshire*, 1809, p 20

92. Young, A. *General view of the agriculture of Oxfordshire*, 1809, p 20; Dickson, R. *General view of the agriculture of Lancashire*, 1814, p 97

93. Brunskill, R. W., *Design and layout of farmsteads in parts of Cumberland and Westmoreland*, RIBA, Neale Bursary 1963, Manchester 1965, sect 8. Presumably for climatic reasons, it was common in certain northern areas. But it was unknown elsewhere except in Devonshire, where the 'pound house' was used for the horses which drove not only the cider press, from the action of which it derived its name, but other barn machinery as well. (Sheldon, L. 'Devon barns', *Transactions of the Devonshire Association*, vol 64, 1932, p 391.)

94. Young, A. *The farmer's guide to hiring and stocking farms*, 1770, vol 1, pp 50–5

95. *Communications to the Board of Agriculture on farm buildings*, 1796. There had been earlier publications on farm buildings. But these were concerned with the imaginary possibilities of *la ferme ornée* and cannot be regarded as agricultural literature. See footnote 72.

96. Loudon, C. J. *An encyclopedia of cottage, farm and villa architecture*, 1836, pp 595–9; Burgess, A. N. *Hops*, 1964, p 8

97. Wedge, T. *General view of the agriculture of the county palatine of Chester*, 1794, p 65

98. Waistell, C. *Designs for agricultural buildings*, 1827, p 2. This

book was published after the end of this period. But it appeared posthumously and represented the views he formed in the course of a lengthy agricultural career which apparently began in the 1770s. The author became a member of the Royal Society of Arts in 1792 and was chairman of the Society's Committee on Agriculture from 1815 to 1825. In 1808 he was awarded the Society's gold medal for a paper on valuing timber. He also invented a corn dibble. (Personal communication from the Librarian of the Royal Society of Arts; *Transactions of the Royal Society of Arts*, vol 26, 1808, pp 19, 45–70; vol 27, 1809, pp 79–84; vol 29, 1812, pp 50–1.)

99. Vancouver, C. *General view of the agriculture of Hampshire*, 1810, p 70

100. Morgan, G. *General view of the agriculture of Cornwall*, 1811, pp 25–6. These 'local circumstances' included the availability of second-hand materials. In his Regency case-study of the modernisation of a Surrey farmstead, Waistell refers to the use in new buildings of materials salvaged from those demolished. (Waistell, C. *Designs for agricultural buildings*, 1827, pp 105–6.)

101. Farey, J. *General view of the agriculture of Derbyshire*, 1815, vol 2, p 17

102. Davies, T. *General view of the agriculture of Wiltshire*, 1811, p 11

103. Davies, W. *General view of the agriculture of North Wales*, 1810, p 182

104. Adam, J. *Practical essays in agriculture*, 1786, vol 2, p 221

105. Farey, J. *General view of the agriculture of Derbyshire*, 1815, vol 2, pp 17–19

106. Wedge, T. *General view of the agriculture of the county palatinate of Chester*, 1794, p 12; Lowe, R. *General view of the agriculture of Nottingham*, 1798, p 9; Rudge, T. *General view of the agriculture of Gloucestershire*, 1807, pp 44–5; Young, A. *General view of the agriculture of Lincolnshire*, 1808, p 39; Hassall, C. *General view of the agriculture of Monmouth*, 1812, p 24; Murray, A. *General view of the agriculture of Warwickshire*, 1813, p 29; Farey, J. *General view of the agriculture of Derbyshire*, 1815, vol 2, p 12. A study of pre-Victorian farmsteads in Shropshire noted the dependence of each area on the materials it produced—triassic marl stone in the north, limestone in the west, poor-quality sandstone, half-timbering and wattle and daub in the south-east, slates near Wales and tiles elsewhere, and rye thatch in a poor land district near Newport. But bricks were used for barns as early as 1700 and by the nineteenth century some of the stone quarries had been abandoned. (Weller, J. B., *Farm buildings of Shropshire before 1837*, 1952, in typescript, kindly lent by the author,

pp 6–7.) At one time, the use of timber was universal in the lowland areas of this county. But this period saw the final replacement of timber by stone or brick. The last dateable example of timber construction was built in 1784. Stone was the original material of the uplands and continued in use there throughout this period. (Davies, D. C. G. *Historic farmstead and farmhouse types in Shropshire*, MA thesis, Manchester University, 1952, pp 47–8, 113.) This period also saw the end of the ancient system of cruck building. A derivative of this system called the 'upper cruck', in which cruck blades were seated in the ends of first floor beams to form trusses, was used in some Worcestershire farm buildings as late as the second half of the eighteenth century. (Charles, F. W. B. *Mediaeval cruckbuilding and its derivatives*, 1967, p 17.)

107. Young, A. *General view of the agriculture of Norfolk*, 1804, p 20
108. Boys, J. *General view of the agriculture of Kent*, 1805, p 32
109. Young, A. *General view of the agriculture of Hertfordshire*, 1804, pp 20–1; Farey, J. *General view of the agriculture of Derbyshire*, 1815, pp 14–15
110. Pitt, W. *General view of the agriculture of Staffordshire*, 1796, p 21
111. Tuke, J. *General view of the agriculture of the North Riding of Yorkshire*, 1800, p 306

Chapter Five

HANOVERIAN FARMSTEADS:
SOME EXAMPLES

In this period the general history of farmstead development can for the first time be illustrated in detail by plans of particular sets of farm buildings and descriptions of the functions they fulfilled. Their appearance in the literature of the late eighteenth century was no accident, for they reflected the spirit of informed improvement which was so typical of the time. The men of the Agrarian Revolution were proudly conscious that they knew better methods of equipping as well as cultivating their land than their forefathers, and they made their principles and techniques clear by demonstrating them on the printed page.

Some of these drawings represented actual farmsteads, others summarised general or local experience. But both types were presented as examples of recommended design. The first drawing of an imaginary model farmstead appeared in 1770, the first plan of a named farmstead 'offered as a mirror in which others may see the advantages and disadvantages of their own farmeries' thirteen years later,[1] and in the next generation these were followed by a variety of plans showing different types of farmstead suitable for different types of farm. (See Figs 8 and 9.) Of course, the sets of buildings thus described were not typical of the time. *Ex hypothesi*, they were better than average. But they were all examples of commercial designs chosen by men with professional reputations to lose for the consideration of men with money to invest. As such, they provide an invaluable series of case-studies illustrating contemporary assumptions and practice.

A STAFFORDSHIRE FARMSTEAD

The first example illustrates Staffordshire practice and was published in 1796,[2] though steadings of this general type were built in most counties throughout this period. (See Fig 10.)

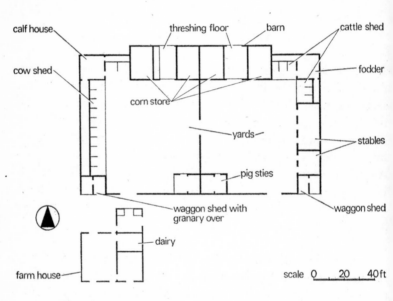

10 Plan of a steading designed in 1796 for a mixed Staffordshire farm of 200 to 500 acres (see p 112)

The steading was described as suitable for 'a respectable farm of 200 to 500 acres' and assumed a mixed-farming system producing corn, milk and meat. It was planned on the familiar U-pattern round two large yards which lay open to the southern sun but provided little protection from the rain that in winter probably turned them into quagmires. The two barns, one for the wheat which was sold off the farm, and the other for the oats and barley which were fed on it, formed the bulk of the north range. Each contained a hard central floor where flailers threshed the corn which was stored in the barn or brought in from the sactkyard to the north of the buildings, the straw going to the livestock houses and the yard, the corn to the granary over one of the cartsheds. The north range was flanked by two ranges of livestock buildings, the east wing housed fattening cattle and working horses or oxen, and the west wing the dairy herd whose milk was processed into butter and cheese in the farmhouse dairy. Waggons and carts were parked in shelters at the south ends of these wings, which was convenient for service in the fields but left them exposed to the warping effects of sun and rain.

These, of course, were all commercial buildings. But the tradition of domestic self-sufficiency was maintained by a few pigs and poultry for family use, housed near the farmhouse where the farmer's wife could feed them on domestic scraps and on the dairy residues.

A YORKSHIRE FARMSTEAD

The Midland steading previously illustrated served a mixed farming system. So did this North Riding farmstead serving a 300-acre holding,[3] though here livestock were more important than corn and fattening cattle than dairy cattle. (See Fig 11.) Again it illustrates the same general principles of design—the barn on the north, the cattle buildings near the barn from which they received their straw, and the pigsties near the dairy in the farmhouse. But the differences in the climate, the size of holding and the economy of the farm were interestingly re-flected in differences in detail. The barn was proportionately smaller and housed livestock as well as corn so that cattle, the main consumers of straw, could be fed and littered without crossing cold and possibly snowbound yards. Yet the basic pattern had not been changed. It had merely been adapted to particular circumstances.

Like its Staffordshire predecessor, this farmstead was de-pendent on human power for all operations. But these were the

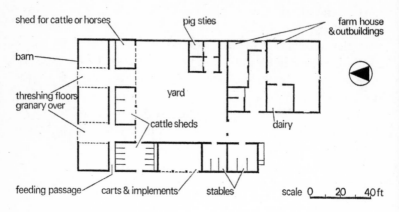

shed for cattle or horses

pig sties

farm house & outbuildings

barn

threshing floors granary over

yard

cattle sheds

dairy

feeding passage   carts & implements   stables   scale 0   20   40 ft

11   Plan of a steading designed in 1800 for a Yorkshire farm of 200 acres
(see p 113)

last years when totally unmechanised steadings could be presented as examples of good practice. From this time onwards one of the themes of farmstead history is the gradual introduction of machinery first for static work, then, much later, for the movement of materials.

LARGE STEADINGS FOR LARGE FARMS

The general standardisation of farmstead design in this period is strikingly illustrated by a comparison of two steadings for large farms, one in the south, one in the north. (See Figs 12 and 13.) The first was built in Sussex, apparently about the year of Trafalgar, to serve the 1,400-acre home farm of a great landowner who paid 'some attention to symmetry and appearance but in general rejected every improvement that could not come within reach of the common farmer'.[4] The second, probably prepared a few years later, was hypothetical. But it represented the views of the experienced Waistell, and may well have been based on a farmstead he had helped to plan.[5]

Both designs assumed mixed farming systems and both accepted the conventional basic pattern, differing only in scale from the smaller steadings of the time, and only in detail from

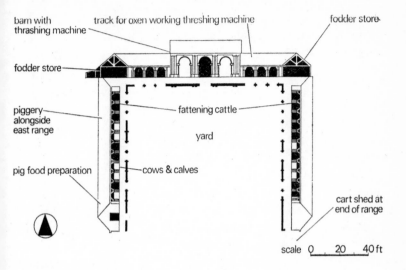

barn with thrashing machine

track for oxen working threshing machine

fodder store

fodder store

piggery alongside east range

fattening cattle

yard

pig food preparation

cows & calves

cart shed at end of range

scale 0 20 40 ft

12 A steading built about 1805 for the home farm of a great landowner in Sussex (see p 114)

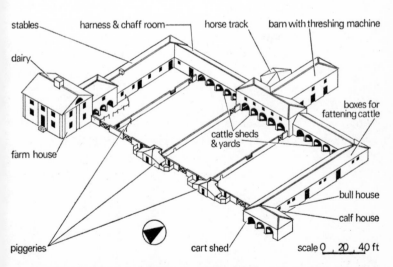

stables

harness & chaff room

horse track

barn with threshing machine

dairy

boxes for fattening cattle

cattle sheds & yards

farm house

bull house

calf house

piggeries

cart shed

scale 0 20 40 ft

13 Steading designed about 1815 for a large northern farm. Note the small circular horsetrack or 'gin gang' which sheltered the horses that drove the threshing machine (see p 114)

each other. In general, these two sets of buildings, planned for areas probably more than two hundred miles apart, are almost interchangeable. The only obvious regional characteristic is the circular shelter, so typical of certain northern areas, which protected the horse and gear that drove the threshing machine.

Both designs include threshing machines driven by animal power, by literal horsepower in the north, by oxen in Sussex which long prized the working qualities of its local breed. But a reference in the description of the southern steading to grinding, chaff-cutting and other food preparation equipment in the barn illustrates an early stage in its change from a building in which corn was stored and threshed to one in which grain and straw, roots and cake were processed with the aid of machines for delivery to livestock. The barn continued to dominate the farmstead. But already, the truth of Arthur Young's prophecy was becoming apparent. Mechanisation was beginning to change its function.

MISSING INFORMATION

Significantly, none of the publications from which these drawings are taken gives any information on the construction of the farmsteads they describe. For their writers knew that all farm buildings were built of local materials and saw no point in detailing the methods of one area for readers elsewhere who could only use such products of woodland, quarry or pit as were available near their homes. So, partly by statement and partly by omission, these case-studies strikingly illustrate the combination of similarity of general design and diversity of particular methods of construction which was so typical of the farmsteads of their age.

NOTES

1. Young, A. *The farmer's guide to hiring and stocking farms*, 1770, vol 2, p 467; Marshall, W. *Minutes of Agriculture*, 1783, pp 21–2. The latter, describing the steading built on his Croydon farm eight years

earlier, referred feelingly to 'the anxieties and attendance which the immediate superintendance (of its construction) occasioned' and his minute of 11 August 1775 records a *cri de coeur* with which many of those concerned with building work on farms will sympathise. 'The carpenters have done building, jobbing, gate-making and tarring and, thank my stars, they are off!' Builders are pleasant people, but their completed work is commonly preferable to their company.

2. Pitt, W. *General view of the agriculture of Staffordshire*, 1796, plate opposite p 18

3. Tuke, J. *General view of the agriculture of the North Riding of Yorkshire*, 1800, plate IV, p 46

4. Young, A. *General view of the agriculture of Sussex*, 1808, pp 464-71, 468-9

5. Waistell, C. *Designs for agricultural buildings*, 1827, plates VII and VIII

Chapter Six

THE AGRICULTURAL REVOLUTION:

THE INDUSTRIAL PHASE, 1820-80

THE INTENSIFICATION OF FARMING

In this period the demand for food increased steadily. The population of England and Wales rose from 12 million in 1821 to 16 million in 1841, 20 million in 1861 and 26 million in 1881; and throughout most of this time it was the responsibility and profitable privilege of the British farmer to feed this growing market with little help or competition from overseas. The result was a major economic achievement of British history, the development of a farming system which raised the art and science of food production to a pitch never before seen, so that visitors from the Old and the New Worlds alike marvelled at the efficiency, the prosperity and the professional pride of the British agricultural industry. Towards the end of the period even this 'High Farming', as it was so rightly called, failed to keep pace with the demands made on it. By 1880 Britain was importing half its bread and a quarter of its meat. Nevertheless, so great was the faith in the continuation of agricultural progress that men as sensible as Caird never doubted that most of Britain's food would continue to come from Britain's farms.

It was, however, clear from the beginning of this period that the resources and methods of the Agrarian Revolution could no longer keep the growing population fed. Reclamation continued; but it could only make a limited and ever-shrinking contribution to the national food supply. Enclosures, too, continued, but here also the end was in sight as Open Field parishes gradually became first anomalies, then rarities. By the time of Queen Victoria's accession it was obvious that any large increases in food production could only come from the more intensive exploitation of existing farmland. So the building of new farmsteads on new farmland, which had been such a conspicuous a feature of George III's time, now dwindled to a minor agricultural theme. A number of new steadings, it is true, were built, some to serve land won from the last areas of the waste, some to serve farms created by belated enclosures, and others to serve farms created by enclosures a generation earlier but worked from village homesteads which were now falling into decay.[1] This, however, was no more than the completion of an inherited task. The new age faced a new need, the development of farmsteads on existing farms to meet the demands of a more sophisticated, more productive and more demanding farming system.

The basic problem was summarised in a letter which Caird wrote to Sir Robert Peel in 1850. 'It would be vain,' he said, 'to drain the land and fit it for the culture of green crops if no suitable housing is provided for economically converting these into a marketable form and for preserving and accumulating manure.'[2] The improvement of fertility by drainage, better tillage, and the use of purchased manures and the residues of purchased feedstuffs; more crops, including more stockfeed; more stock and therefore more corn, meat, butter and cheese to sell; and more by-products of stock and crops to go back to the land to maintain and improve fertility—such was the circle of Victorian farming. So the farmstead became the workshop wherein an increasing weight of crops was either prepared for market or converted by increasing number of stock into saleable products and manure.[3]

But the growing demands on the farmstead reflected an improvement in the quality as well as an increase in the quantity of the variety of equipment, crops and stock housed, stored or processed there. The point was neatly illustrated in a question raised in 1841. 'As the cost and wear and tear of implements have now become a serious consideration in the farmer's outlay ... might not every farmer have a suitable shed with a hard, clean floor ... within which each implement should have its proper place?'[4] Clearly, the complicated and expensive equipment which the farmer was now buying from the manufacturer merited better protection than the cruder products of the old order. Equally clearly, the same argument applied more forcibly in the wider world of livestock, which are inherently likely to respond to better treatment than inorganic equipment. The improved cattle of the period required improved housing if they were to repay the time and skill which had been invested in them.[5] And obviously such needs could not be met by the traditional type of steading with its obsolescent barn, dark, dirty and ill-ventilated stables and cowhouses, inadequate implement housing and open central yard where water from the spoutless buildings washed away so much of the value of the manure which accumulated there.[6]

THE INDUSTRIAL FARMSTEAD

The Victorian farmer met the new problems of the farmstead in the same way as he met the new problems of the farm. He sought new technical allies who could provide him with means of producing more food from a limited acreage. He found them in the new urban economy created by the Industrial Revolution. As the years passed, he came to rely increasingly on the engineer for the new techniques of deep drainage, on the manufacturer for implements, on the chemist and the merchant for the guano, superphosphate and other purchased plantfoods which were beginning to reinforce the traditional dung-heap. So the farmer turned specialist, a specialist in the growing of crops and rearing of stock, and delegated to other specialists many of the new forms of old technical responsibilities once undertaken on the farm or in the village.

In particular, he delegated many of his traditional responsibilities for the design, equipment and erection of the more com-

Page 121 (above) Early Victorian horse threshing gear. In some northern counties it was customary to house the horsetrack in a small circular building locally called a 'gin gang'; (below) steam-engine built in 1811 by Richard Trevithick to drive a threshing machine on a Cornish farm (see p 108)

Page 122 (above) The first concrete farm building, on right. It was erected in Berkshire by Robert Campbell about 1870. The walls are of mass concrete (see pp 136, 155) (below) a silo built by a pioneering Herefordshire farmer in 1885

plicated buildings demanded by a more exacting farming system to the specialist who provided some of his knowledge, to the engineer who provided much of his equipment, and to the manufacturer who provided most of the building materials he required. The implications were obvious and accepted. The farmer who called to his aid the resources of industry came to consider the problems of his farmstead in industrial terms. It was, therefore, in the early Victorian period that the familiar modern concept of the farmstead as an agricultural factory was first consciously established.

'Agriculture has most properly come to be regarded as a manufacture and the benefits arising from a perfect adaptation of the farm buildings to the various operations conducted in them are now generally admitted. . . . In other mechanical arts we find no difficulty in distinguishing one building from another. Nobody would mistake a flour mill for a spinning mill or a factory for a warehouse. So ought we to be able to distinguish the system of farming by the structure of the steadings.' This passage combines quotations from two textbooks of the 1860s.[7] But its cohesion illustrates the strength of the common doctrine. Contemporaries repeated the same assumptions in different words, referring to the homestead as 'the farmer's manufactory'[8] and urging the use of the machine 'to make the business of the farm approximate more closely to that of the factory.'[9] The men of the steam age were proudly conscious of the improvements which the developments of their time made possible and their buildings still bear witness to the conviction and skill with which they applied the equipment and techniques made available to them by expanding industry.

Nevertheless, the new approach did not change the general principles of farm buildings design. Caird's criteria of a good farmstead—the degree to which it provided stock with warmth and shelter, allowed ease of working and made possible the conservation of rich manure[10]—were those of his grandfather, though the next generation gave rather higher priority to economising labour.[11] Neither did it revolutionise the application of these principles.

H

Thus, it made little difference to the siting of new farmsteads. 'Centricity' was still as important as it was in the days of the Hanoverians, and the need for a reliable supply of water as vital as it was in the days of the Heptarchy. Neither did it affect the basic needs and relationships of men, materials and livestock. It was still necessary to convert stacked corn into grain and straw, it was still necessary to store the grain safely and pass the straw to the yards and stockbuildings for conversion into manure. It was still necessary to face yards south to catch the sun, and cartsheds north to protect timber from sun and rain. It was still convenient to site stables near cartsheds and piggeries near the farmhouse on dairy farms. Even the changes in the function of the barn were not sufficient to affect its proud inherited position. Many eighteenth-century arguments and recommendations on planning were repeated in nineteenth-century books, many eighteenth-century decisions in nineteenth-century steadings. So the Victorian farmstead was essentially an industrialised version of its predecessors. It was fitted with industrially-produced equipment and built with industrially-produced materials, but it served familiar needs in a familiar way and the old pattern of north range and south-facing yards continued unchanged into the new age.[12]

NEW MEN, NEW BOOKS

Yet the implications of this industrialisation were considerable. In particular, the pressure of technical change and the possibilities and problems involved soon made it increasingly clear that local experience and inherited lore were no longer sufficient qualifications for the designer of farm buildings. There were too many new ways of building and equipping farmsteads, too many new ideas and proprietary products, too many decisions on new issues requiring new technical knowledge for the traditional estate manager to remain master of the subject. More specialised men were needed, more specialised men duly appeared, and changes in their professional characteristics and in the technical literature they produced for the guidance of their more general-purpose brethren illustrated the growing complexity of the subject they served.

Thus Waistell, whose posthumous treatise on farm buildings appeared in 1827, was the last representative of old tradition. He was a farmer giving other farmers the benefit of his personal experience and observations.[13] In the next decade, Loudon combined the old and the new. He was a farmer and a land agent, but he enlisted the services of a team of architects, engineers, farmers and surveyors in compiling the massive encyclopedia of rural buildings he published in 1833.[14] A generation later the change was complete. In 1861, Burn, co-author of a substantial volume which included illustrated descriptions of ten model and five actual farmsteads, described himself as an engineer.[15] Two years later, Denton appeared on the title page of his classic series of studies of *The farm homesteads of England*, which ended with a sixty-page 'description of the principles recognised in the construction and arrangement of approved farm buildings', in full formality as MInst CE and 'Engineer to the General Land Drainage and Improvement Company'.[16] Agriculturists who specialised in farm buildings were replaced by technical men who specialised in agriculture.

Traditional local skills, like traditional local materials, were no longer sufficient to meet the needs of the farmstead, for the cost and complication of the work now necessitated a far more rigorous and informed analysis of the problems involved and a far more conscious application of established principles to obtain specified results. So the new literature set forth with a mass of detail the grammar of the subject from the determination of building requirements via the procedures for siting and planning farmsteads to the criteria for choosing building materials. In so doing, it equipped the farming industry with its first sound and comprehensive guides to the design and construction of farm buildings.[17] Denton was over-optimistic in his conclusion that, 'under the stimulation of an imperious necessity', local tradition and casual empiricism had been replaced by 'a collection of well-recognised axioms'.[18] No technology serving such a complex of variables as the needs of the farm can be completely or decisively codified. But, like James Small's famous treatise on the plough half-a-century earlier, these new textbooks 'concentrated and clarified what other men had been thinking in a muddled and indefinite manner'.[19] They also marked the end of an age. Here as elsewhere, the farm was no longer technically sufficient unto itself.

THE LANDOWNER AND FARMSTEAD DEVELOPMENT

The new technology, however, operated within the framework of the old rural order. It was the landlord, working through his agent or other professional advisor, who made the final decisions and, as in the past, he exercised his power according to his personal character, abilities and resources. Individually, landlords were responsible for the buildings on their farms. Collectively, therefore, they controlled the course of farmstead development.

The task before them was considerable, for the steadings inherited from the Agrarian Revolution were no more capable of meeting the needs of the changed times than those inherited by the Agrarian Revolution had been a century earlier. Nothing less than a general modernisation was required. Some landowners, notably such leaders of the industry as the Duke of Bedford and the Duke of Northumberland, who employed skilled staff to build and repair their farmsteads, demonstrated model buildings in the massive steadings they erected in their home farms, maintained large and highly-equipped estate yards[20] and over the years invested huge sums in farm buildings and other improvements, were both equipped and prepared to meet their responsibilities. In particular, they appreciated that the right sort of buildings were necessary to attract the right sort of tenants on whom depended the long-term prosperity of their estates.[21] But others, such as the Buckinghamshire landowner who received £1,500 a year in rent from a farm yet refused to provide proper accommodation for his tenant's cattle,[22] were less able or less willing to meet their responsibilities. The latter was exceptional, but unfortunately, as Caird's report of

1852 on his agricultural tour of the country made clear, the former were not typical. He saw many new farmsteads, well designed, well built and well equipped, the rural equivalent of the factories which were making his country the workshop of the world, and he gave praise where praise was due. But in his final judgement he quoted the general state of the buildings he had seen as evidence of the low standards of estate management that prevailed.

'The inconvenient, ill-arranged hovels', he wrote, 'the rickety wood and thatch barns and sheds devoid of any known improvement for economising labour, food and manure, which are to be met with in every county in England and from which anything else is exceptional in the southern counties, are a reproach to the landlords in the eyes of all skilful agriculturists who see them. One can scarcely believe that such a state of affairs is permitted in an old and wealthy country.' The British farmer, he concluded, was meeting the necessities of the present with the equipment of the past.[23] Nearly thirty years later the more generalised review of landowners and landownership which he gave to an international congress was considerably more favourable. He referred to a general improvement in farm buildings and his main criticism was not neglect but the extravagant expenditure caused by insufficient assessment of agricultural needs and poor planning.[24] Even so, the year after he spoke, another prominent agriculturist commented on the landlords' responsibility for the 'want of adequate buildings which at present impedes the progress of improved dairy husbandry'.[25] The farmsteads of Victorian England reflected the shortcomings as well as the virtues of the landlord-and-tenant system of the time.

In principle, of course, there was nothing new in this. From the earliest times, men have made their individual decisions on the equipment of the farms and the differences which resulted have been plain for all to see. But in this period a new type of difference results from such decisions. Formerly, farmsteads were well or badly built, well or badly planned, adequate or inadequate for their purposes. But, on the whole, the distinction between old and new was physical, not technical. Development had been insufficient to create more than the prophecy of the familiar contrast between 'modern' and 'old-fashioned'. Now, however, the farmsteads of men who exploited the resources of their age incorporated and proclaimed technologies unknown on the farms of those who continued with inherited buildings and equipment.

It was in this period, therefore, that the differences between advanced and traditional farmsteads increased and developed until they became an obvious and accepted factor in the rural economy. From this time onwards we must remember that 'technical change in the farmstead' means technical change in a certain proportion of farmsteads, and that farms are served not merely by new and old but by up-to-date and obsolete buildings. And for every Victorian farmer who worked in a Victorian farmstead there were a dozen who worked in steadings built in the days of the Hanoverians, the Stuarts, or the Tudors.

MORE HOUSING FOR MORE CATTLE

The most obvious weakness of the early Victorian farmstead was insufficient accommodation for cattle, for expansion had failed to keep pace with the increase of horned stock made possible by the new cropping systems. 'There is scarcely a farmer of stability in the country,' wrote Dean, an experienced agricultural architect, in 1851, 'who would not pay an additional rent of from 7 to 9 or, in some instances, 10 per cent on the cost of a first-rate homestead, provided the outlay be judicious, rather than have a miserable one such as farmers are now compelled to put up with. . . . It would pay him well to give such a percentage, as the homestead would enable him to feed a large number of livestock through the winter.'[26] A mass of local evidence provides a detailed commentary on his generalised conclusion. In the north and the south, on the arable and pastoral districts alike, the general story is the same—too few buildings for too many cattle. The consequences for both stock and soil were plain to see, for the outwintering of cattle in the fields meant the loss of condition in wet and cold, the poaching of soggy pasture and the dropping on grassland of manure more urgently required by the hungry ploughlands.[27]

Here, indeed, was one of the limiting factors in contemporary agricultural development. At one end of the scale, it prevented progressively-minded farmers from adopting improved techniques. The conservation of manurial values remained one of the primary functions of the farmstead yet, for example, a visitor to Northamptonshire in 1852 lamented that 'it was vain for the tenant to endeavour to improve the quality of his manure' by the intensive indoor feeding of cattle, for he lacked bullock hovels.[28] At the other, it enforced almost archaic standards on the less advanced. Half a century after the turnip had helped to revolutionise the system of fodder production, the farmers of South Wales answered those who recommend this crop to them with a simple question. 'What is the use of growing turnips when we have no sheds to feed them in?'[29] Seldom has the importance of buildings in the agricultural economy been more succinctly illustrated.

But it was not just a question of more accommodation. It was also a question of better accommodation. In Napoleonic times, progressive men had argued that cattle should be wintered in buildings and not left to fend for themselves in fields. Half a century later, their successors were arguing that cattle should be kept not in open yards but under cover. The change reflected important advances in their methods and managerial standards. For one thing, the growing use of expensive oilcake and other purchased concentrates for fattening cattle increased the incentive to provide stock with conditions which encouraged the efficient conversion of feed into meat. It was noted in this period that farmers were 'beginning to see that warmth and shelter are equivalents to food' and one enthusiastic pioneer even suggested that a thermometer should be fitted in every cattleyard.[30] For another, this new form of expenditure made necessary the better protection of manure to prevent the wastage of the residues of these rich rations by exposure to rain. Once again, improved techniques required improved buildings if the full benefits they offered were to be secured.

So the development of cattle accommodation was a major feature of this period. In particular, the yards grew in size until they often covered far more floor space than all the rest of the farmstead. At first, they were either open or, at most, provided with shelters. Under pressure of informed opinion, however, covered yards gradually became more common. Open yards continued to hold their own in rearing districts, since young stock require sunshine, in areas such as East Anglia, where rainfall was light and straw for litter plentiful and, inevitably, on the less advanced farms elsewhere. But by the 1860s the roofing of yards was established or at least approved practice in most parts of the country.[31]

The provision of roofing enabled the yard to provide both cattle and manure with better protection. But it did not alter its essential character. It remained a mass-production unit, housing a large number of animals in a manner which enabled the master cattle 'to drive the weak about and allow them little rest' and rendered feeding 'slovenly, wasteful and imperfect', since the stronger 'consume the choicest parts of the food'.[32] The improvement of yards, therefore, was accompanied by an increase in more intensive systems of boxes or stalls which made possible the individual treatment of stock, each animal being confined or tethered in 'a place of its own' so that bullying was eliminated and the cattle allowed to eat and rest undisturbed, while feed could be carefully rationed and manure properly conserved.[33]

Such a system provided cattle with the most favourable conditions for meat production, and the farmer with the most effective methods of manure conservation so far devised. But these were achieved only at heavy cost in both capital and labour, and, in particular, they involved expensive buildings which continued in their own way the tradition of the specialised 'oxhouses' of the later eighteenth century. The fattening-house which Read visited in Buckinghamshire in 1855 differed little in principle from that which Young visited in Nottinghamshire in 1771.[34] But it was very different in detail. In the Victorian building the cattle were fed from trolleys running on a small railway up the central gangway and their water was pumped by steam. Of course, few houses were as elaborate as this, but the degree of investment in this particular building illustrated in extreme form the general level of capitalisation which such intensive systems made necessary.

Normal practice, however, lagged far behind the advances of the enterprising minority and, though on the whole the cattle of 1880 were considerably better housed than those of 1820,[35] the general deficiency in the quantity and quality of cattle accommodation continued. Meanwhile, the cattle population of the country was steadily rising—in the final decade of this period, the first years for which official statistics are available, it rose from four and a quarter million to over four and three-quarter million—and there must have been many areas like Westmorland where it was clear by 1878 that building was failing to keep pace with breeding.[36]

Deficiencies in quality were equally obvious, though more difficult to assess. But the provision of guttering and downpipes can be taken as a practical index of the varying standards of accommodation, since yards and the cattle in them are the principal beneficiaries of such protection against the concentrated fall of rainwater from the roofs of surrounding buildings. In some areas, guttering came to be regarded in the later years of this period as normal equipment. In others, 'spoutless buildings' bore witness to the general inefficiency of the local farmsteads which was reflected in the poor condition of the stock they housed.[37] So great, even in such a relatively simple matter as the housing of cattle, was the difference between farmer and farmer, area and area.

At first sight, the story of the cattleyard in this period continued the familiar tradition of practical men meeting practical needs with such resources as were readily available. In general, this was true. But the mid-Victorian covered yard also reflected the coming of a new and revolutionary form of knowledge, for it was the first type of agricultural building to be influenced by the findings of scientific research.

Thus, farmers had long known that unprotected manure lost

much of its value. But the Victorians were the first who could measure this loss and draw informed financial and structural conclusions from it. In the 1850s, Voelcker had shown in detail by a series of experiments the degree to which cover preserved the nutritive value of farmyard manure,[38] and a few years later Denton in his textbook on farm buildings quoted the finding of chemical analysis on this point as well as Voelcker's generalised opinion that 'manure made in covered yards was worth fully half more than manure made in open yards'.[39] Significantly, too, one of the champions of the covered yard was Sir Henry Thompson, the railway magnate and improving landlord, who was apparently led to a belief in its advantages by his interest in soil-chemistry.[40] Here, indeed, was prophecy. Traditionally, the designer of farm buildings had relied exclusively on experience and observation. Now, for the first time, he was beginning to pay heed to the findings of scientific research.

Indeed, he was even beginning to call for research on problems created by new developments. The first such suggestion dates from 1857. 'The writer regards the subject (of the comparative advantages and disadvantages of yard and box systems for fattening cattle) as sufficiently important to warrant a suggestion that the Royal Agricultural Society of England should get some well-attested experiments on the subject.'[41] Admittedly, this was no more than prophecy, for it was long before the scientist made a substantial and continuing contribution to the knowledge required in farmstead planning. But Voelcker and Thompson showed the way which many were to follow in due process of time and the historical importance of their work is as obvious to later generations as its practical importance was to their contemporaries.

DAIRY BUILDINGS IN COUNTRY AND TOWN

Until the middle years of the nineteenth century, the inherited dairy system continued unchallenged. The milk-producing farm sold its milk as butter or cheese and the urban cowkeeper provided the townsman with his liquid milk.

In early Victorian times, as in Hanoverian times, the traditional dairy areas produced their traditional specialities—
butter in the Vale of Aylesbury, for instance, cheese in Cheshire
and Leicestershire—in traditional types of building. The familiar cowhouse, with its rows of individual stalls in which cows
were tied in the winter and milked all the year, was now the
accepted and satisfactory form of housing. It was found, with
endless local variations, in all milking areas and the designs
recorded by Loudon in the 1830s and Denton in the 1860s were
merely improved versions of those which the Board of Agriculture's surveyors had found in advanced farms a generation
earlier. Reformers like Joseph Harding might complain in detail of damp, badly-ventilated dairies standing too close to the
farmyard, and occasional enterprising farmers might attract
attention by harnessing horsepower to the cream churn,[42] but
there was no suggestion that the principles on which the dairies
were planned and built needed more than sensible and con-
scientious application.

Neither at first was there any great change in urban dairying.
The number of cows in London increased as the population
grew until in the early 1860s they totalled some 24,000.[43] But
the general standards of urban milk production remained those
of the eighteenth century, as descriptions in the 1840s of 'the
half-underground dens and cellars in which cows were kept for
the greater part of the year, standing knee-deep in filth, with
little or no ventilation' and the condemnation of the London
milk supply by the *Lancet* in 1847 showed.[44] Nevertheless, the
shape of things to come was already apparent. In 1844 the first
milk to be transported by rail reached Manchester and shortly
afterwards the railways started bringing milk to London. As
early as 1846, a Romford farmer, who sent his milk to London
on the Eastern Counties Railway, won from a London dairy-
man the contract for supplying St Thomas's Hospital by quot-
ing a price of 9d to 10d a gallon against his rivals' 1s a gallon.[45]
For the first time the urban milk producer faced competition
from his country cousin. Even so, the amount of 'railway milk'
reaching the cities was small and the rate of increase slow until

1865, when the cattle plague devastated the cattle population of this country. Within a year, nearly a quarter of a million cattle died of this plague or were slaughtered to prevent its spread, and losses were proportionately higher among the crowded herds of the towns than on the farms.[46]

The first effect of this was, of course, a great increase in the volume of milk brought to London by rail to make good the deficiency. The second was less predictable but equally important. For the inspectors appointed to supervise the measures taken to control the cattle plague were the first officials to penetrate the London cowhouses and their revelations encouraged both the consumption of railway milk by the urban public and the enactment of sanitary legislation by the municipal authorities. Within a year or two, such effects of the new regulations and the inspections which enforced them as the exclusion of cowhouses from the more congested areas and the establishment of minimum space requirements per beast, were noted as welcome novelties.[47] Thus did the legislative control of building design come to the London cowhouse. It was soon to come to all cowhouses and ultimately, in various forms, to all types of farm building. The inspectors appointed under the Cattle Disease Prevention Act of 1866 had many successors and from this time onwards 'the requirements of the regulations' were among the factors affecting the planning and construction of farm buildings.

But this was for the future. The immediate consequence was a general improvement in standards. There were still plenty of 'filthy holes' but the changing times favoured such 'patterns of neatness and convenience' as Mr Drewell's establishment in Upper Weymouth Street, Marylebone, which included a quarantine room for newly-arrived cows, and Mr Veale's 'clean, dry, warm and airy' cowsheds in Acacia Road, St John's Wood.[48] Nevertheless, the days of even the best urban cowhouses were numbered.

At the height of the cattle plague, milk came to London by rail from as far away as 200 miles. When the plague ended the London cowhouses were restocked and the maximum distance fell to ninety-five miles.[49] But the lesson had been learnt and the rattle of the milk trains sounded the knell of the old order. By the late 1870s, the figure was back to 150 miles.[50] Caird, who as early as 1851 foresaw the possibility of farms in Hampshire and Essex providing London with liquid milk, proved a true prophet.[51]

The railways had enabled the Victorian farmer to take the first step towards the modern dairy system. A combination of foreign competition and industrial development compelled him to take the second. For in the 1860s American factory-made cheese began to beat the produce of the English farmhouse so decisively in both price and quality that the Royal Agricultural Society of England, after due inquiry, sponsored the establishment of a cheese factory under an American manager. This opened in 1870 and within six years ten such factories were in operation, between them processing the milk of seven to eight thousand cows.[52] The economic advantages of the new order were obvious and, as one of the last rural survivals of the domestic system yielded to the factory system, it did not need much prescience to see that butter-making would soon follow.[53] The farmer of the coming age would no longer process milk. He would sell it as a liquid, and new types of dairy would bear witness to the change.

OTHER LIVESTOCK BUILDINGS

Like the yard and the cowhouse, the stable in these years changed little in principle but greatly in detail and its higher standards of flooring, drainage and ventilation illustrated both the application of new materials and fittings and the growing appreciation of livestock needs. Typically, it is in this period that we meet the first detailed advice on desirable environments in animal houses to appear in technical literature. Loudon's recommendation that the temperature in stables should be 50° F in winter and from 60° to 65° F in summer was based on experience rather than research.[54] Yet it foreshadowed the development of that codified knowledge of the physiological requirements of livestock which is the scientist's greatest contribution to farmstead development.

There was, however, little interest in new forms of piggery. The days of the woodland herd were now past and most pigs farrowed and fattened in variations of the traditional sty, though there were occasional and prophetic references to intensive and labour-saving pig fattening-houses 'which have some resemblance in form and disposition to cattleboxes on a smaller scale'.[55] Similarly, apart from premature mention in the 1860s of the large-scale production of eggs and table poultry in 'a greenhouse-looking affair' over 300ft long,[56] poultry were generally expected to continue their immemorial practice of finding their own homes among the buildings of the farmyard. There was even less interest in any form of sheephousing, for the sheep was now almost wholly an animal of the fields. The fattening of lambs for the Christmas market in buildings which had once been such a feature of agriculture in Middlesex had now ceased and only a few experimentally-minded farmers, among then J. J. Mechi and 'Mr Lawes of Harpenden in Hertfordshire', housed either breeding or fattening sheep.[57]

INTENSIVE LIVESTOCK HOUSING

So the general intensification of agriculture was not accompanied by any general intensification of livestock housing. In his report on his agricultural tour, for instance, Caird mentions only one or two cases of soilage systems,[58] and there are no further references to the London fattening houses, which had presumably closed by Victorian times. Such traditions, it is true, were continued in the 1870s by an enterprising Berkshire landowner who built a large concrete shed for fattening tied cattle on the waste products of the sugarbeet he grew for his distillery. (See illustration, p 122, top.) But this was the highly exceptional system of a highly exceptional man.[59] Throughout this period, the town cowhouse remained the only common example of the use of a building to make possible an intensive system of livestock husbandry divorced from the fields.

THE STEAM-ENGINE AND THE BARN

After a lifetime of change, therefore, livestock houses were still immediately recognisable versions of the types of building from which they were descended. But the traditional barn was required to adapt itself to the more radical demands of new equipment and new processes, and it could only do so by abandoning its traditional assumptions and designs. Thus, in one generation, an ancient type of building became obsolete and its epitaph was written by the mid-Victorian farmers who lamented the superfluous barns inherited from the past or, more practically, converted them to cattle sheds.[60] On many farms the new technologies could, in practice, be fitted into existing barns with reasonable efficiency and economy. But in principle they demanded a new type of building.

The cause of this drastic change was the combination of an eighteenth-century invention and a nineteenth-century power-unit. By the 1820s, mechanical threshing was widespread practice, as the Luddite riots of the labourers whom it deprived of their precious winter work as flailers showed so pathetically.[61] But it was not until early Victorian times that steam power began to replace four-legged horsepower as the prime mover of the process and the steam-engine became normal equipment on the larger arable farms. To this day, many of the factory-type chimneys of this new technical order stand with apparent incongruity in the farmlands as memorials to the acceptance by the oldest of trades of the first great achievement of the new mechanical age.[62]

The appearance on the farm of the sweet and mighty power of steam fascinated the men of the time and the new chimneys achieved an almost aggressively symbolical importance. Loudon, who in 1836 had commended the 'remarkable elegance' of Glasgow factory-stacks to the attention of the rising generation of agricultural architects and dreamed of chimneys enriching the landscape of Northumberland,[63] foresaw the kind of delight with which Ruegg ten years later hailed 'the tall chimney and extensive range of buildings' of an advanced farm that brought 'activity and animation to a somewhat desolate district' of Dorset.[64] The contemporary hope of repeating in agriculture the steam-driven triumphs of the Industrial Revolution was epitomised by the smoking chimney which dominated the idyllically aristocratic estate shown in the frontispiece of a textbook of the 1860s.[65]

At first, the new power more than fulfilled the prophecies made on its behalf. Predictably, it threshed corn more cheaply than the old system—Wilson in 1862 reckoned it reduced the cost by three-quarters.[66] Less predictably, it soon began to serve the stockman as well as the corngrower by continuing in new form the minor processing revolution which sought to make the varied range of fodders available for the growing livestock population more digestible and palatable. Grey was not the only farmer of the time to see that 'the erection of a steam-engine affords a good opportunity for constructing apparatus for steaming potatoes and other foods for cattle'.[67] For the power of the steam-engine could grind or crush corn and beans, break oil cake and cut chaff and roots, while its heat could steam potatoes and chaff, boil linseed and cook pigfeed. So the machinery introduced for one major task was additionally harnessed with equal success to a number of minor ones.[68]

Few farmers could attain the complicated and expensive efficiency of the Yorkshire manufacturer turned farmer 'within whose barn are fitted every imaginable machine for converting the corn and vegetable produce of the farm into food for man and beast'.[69] But by the 1850s there must have been a number like Sir John Conroy of Berkshire whose barn contained steam-driven equipment for breaking cake, grinding corn and slicing roots.[70] A more general tribute to the consequences of the introduction of the steam-engine to the farmstead came a few years later from Nottinghamshire, where 'the erection of suitable buildings for cutting fodder and straw, pulping roots and grinding corn for consumption by livestock' was classed among major recent improvements in agriculture.[71] The new equipment and the new processes made necessary new buildings.

Page 140 (above) The end of a tradition; this West Country yard with the familiar overhead 'tallet' for storing hay awaits demolition; (below) the beginning of a tradition the first milking-parlour, built in Wiltshire by Arthur Hosier in 1932 (see p 182)

Contemporary interest in the possibilities of mechanising farmstead processes was considerable.[72] But the steam-engine did not prove a satisfactory agent for such mechanisation. In particular, it could not readily distribute the power it produced or apply it to haulage work. Consequently it remained harnessed to certain limited operations, and in the rest of the steading human arms and legs continued to provide the power for transport and handling. Indeed, within a decade of its general appearance in the farmstead, it began to lose its major responsibility there, for the obvious convenience of taking the threshing machine to the corn stacks instead of bringing all the corn into the barn encouraged the development of portable threshing tackle hauled and driven by portable steam-engines. As the years passed, therefore, more corn was threshed in the fields, and fewer steam-engines were installed in the buildings. The change is illustrated by a comparison of the entries in the farmstead competitions organised by the Royal Agricultural Society of England in 1849 and 1879. In the former, the steam-engine dominated the farmstead from the barn. In the latter, steam was seldom more than an agent for the processing of fodder, for the competitors assumed that corn was threshed in the fields.[73]

Thus the steam-engine mechanised certain farmstead chores and, in so doing, influenced farmstead design. But it did not, as was at one time confidently hoped, revolutionise farmstead planning. It did, however, illustrate one valuable technical truth. It was introduced as a means of substituting inorganic for organic power in one form of barnwork. Further development made this particular improvement obsolete. But in the meantime the new power was applied to other forms of barnwork in a manner which transformed and extended the functions of the barn. Thus it repeated the lesson first taught by the threshing machines of George III's time. New ways of doing old jobs seldom limit themselves to the improvement of existing routines. It is not just a question of fitting new equipment into old buildings, for the possibilities offered and the demands made by the new techniques combine to form around them new opera-

I

tional systems which, in due course of time, require new types
of building to house them.

BUILDINGS FOR STORAGE AND PROCESSING

Even the humble storage buildings illustrated the intensification and complication of Victorian agriculture. Thus, rising
values encouraged expenditure on the protection of farm produce, as references to Dutch barns show.[74] Again, implements
received greater care and attention—the shed on a progressive
Berkshire farm where 'the more intricate machines are kept
under lock' was an extreme instance of this tendency[75]—and the
fertiliser store made its first appearance on farmstead plans.[76]
Greater production per acre meant increased reliance on purchased resources and this, in turn, meant more capital outlay
on buildings.

It also meant greater attention to the various processing
enterprises of the farm. New forms of cider-mill appeared[77] and
on hop farms the last of the old cockle kilns were replaced by
the familiar square or circular oasthouses topped with revolving
cowls.[78] The same general pressures were reflected in the
various efforts made at the end of this period to develop crop-
drying equipment.[79] None of these was successful but they foreshadowed the future reliance of the farmer on the industrialist
for the mechanical means of conserving his harvested crops
which brought so much change to the operations and appearance of the farmstead in the next century.

BUILDING MATERIALS AND EQUIPMENT

The industrial age wrought even greater changes in the
fabric and fittings of farm buildings than in their design. The
brickfield and the slate quarry greatly increased the production
of familiar materials, the factory added a steady flow of new
types of material and equipment, and the railways, fulfilling the
promise made by the canals in the previous century, carried
old and new alike throughout the length and breadth of the

land. It was in this period, therefore, that the ancient dependence on local resources came to an end.

The change was rapid. In 1836, for instance, Loudon could still write that 'the materials with which farm buildings are constructed are commonly those which are most abundant in the locality'. Significantly, however, he added in a later paragraph that 'in all the more advanced districts of Britain, thatched roofs have given way to tiles and slates.[80] A generation later the emphasis was very different. In 1863 Denton thought it necessary to warn his readers against the assumption that purchased materials were invariably better than home-produced ones, adding magisterially that 'local materials should not hastily be set aside'. But he emphasised that purchased bricks were sometimes better and cheaper than local stone and imported timber better and cheaper than home-grown, while few of the materials he recommended could have been provided from local sources or manufactured by local skills.[81] The general point was aptly illustrated in the 1840s by Frederic Knight when building farmsteads to serve the new land he was so laboriously reclaiming from the Exmoor wilderness. 'No English fir for me,' he wrote on the bottom of one of his specifications. Even in one of the most remote of all farming areas in the kingdom, the timber used in new farmsteads came from the Baltic.[82] By the same token, stone was plentiful in Staffordshire, but by the 1860s landlords preferred to build in brick because it was cheaper.[83]

The most obvious consequence of these changes was the widespread use of the better traditional materials. Brick, tiles and slates, hitherto only available in areas which produced them or which happened to lie convenient to river or canal, began to replace the less durable mud, timber and thatch of the older tradition. As early as the 1840s slates were becoming the normal material for roofing in areas as different as Northumberland and Devon[84] and in the next decade Caird frequently contrasted the barns and hovels of local materials 'requiring constant repair, a fruitful source of inconvenience and waste',[85] with the new buildings of neater and more lasting type erected

by such landowners as Lord Derby, the Duke of Wellington and
Sir James Graham. Already, therefore, the new system was
establishing itself. The days when farm buildings appeared to
grow out of the soil of their parish were passing. From this time
onwards, the materials of which they were built had no necessary connection with the land on which they stood.

Less immediately important but more prophetic was the
appearance on the farm of new materials created or developed
by the factory system. Creosote was used for preserving timber
in the 1840s,[86] asphalt for damp-proof courses and flooring in
the 1860s,[87] and, more important, in the same period glazed
windows became normal practice.[88] Two basic materials of the
future, galvanised corrugated iron sheeting and concrete, also
entered agricultural service in these years. The former established itself as a recognised roofing material, appreciated for its
cheapness and lightness but disliked for the poor insulation it
provided and its liability to rust,[89] while the latter soon became
'the invariable material for the foundations of all good buildings'.[90] A little later, it was also used for walls. But the failure of
attempts to make it available in the convenient form of concrete blocks limited its uses for above-ground work, and it
seems to have remained to the end of this period 'an auxiliary
material to use when usual building materials must be brought
from a distance and those adapted to making concrete are
readily obtained on the spot[91]'.

Many other factory products, too, were now influencing the
construction and equipment of farm buildings. Some, such as
metal heelposts, stall divisions and mangers, were new forms of
traditional fittings.[92] Some, such as ventilation cowls, hollow
bricks to improve insulation, and rails and rollers for sliding
doors, were new devices from the technical world beyond the
village workshop.[93] Some, such as cast-iron pillars and the iron
trusses which bridged wide spans more economically than
timber, were structural parts which foreshadowed prefabrication systems to come.[94] Others, more novel, offered new ways of
doing old jobs. There was no precedent on the farm for the gas-
lighting which appeared in occasional advanced steadings in

the 1860s,[95] or for the iron railways on which trollies carried stacks to the threshing machine or fodder to the troughs of housed cattle.[96]

Indeed, one of the signs of the times was the increasing frequency with which proprietary names and illustrations of proprietary products appeared in the technical literature. The cast-iron stalls of Messrs Cottam & Hallen,[97] the pig-troughs of the Shotts Iron Company,[98] Dean's linseed mill[99] and Beedon's patent eaves tiles,[100] all showed that the age of local craftsmen and local materials was passing. The day of the manufacturer and the merchant had come.

NOTES

1. Hoskins, W. G. *Leicestershire*, 1957, p 99

2. Spring, D. *The English landed estate in the 19th century—its administration*, 1963, p 117. Coke of Holkham put the same point in more particular terms when he said to a tenant 'if you will keep an extra yard of bullocks I will build you a yard and sheds free of expense'. (Bacon, R. N. *Report on the agriculture of Norfolk*, 1844, p 394.)

3. The importance of the farmstead in this period as a 'manure-factory' is illustrated by the considerable interest in the possibilities of conserving and using liquid manure. See, eg, Love, P. 'On the best method of applying liquid manure to the land in a liquid state', *Journal of the Royal Agricultural Society of England*, vol 20, 1859, pp 22–30; Blackburn, J. T. 'On the economical application of the liquid manure of a farm', ibid, vol 23, 1862, pp 1–15. Schemes for the collection of liquid manure in tanks and its distribution to the fields by pipes or carts were included in a number of advanced farmsteads but results were seldom satisfactory. 'Great disappointment has been experienced by farmers generally in the want of profit resulting from the distribution of liquid manure; experience and careful calculation having proved that where it necessitates the several operations of raising, carting and spreading, the benefit does not equal the cost of application.' (Denton, J. B. *The farm homesteads of England*, 1863, p 158.) The subject occurs frequently in the literature of the time but the practice never became general.

4. Crosskill, W. 'On the necessity of care in the preservation of agricultural implements', *Journal of the Royal Agricultural Society of England*, vol 2, 1841, p 150

5. The consolidation of the new breeds of cattle was a major

feature of the times. The Shorthorn Herdbook appeared in 1822, the Hereford Herdbook in 1846, the Devon Herdbook in 1851, the Aberdeen-Angus Polled Herdbook in 1862. The publication of a herdbook, of course, implies both a considerable degree of development and a desire for further improvement.

6. Andrews, H. G. *A rudimentary treatise on agricultural engineering. I. Buildings*, 1852, pp 2-4, 75-7, 105

7. Stephens, H. and Burn, R. S. *The book of farm buildings*, 1861, p vi; Denton, J. B. *The farm homesteads of England*, 1863, p vi. The same point was later repeated even more forcibly by a commentator on the plans submitted in a farm buildings competition. 'Until a competitor can put himself in the position of a manufacturer wanting the best for his factory, totally regardless . . . of any considerations beyond the best and cheapest way of manufacturing his goods, he will be unlikely to succeed as a planner of farm buildings.' ('Salt', *The Builder*, vol 37, no 1903, 26 July 1879, p 840.)

8. Wilson, J. *British farming*, 1862, p 83

9. Thompson, —. 'Farm Buildings'. *Journal of the Royal Agricultural Society of England*, vol 2, 1850, p 187

10. Caird, J. *English agriculture in 1850-1*, 1852, p 489

11. Throughout this period wages remained low. But after 1850 they rose perceptibly and regularly. Hence the mid-Victorian comment that 'so much of the cost of all farming operations is reducible to labour, and so much of this labour is connected with the homestead, that the arrangements of the latter should be especially framed to economise time'. (Elliott, J. 'Farm buildings', *Journal of the Royal Agricultural Society of England*, vol 23, 1862, p 473.) The general improvement in rural standards was reflected in the difficulty of obtaining stockmen for the outlying barns and yards on the big Downland farms. Respectable men were not prepared to live in such isolated cottages, particularly as their children would lose any chance of education. 'This state of affairs (ie, the continuation of these outlying units served by a resident stockman) . . . must undergo a change as the condition of the poor improves.' (Spearing, J. B. 'On the agriculture of Berkshire', ibid, vol 21, 1860, p 33

12. For a contemporary analysis of this basic pattern see Morton, J. C. *Cyclopedia of Agriculture*, 1855, vol 1, pp 790-1

13. See footnote 98 to Chapter Four.

14. It is, however, only fair to add that the astonishing J. C. Loudon (1783-1843) the only designer of farm buildings to win a place in *The Dictionary of National Biography*, would have found no particular technical difficulty in replacing any or all of his contributors. He was an agriculturist and horticulturist, an architect and

a town-planner; he wrote his way through the entire corpus of rural knowledge, at one time editing no less than five journals simultaneously; he found time for a form of professional Grand Tour during which he accompanied the Russian forces which followed the despairing *Grande Armée* on the retreat from Moscow; and he left as his memorials five massive encyclopedias and much of the enduring delight of Great Tew in Oxfordshire, one of the most beautiful of all English villages, where he replanned the landscape as well as the farming system when he was agent for a local landowner.

15. Stephens, S. and Burn, R. S. *The book of farm buildings*, 1863

16. J. B. Denton (1814–1893) trained as a surveyor under a land agent and began his career as a surveyor for enclosure schemes. He later became a civil engineer concerned with railway construction, water supplies and sewage disposal. But he maintained an interest in agriculture throughout his professional life and was for a time a director of a land company as well as a land-drainage engineer. (*Minutes of Proceedings of the Institution of Civil Engineers*, vol 15, 1894, pp 386-9.)

17. It also recorded the end of the unhappy tradition of *la ferme ornée*. In this period Loudon was influenced by this curious fashion, though it affected the domestic rather than the agricultural sections of his *Encyclopedia of cottage, farm and villa architecture*. But its epitaph was written crushingly in 1863 by Denton, who dismissed in a phrase those who 'regarded farm architecture as a mere matter of taste' before turning to the adult and practical question of 'the adaptation of farm buildings to the various operations conducted within them'. (Denton, J. B. *The farm homesteads of England*, 1863, p vi.) The Victorians stood no nonsense from Regency affectations.

18. Denton, J. B. *The farm homesteads of England*, 1863, p vi. Few of his contemporaries, however, would have quarrelled with the twelve 'golden rules . . . generally recognised in the arrangement of the best buildings' which he listed on pp 145-7

19. Fussell, G. E. *The farmer's tools*, 1952, pp 48-9

20. Little systematic information is available on the origins and development of estate yards and their associated brickworks, quarries and woodlands. But the importance in farmstead and other rural building work of these numerous and sometimes very substantial centres must have been considerable. In early Victorian times, the Duke of Bedford's yard employed a hundred men (Caird, J. *English agriculture in 1850-1*, 1852, p 439), the Marquess of Bath's yard at Longleat more than sixty (Thompson, F. M. L. *English landed society in the nineteenth century*, 1963, p 171.) The former, which included steam-driven machinery for sawing timber, was described by

Peel in 1849 as 'more like a dockyard than a domestic office'. (Spring, D. *The English landed estate in the nineteenth century*, 1963, p 45.) A history of estate yards would fill a noticeable gap in rural history.

21. Grey, J. 'On farm buildings', *Journal of the Royal Agricultural Society of England*, vol 4, 1843, p 3; Spring, D. 'A great agricultural estate. Netherby under Sir Charles Graham, 1820–1845', *Agricultural History*, vol 29, no 2, April 1955, p 76

22. Caird, J. *English agriculture in 1850–1*, 1852, p 2

23. Caird, J. *English agriculture in 1850–1*, 1852, pp 490–1

24. Caird, J. 'British agriculture'. *Journal of the Royal Agricultural Society of England*, vol 14, 2nd ser, 1878, p 312. It is difficult to establish the professional qualifications and experience of the men who designed the farm buildings of this period and supervised their construction. The land agent, acting on behalf of the landowner, was, of course, ultimately responsible. It is probable that in many cases, perhaps in most cases, he designed the buildings himself and arranged for their construction by his estate staff. Sometimes, presumably on the larger jobs, he employed an architect and for certain types of work he must also have required the services of an engineer. Ewart in 1851 recommended that the construction of big steadings should be supervised by 'an architect or a competent building surveyor'. (Ewart, J. *A treatise on the arrangement and construction of agricultural buildings*, 1851, p 1.) But the only systematic evidence on this point, the designers listed in Denton's series of case-studies in *Farm homesteads of England*, 1863, shows that some land agents at least were capable of undertaking very considerable projects without architectural assistance. It is noteworthy, too, that the dozen farmsteads built by Frederic Knight to serve the reclaimed Exmoor uplands in early Victorian times were 'designed by Knight himself or his agents'. (Orwin, C. S. *The reclamation of Exmoor Forest*, 1929, pp 54–5, 57.) Few architects, it seems, took much interest in this type of work (*The Builder*, vol 7, no 352, 3 November 1849, p 517; Wilson, J. *British farming*, 1862, p 84; *The Builder*, vol 23, no 1152, 5 March 1865, p 146; Dean, G. A. *The land steward*, 1851, p 183, who suggests rather than assumes the appointment of an architect to supervise construction). A study of the various professional men concerned with the substantial technical and financial investment in the farm buildings of Victorian England would make a useful contribution to social history.

25. Murray, G. 'Report on the trial of dairy implements and machinery at Bristol'. *Journal of the Royal Agricultural Society of England*, vol 15, 2nd ser, 1879, p 136

26. Dean, G. A. *The land steward*, 1851, p 177

27. Raynbird, H. 'On the farming of Suffolk', *Journal of the Royal Agricultural Society of England*, vol 8, 1848, p 320; Ackland, T. D., 'On the farming of Somerset', ibid, vol 11, 1850, pp 743, 745; Rowley, J. J. 'On the farming of Derbyshire', ibid, vol 14, 1853, p 49; Read, C. S. 'On the farming of Oxfordshire', ibid, vol 15, 1854, p 255; Moscrop, W. J. 'On the farming of Leicestershire', ibid, vol 2, 2nd ser, 1866, p 334; Bowstead, T. 'Report on farm prize competition' (in South Wales), ibid, vol 8, 2nd ser, 1872, p 279; Harding, J., 'Recent improvements in dairy practice', ibid, vol 21, 1860, p 84, commented on the increase in the yields of grass and hay which followed investment in yards and other stockbuildings which kept cattle off the land in winter.

28. Bearn, W. 'On the farming of Northamptonshire', *Journal of the Royal Agricultural Society of England*, vol 13, 1852, p 86

29. Read, C. S. 'On the farming of South Wales', *Journal of the Royal Agricultural Society of England*, vol 10, 1849, p 147

30. Bravender, J. 'The farming of Gloucestershire', *Journal of the Royal Agricultural Society of England*, vol 11, 1850, p 176; Mechi, J. J. *A series of letters on agricultural improvement*, 1845, p 70

31. Blundell, J. 'Farm buildings', *Journal of the Royal Agricultural Society of England*, vol 23, 1862, pp 475–6

32. Glover, —. 'On box-feeding cattle', in *The farmer's friend*, 1847, p 21

33. Almack, B. 'On the agriculture of Norfolk', *Journal of the Royal Agricultural Society of England*, vol 5, 1845, p 319; Bell, T. G. 'A report upon the agriculture of the county of Durham', ibid, vol 17, 1856, p 109; Read, C. S. 'Recent improvements in Norfolk farming', ibid, vol 19, 1858, p 295

34. Read, C. S. 'Report on the farming of Buckinghamshire', *Journal of the Royal Agricultural Society of England*, vol 16, 1855, p 297. See also p 84

35. Readers of Jefferies will remember his incidental references to the improvement of cattle housing. 'In those days (the 1820s) cattle for the most part—except those that were fattening—remained in the fields throughout the winter, roughing it in the shelter of great hawthorn bushes. Cattle are now sheltered far better than they ever were before. . . . For modern scientific farming (in 1883) depends much upon improved sheds and careful housing of cattle. The old farmers preferred cattle that could stand any weather out of doors.' (*Field and farm*, ed Looker, S. J., 1957, pp 32, 80, 85.)

36. Garnett, F. W. *Westmorland agriculture*, 1912, p 191

37. In 1845, J. J. Mechi listed guttering and downpipes among

the items of expenditure against which he was 'warned, entreated and dissuaded' by his farming friends. Early in the next decade Caird made special reference to 'the spouting to carry off rainwater' on a model farm in Berkshire, so presumably regarded it as exceptional and Andrews remarked that 'nine-tenths of the farm steadings of England are without guttering'. (Mechi, J. J. *Letters on agricultural improvement*, 1845, p 1; Caird, J. *English agriculture in 1850–1*, 1852, p 106; Andrews, W. G. A. *Rudimentary treatise on agricultural engineering. I. Buildings*, 1852, p 2.) A few years later, however, Read found that spouting was normal practice in Norfolk. (Read, C. S. 'Recent improvements in Norfolk farming', *Journal of the Royal Agricultural Society of England*, vol 19, 1858, p 295.) But it was not normal practice everywhere, for Wilson found it necessary to urge the importance of providing farm buildings with spouting. (Wilson, T. *British farming*, 1862, p 96.) Such variations continued in the next decade. A committee awarding prizes in a farm competition specifically commented on the lack of guttering on a Shropshire farm and ascribed it to a whim of the owner, whereas a similar committee a year later reported that 'spoutless buildings' were common in South Wales. (Wheatley, J. 'Report of the farm prize competition', *Journal of the Royal Agricultural Society of England*, vol 7, 2nd ser, 1871, p 319; Bowstead, T. 'Report on the farm prize competition', ibid, vol 8, 2nd ser, 1872, p 322.)

38. Voelcker, A. 'On the composition of farmyard manure', *Journal of the Royal Agricultural Society of England*, vol 17, 1856, pp 213–59

39. Denton, J. B. *The farm homesteads of England*, 1863, pp 130–1. The first reference to the findings of research as a factor in the design of buildings for the farm, however, occurred a few years earlier, when J. C. Morton quoted the opinion of 'the French Academicians' on the desirable cubic airspaces for horses and cattle. (*Cyclopedia of agriculture*, 1855, vol 1, p 798.)

40. Fussell, G. E. 'Sir Harry Stephen Moysey Thompson', *Journal of the Land Agents Society*, vol 49, no 12, December 1950, p 541

41. Bennett, W. 'The farming of Bedfordshire', *Journal of the Royal Agricultural Society of England*, vol 18, 1857, p 25

42. Cheke, V. *The story of cheesemaking in England*, 1959, p 162; Caird, J. *English agriculture in 1850–1*, 1852, p 4

43. Morton, J. C. 'Dairy farming', *Journal of the Royal Agricultural Society of England*, vol 14, 2nd ser, 1878, p 670

44. Drummond, J. C. *The Englishman's food*, 1957, p 299–300

45. Burnett, J. *Plenty and want*, 1966, p 6

46. 5,357 of the 9,531 cows in the Metropolitan Board of Works

area were attacked by the plague. Of these, only 325 recovered. Burnett, J. *Plenty and want*, 1966, p 156

47. Whetham, E. H. 'The London Milk Trade, 1860–1900', *Economic History Review*, vol 17, 2nd ser, 1964, p 372; Morton, J. C. 'Town milk', *Journal of the Royal Agricultural Society of England*, vol 4, 2nd ser, 1868, p 85; Clutterbuck, J. C. 'The farming of Middlesex', ibid, vol 5, 2nd ser, 1869, p 21

48. Morton, J. C. 'Town milk', *Journal of the Royal Agricultural Society of England*, vol 4, 2nd ser, 1868, p 83–6

49. Morton, J. C. 'Town milk', *Journal of the Royal Agricultural Society of England*, vol 4, 2nd ser, 1868, p 97

50. Morton, J. C. 'Dairy Farming', *Journal of the Royal Agricultural Society of England*, vol 14, 2nd ser, 1878, p 670

51. Caird, J. *English agriculture in 1850–1*, 1852, pp 94, 142, 227–8

52. Morton, J. C. 'On cheesemaking', *Journal of the Royal Agricultural Society of England*, vol 2, 2nd ser, 1875, pp 261–300

53. Chester, H. 'The food of the people', *Journal of the Royal Agricultural Society of England*, vol 4, 2nd ser, 1868, p 119

54. Loudon, C. J. *An encyclopedia of cottage, farm and village architecture*, 1836, p 375

55. Dean, G. A. *The land steward*, 1851, p 205. See also Stephens, H. and Burns, R. S. *The book of farm buildings*, 1861, p 493

56. Clarke, J. A. 'On increasing our home production of poultry', *Journal of the Royal Agricultural Society of England*, vol 2, 2nd ser, 1866, pp 356–7

57. Clutterbuck, J. 'On the farming of Middlesex', *Journal of the Royal Agricultural Society*, vol 5, 2nd ser, 1869, p 19. Mechi housed his sheep in yards with sheds for shelter (Mechi, J. J. *A series of letters on agricultural improvement*, 1845, p 71). Lawes used portable houses with slatted floors run on rails laid in the fields to save treading on the soil and provide the sheep with a dry bed. (Caird, J. *English agriculture in 1850–1*, 1852, pp 463–4.) Moveable sheds were also used on the Quantocks (Ackland, T. D. 'On the farming of Somerset', *Journal of the Royal Agricultural Society of England*, vol 11, 1850, pp 694–5). The Prince Consort used a more intensive system on one of his Windsor farms. He housed fattening sheep in a building with a slatted floor and found that they 'throve fast compared with the progress made out of doors' (Morton, J. C. *The Prince Consort's Farms*, 1863, p 87). But the practice was exceptional. It was, however, found in Derbyshire in this period. (Rowley, J. J. 'The farming of Derbyshire', *Journal of the Royal Agricultural Society of England*, vol 14, 1853, p 47.)

58. He also mentions slatted floor systems, which are now some-

times regarded as intensive forms of livestock housing. But these, too, were confined to the farms of occasional pioneers. (Caird, J. *English agriculture in 1850–1*, 1852, pp 69, 121, 141, 271, 375.)

59. Robert Campbell built this house on his Faringdon estate about 1870. (Gray, J. 'An industrialised farm estate in Berkshire', *Bulletin of Industrial Archaeology in CBA Group 9*, no 7, January 1969, pp 2–3.) From internal evidence it seems possible that this was the farmstead where Taine saw a slatted floor installation—'a system of byres in which the floor is a grating. . . . Beasts being fattened remain there for six weeks without moving'. (*Taine's Notes on England*, ed Hyams, E., 1957, p 132.)

60. Read, C. S. 'On the farming of Oxfordshire', *Journal of the Royal Agricultural Society of England*, vol 15, 1854, p 255; Blundell, J. 'Method of converting old barns into cattleboxes', ibid, vol 25, 1864, pp 250–3; Read, C. S. 'On the farming of Buckinghamshire', ibid, vol 16, 1853, p 309

61. By 1827 attacks on threshing machines were sufficiently common to make necessary an Act imposing a penalty of seven years transportation on those who damaged them. Nevertheless their destruction was 'a prominent feature' of the labourers' rising of 1830 (Hammond, J. L. and B. *The Village Labourer 1760–1832*, 1911, pp 249, 273). See also Hobsbawm, E. J. and Rudé, J. *Captain Swing*, 1969, pp 74, 198, 288–99, 359–65

62. See note 83 to Chapter 4. The unpublished thesis on *The New Bingfield Project* mentioned there described the reconditioning of a 10hp steam-engine erected between 1840 and 1845 on a Northumberland farm to drive a threshing machine, a grinder and possibly also a chaff-cutter. This engine continued in use until shortly after the First World War. (Personal communication and loan of typescript thesis from Mr John Moffitt, Peepy Farm, Stocksfield, Northumberland, who was responsible for preserving this engine in his collection of historical agricultural machinery.)

The spread of steam threshing was rapid and in 1867 the machinery judges of the Royal Agricultural Society of England recommended the discontinuation of prizes for horse-threshers, which they regarded as obsolete (Long, W. H. 'The development of mechanisation in English farming', *Agricultural History Review*, vol 11, 1963, p 19). Nevertheless, the victory of steam over the older forms of power was neither immediate nor absolute. As late as 1902 it was noted by a northern writer that horse-threshers were 'now being often left to fall into decay'. (Henderson, S. *The modern farmstead*, 1902, p 226) and in certain northern areas horse-driven machines continued in use till the 1930s when they were converted to tractor-power or electric drive without passing through the steam-power stage. (Pawson, H. C. *A survey of the agriculture of Northumberland*, 1961, p 37; Brunskill, R. W. *Design and layout of farmsteads in parts of Cumberland and Westmorland*, RIBA Neale Bursary 1963, Manchester 1965, sec 8.) In 1967 it was still possible to meet a Northumberland farmer who, as a young man, had trained horses for driving a threshing mill in the circular 'gin gangs' which are such a feature of that county. He remembered particularly the ease with which they learned to step over the revolving shaft on the floor which carried the power to the machine in the barn. (Personal experience.) Waterwheels, where the flow of water allowed them, continued in use throughout this period. Two enterprising landlords, one in Shropshire, the other in Berkshire, even installed water turbines to drive farmstead machinery. ('Modern houses reared beef before Waterloo', *Farmers Weekly*, vol 64, no 22, 3 June 1966, p 49; Gray, J. 'An industrialised farm estate in Berkshire', *Bulletin of Industrial Archaeology in CBA Group 9*, no 7, January 1969, p 3.)

63. Loudon, C. J. *An encyclopedia of cottage, farm and villa architecture*, 1836, p 662

64. Ruegg, L. H. 'Farming of Dorsetshire', *Journal of the Royal Agricultural Society of England*, vol 15, 1854, p 410

65. Stephens, H. and Burn, R. S. *The book of farm buildings*, 1861

66. Wilson, J. *British farming*, 1862, p 155

67. Grey, J. 'On farm buildings', *Journal of the Royal Agricultural Society of England*, vol 4, 1843, p 7

68. The waste heat of the steam-engine could also be used to dry corn either as sheaves or as grain. (Stephens, H. and Burn, R. S. *The book of farm buildings*, 1861, pp 494–507.) But it seems that in this period grain drying in any form was a highly exceptional practice. These authors also discussed on pp 507–8 a prophetic contemporary suggestion that grain could be stored safely in airtight containers, apparently unaware of French experiments with this technique a generation earlier. (Jenkins, H. M. 'Report on the practice of ensilage', *Journal of the Royal Society of England*, vol 20, 2nd ser, 1884, pp 129–32. See also *Silos for preserving British fodder crops*, by the sub-editor of *The Field*, 1884, pp 1–18.)

69. Caird, J. *English agriculture in 1850–1*, 1852, p 305

70. Caird, J. *English agriculture in 1850–1*, 1852, p 104

71. Parkinson, J. 'On improvements in the county of Nottingham since 1800', *Journal of the Royal Agricultural Society of England*, vol 22, 1861, p 165

72. Ritchie, R. *The farm engineer*, 1849, pp 209, 213, 223, 257. Significantly the volumes on *Motive powers and machinery of the farm-*

stead and on *Buildings* in Andrews, G. H., *A rudimentary treatise on agricultural engineering*, 1852, were of equal length.

73. 'Essays on the construction of farm buildings', *Journal of the Royal Agricultural Society of England*, vol 11, 1850, pp 186–310; Report by judges of the farm buildings competition, ibid, vol 15, 2nd ser, 1879, pp 774–836

74. 'If there is one improvement required more than another at the present time, it is the use of Dutch barns instead of ricks.' Spearing, J. B. 'On the agriculture of Berkshire', *Journal of the Royal Agricultural Society of England*, vol 21, 1860, p 34. Denton, J. B., *The farm homesteads of England*, 1863, p 162, described Dutch barns as 'deservedly growing in favour, though at a slow rate'.

75. Caird, J. *English agriculture in 1850–1*, 1852, p 104

76. Plan illustrating article by T. Sturgess on 'Farm buildings', *Journal of the Royal Agricultural Society of England*, vol 11, 1850, pp 288–91

77. Cadle, C. 'Essay on the manufacture and preservation of perry and cider', *Journal of the Royal Agricultural Society of England*, vol 25, 1864, pp 78–81

78. Whitehead, C. 'On recent improvements in the cultivation and management of hops', *Journal of the Royal Agricultural Society of England*, vol 6, 2nd ser, 1870, pp 363–5; Whitehead, C. 'Fifty years of hop farming', ibid, vol 1, 3rd ser, 1890, pp 336–7

79. Fussell, G. E. *The farmer's tools*, 1952, p 179

80. Loudon, J. C. *An encyclopedia of cottage, farm and villa architecture*, 1836, pp 416, 418

81. Denton, J. B. *The farm homesteads of England*, 1863, p 147

82. Orwin, C. S. *The reclamation of Exmoor Forest*, 1929, p 54. See also Low, D. *Landed property*, 1844, p 119; Ewart, J. *Treatise on the arrangement and construction of agricultural buildings*, 1851, p 5; Denton, J. B. 'On the use of homegrown timber', *Journal of the Royal Agricultural Society of England*, vol 4, 2nd ser, 1868, p 208; and Denton, J. B., ibid, vol 15, 2nd ser, 1879, p 783

83. Evershed, H. 'The agriculture of Staffordshire', *Journal of the Royal Agricultural Society of England*, vol 5, 2nd ser, 1869, p 304

84. Grey, J. 'A view of the past and present state of agriculture in Northumberland', *Journal of the Royal Agricultural Society of England*, vol 2, 1841, p 190; Tanner, H. 'The farming of Devon', ibid, vol 9, 1849, p 488. The slates used in Northumberland came from Westmorland and Wales. The sources of those used in Devon is not given. Probably they were shipped across from Wales, like those which roofed John Knight's new farmsteads on Exmoor. (Orwin, C. S. *The reclamation of Exmoor Forest*, 1929, p 52.)

85. Caird, J. *English farming in 1850–1*, 1852, p 152

86. In this period a variety of substances and processes for the preservation of timber were suggested and a number were patented. The only one to survive was creosoting, which was patented by Bethell in 1838. (Richardson, N. A. 'Creosote as a wood preservative', *The Journal of the Chartered Land Agents Society*, vol 65, no 3, March 1966, p 112.)

87. Denton, J. B. *The farm homesteads of England*, 1863, p 157

88. Loudon, C. J. *Encyclopedia of cottage, farm and villa architecture*, 1836, pp 376, 386; Low, D. *Landed property*, 1844, p 125; and Stephens, H. and Burn, R. S. *The book of farm buildings*, 1861, pp 346, 352. The first refers to glazing in stables and cowhouses only, the second and third to glazing in granaries and barns as well.

89. Ewart, J. *A treatise on the arrangement and construction of agricultural buildings*, 1851, p 6; Elliott, J. 'Farm buildings', *Journal of the Royal Agricultural Society of England*, vol 23, 1862, p 475; Evershed, H. 'Agriculture of Hertfordshire', ibid, vol 25, 1864, p 301; Denton, J. B. 'On the comparative cheapness and advantages of iron and wood in the construction of roofs for farm buildings', ibid, vol 2, 2nd ser, 1866, p 120; Tuckett, P. D. 'On the comparative cheapness and advantages of iron and wood in the construction of roofs for farm buildings', ibid, vol 2, 2nd ser, 1866, p 140
The land steward, 1851, p 195

90. Denton, J. B. *The farm homesteads of England*, 1863, p 147. See also Caird, J. *English agriculture in 1850–1*, 1852, p 439; Tebbutt, C. P. 'On the construction of farm buildings', *Journal of the Royal Agricultural Society of England*, vol 11, 1850, p 303; and Dean, G. A.

91. Hunt, G. 'On concrete as a building material for farm buildings and cottages', *Journal of the Royal Agricultural Society of England*, vol 10, 2nd ser, 1874, pp 211–32. Concrete blocks were used experimentally in the 1860s and proved cheaper than brickwork (Clark, F. J. 'A cheap material for farm buildings', ibid, vol 24, 1863, pp 552–3). But some at least proved 'very deficient in durability of transverse strength'. (Stephens, H. and Burn, R. S. *The book of farm buildings*, 1861, p 142), and there is no mention of such blocks in Hunt's general article quoted above. The first concrete farm building in this country was probably the highly unusual feeding shed, 162ft long, 60ft wide and 12ft 6in to the eaves, with mass concrete walls and an insulated tile roof, which Robert Campbell built about 1870 for an intensive cattle fattening enterprise on his Faringdon estate. (Gray, J. 'An industrialised farm estate in Berkshire', *Bulletin of Industrial Archaeology in CBA Group 9*, no 7, January 1969, pp 2–3.) See illustration p 122, top.

92. Stephens, H. and Burn, R. S. *The book of farm buildings*, 1861, pp 336, 419, 422

93. Andrews, H. G. *A rudimentary treatise on farm buildings, I. Buildings*, 1852, pp 135–40; Morton, J. C. *Cyclopedia of agriculture*, 1855, vol 1, p 797; Stephens, H. and Burn, R. S. *The book of farm buildings*, 1861, p 418; Denton, J. B. *The farm homesteads of England*, 1863, p 152

94. Tebbutt, C. P. 'On the construction of farm buildings', *Journal of the Royal Agricultural Society of England*, vol 11, 1850, p 309; Dean, G. 'On the cost of agricultural buildings', ibid, vol 11, 1850, p 568

95. Moscrop, W. J. 'On the farming of Leicestershire', *Journal of the Royal Agricultural Society of England*, vol 2, 2nd ser, 1866, p 312; Jenkins, H. M. 'Eastburn Farm, near Driffield, Yorkshire', ibid, vol 5, 2nd ser, 1869, p 415

96. Read, C. S. 'Report on the farming of Buckinghamshire', *Journal of the Royal Agricultural Society of England*, vol 16, 1855, p 309; Elliott, J. 'Farm buildings', ibid, vol 23, 1862, pp 43, 473; Denton, J. B. 'Report of the judges of farm plans sent in for competition', ibid, vol 5, 2nd ser, 1879, pp 780–1

97. Dean, G. A. *The land steward*, 1851, p 202

98. Stephens, H. and Burn, R. S. *The book of farm buildings*, 1861, p 422

99. Marshall, J. 'A report on the feeding of stock with prepared food', *Journal of the Royal Agricultural Society of England*, vol 7, 1847, p 392

100. Denton, J. B. *The farm homesteads of England*, 1863, p 152

(*above*) Post-war mechanisation: a graindryer stands in the old barn, a tractor fuel store outside it; (*below*) post-war improvisation: a cheap but effective system of storing concentrate fodder for feeding a piggery

Page 158 (above) The old order: a yard formed by buildings of local materials; (below) the new order: a yard built of prefabricated concrete members and asbestos-cement sheeting

Chapter Seven

VICTORIAN FARMSTEADS:
SOME EXAMPLES

NEW TIMES, NEW STANDARDS

The Victorians, like the Hanoverians, published their farmstead case-studies to illustrate practical examples of good commercial design. But their task was more difficult for they were
concerned with the introduction of new equipment and techniques as well as the application of agreed principles. Moreover,
their readers were considerably more sophisticated and critical
than those of Arthur Young's time, so that their work was
different in form as well as in content. It was more detailed, more
technical, more professional both in preparation and presenta-
tion, and its quality and character remind us immediately that
we are in the age of the engineer. Farmsteads were now industrial
installations designed on industrial principles, and those who
described them conformed to industrial standards.

A CORN-AND-MEAT FARMSTEAD

The farmstead shown in Fig 14 was planned in 1849 for a
typical corn-and-meat farm of 250 to 300 acres.[1] In basic design, it continued the traditions of the Agrarian Revolution, but
the improvements in detail it included were numerous.

Thus, the yards were better planned than those previously
illustrated, allowing the easier distribution of fodder and the
housing of cattle in small groups. The fattening shed was fitted
with a tramway for trollies to reduce the labour of feeding.
Louvred ventilators were provided for the enclosed livestock

K   159

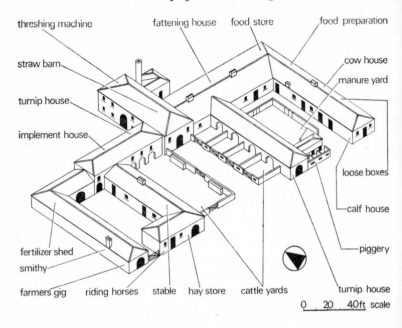

threshing machine   fattening house   food store   food preparation

straw barn

turnip house

implement house

cow house

manure yard

loose boxes

calf house

piggery

fertilizer shed

smithy

farmers gig   riding horses   stable   hay store   cattle yards   turnip house

0   20   40ft   scale

14   Steading designed in 1849 for a mixed farm of 200 to 300 acres
(see p 159)

buildings. Drainage, too, was carefully considered and an underground tank provided for liquid manure storage, while one of the sheds was used as a store for the fertilisers which advanced farmers were now beginning to buy in increasing quantities. Still, there was no drastic change in the system and, typically, the most conspicuous innovation, the introduction of steam threshing, did no more than substitute a more efficient for a less efficient form of prime mover. The barn altered its position to suit the new routine, but there was little attempt in this particular steading to use the new power to create a feed-preparation centre—the buildings contained five separate rooms for storing and processing fodder, each serving a particular group of animals. Essentially, therefore, this farmstead is a Victorian version of its predecessors.

A DAIRY FARMSTEAD

The needs of the dairy farm were very different from those of the corn-and-meat farm. Nevertheless, as this dairy farmstead (see Fig 15), designed in 1851 for a farm of 100 to 150 acres carrying a herd of twenty-eight milkers, showed, its buildings conformed to the same general pattern.[2]

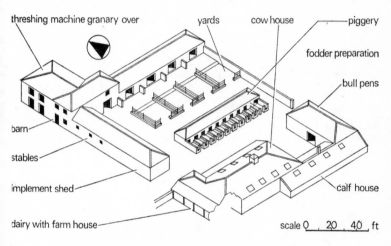

15   Steading designed in 1851 for a dairy farm of 100 to 150 acres carrying a herd of twenty-eight milkers (see p 161)

There were, of course, modifications. In particular, the barn decreased in importance and size and, since there was little corn to thresh, horse-gear was preferred to the more efficient but more expensive steam-engine. Again, a farm of this type needed only a small stable and implement shed. More generally, the dairy enterprise added a southern range, consisting of a cowshed adjacent to the farmhouse where the milk was made into butter, a calfhouse and bullpens, which in turn made necessary a row of sties for the pigs that fattened on the dairy wastes. But there was no radical change in plan. The steading remained a recognisable version of that found on the mixed farm previously illustrated.

AN ADVANCED FARMSTEAD OF THE STEAM AGE

One of the most remarkable sets of buildings of this period was erected in Herefordshire in 1861 to serve an arable and fattening farm of 614 acres which reared its own young stock.[3] (See Fig 16.) In general plan, it followed tradition, though the roofing of the yards to protect the cattle and manure was advanced rather than general practice. But its aggressively industrial equipment and manner of operation illustrated the degree to which a wealthy and progressive landowner could adapt the technology of the steam age to the purposes of the farm.

The mechanical heart of the farm was a 12hp steam-engine 'in a handsome Doric frame'. Its main task was driving the threshing machine, which was served by a miniature railway terminus of tramlines down which the stacks rolled by gravity

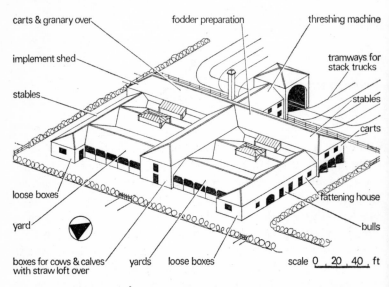

16　An advanced farmstead built in 1861 to serve a mixed farm of 614 acres in Herefordshire (see p 162)

on their timber trucks when the time came, and handling the grain and straw thus produced. After threshing, the grain went either to a sacking apparatus 'actuated by the beam of the weighing-machine', which not only ceased to pour when the sack was full but obligingly rang a bell as well, or else was carried to the granary by an auger and poured into any one of sixteen bins from swivel spouts. The straw was mechanically elevated and transported along a passage under the roof of the central range and dropped where required to the boxes and yards below.

In addition to processing the corn harvest, the engine also served the cattle enterprise. Its power was harnessed to a variety of cutting and grinding equipment, and its heat to cooking apparatus, so that the barn area included a central workshop for fodder preparation. Indeed, this steading represents one of the most ambitious attempts ever made to exploit the power of steam for farmstead work. But it illustrates the limitations as well as the achievements of the new prime mover. The steam-engine could not readily transmit power around a range of buildings and so failed to provide a basis for a satisfactory system of materials-handling. The grain in its auger and the straw on its conveyor emphasised by contrast the dependence of even so mechanised a farmstead as this on manual effort for the bulk of its internal transport.

CHOICE OF BUILDING MATERIALS

These case-studies show that the industrial age brought many improvements but few fundamental changes to farmstead design. They also show, however, that its effects on farmstead construction were more revolutionary, more comprehensive. The references in the specifications and descriptions of these buildings to cast-iron spouting, cast-iron pillars, asphalt, and galvanised-iron sheeting demonstrated the use the builder was now making of factory products. But the wider and more decisive implications of the Industrial Revolution were illustrated by the summaries of the advantages and disadvantages of such major materials as brick or stone for walling, and tiles or slates for roofing, given by the authors of the first two examples. For it was the railway age which, by ending dependence on local materials, first made such choices standard practice.

NOTES

1. Sturgess, T. 'Farm buildings', *Journal of the Royal Agricultural Society of England*, vol 11, 1850, pp 288–300
2. Ewart, J. *A treatise on the arrangement and construction of agricultural buildings*, 1851, pp 5–6, 18–20
3. Denton, J. B. *Farm homesteads of England*, 1863, pp 57–9, 92–4

Chapter Eight

DEPRESSION, ADAPTATION
AND IMPROVISATION:

1880-1939

COMPETITION FROM OVERSEAS

In 1866, some 16,000 lb of canned meat from Australia reached British ports. In 1871, the figure was 22 million lb.[1] This sudden appearance of a new source of food for the British consumer foreshadowed the more general combination of two factors which were soon to overthrow the traditional farming system of this country. The first was the exploitation of new lands overseas by colonising farmers, the second the development of cheap and reliable means of bringing their products to the British market.

The next generation saw the fulfilment of this prophecy. The mechanical reaper redeemed the prairie wheatgrower's lack of human labour, the wire fence came to the aid of the rancher on the treeless plains, and the railway was reinforced by the steamship equipped with refrigerated chambers. By the end of the century, the British farmer's ancient monopoly of the home market had gone down into history and he was striving to justify an economic activity whose obvious necessity had never before been questioned. The overseas producer, whom Caird in 1878 had welcomed as an ally in the task of feeding a growing population of these crowded islands where little land of agricultural value remained unoccupied, had turned rival, and for a lifetime there was little respite for the British farmer.

The flood of cheap corn from North America which reduced

the average price of wheat from 120s a cwt in the 1860s to 68s a cwt in the 1890s was merely the precursor of a steadily increasing mass of imports. Grain and meat, butter and cheese, from countries as varied as Australia and the Argentine, Denmark, New Zealand and the USA, undersold the British farmer in his home market. The Englishman's economic adversaries were powerful and he could expect little encouragement and few favours from his Free Trade countrymen. In the 1870s, the home farmer had supplied the home market with some three-quarters of its food. In the first decades of the present century, he supplied about a quarter, and it was the imports which fixed the prices he received. The pressure of foreign competition had replaced the needs of a growing population as the decisive factor in agricultural development. The depression times had come.

AGRICULTURAL ADJUSTMENT

So this period saw the gradual and painful adaptation of the farming system to the new conditions. Hence the change from brown to green as the farmer abandoned an arable system whose costs and losses were becoming intolerable and allowed the defeated ploughland to go down to grass. Hence a steady rise in the importance of the livestock with which the farmer exploited the new pastures and the cheap grain which had suddenly been thrust upon him. Hence, above all, the development of the liquid-milk industry for, alone among farmers in Great Britain, the milk-producer feared no competition from overseas. The extent of the change is shown in the figures. In the later 1860s, it has been estimated, the British farmer derived some 45 per cent of his income from his arable crops and 55 per cent from his livestock. By the later 1930s, the figures were 27 per cent and 73 per cent respectively. More particularly, in the same period, the proportion provided by wheat sank from 15 per cent to 2 per cent, the proportion provided by milk rose from 15 per cent to 29 per cent.[2] By the end of this period the farmer earned more from his milk than from all his arable cash crops put together, and the establishment in 1933 of the Milk Marketing Board, the farmer's first appearance in the unfamiliar world of Big Business, reflected the new agricultural order.

But the growing predominance of livestock brought with it other economic changes. Grass and its winter version, hay, could not feed all the animals all the time. So the farmer came to rely increasingly on imported fodders, particularly on imported concentrates which provided the protein necessary for the efficient production of meat and milk. This was nothing new in principle. But, as the volume of imported feedstuffs grew until by the late 1920s they provided about half the food, except for grass, consumed by British livestock, the change in scale produced a new form of agricultural industry. The farmer, who bought so much of his raw materials from overseas and converted them via the stomachs of his stock into human food, was turning manufacturer. By 1939 it was easy and even necessary to describe our farming system in crudely industrial terms of input, output and end-products.

NEGLECT AND DETERIORATION IN THE FARMSTEAD

Such changes in the farming system implied corresponding changes in the farmstead to meet the new technical needs. But the fall in agricultural prices was inevitably followed by a fall in the rent of agricultural land. The income on which the landlord depended to maintain and improve his property shrank—the rents of the depression times were commonly 10 per cent to 20 per cent lower than those of the mid-Victorian decades, yet building costs steadily increased with the general rise of prices.[3] There was now little point in reclaiming such small areas of the waste as remained, so no new farmsteads were required to save new farmland. The only class of new homestead built in this period served the smallholdings created for social rather than economic reasons under the 1892 Act and later legislation.[4] There was no incentive to reconstruct existing farmsteads to meet the new needs, soon there was no economic possibility of doing so. And finally, as hopes and resources slowly failed, even their maintenance was neglected. This was an age of steady deterioration, at best checked by patchwork and repairs on the cheap.

So the first general theme of this period was the end of a century's continuous development, the second the steady decay of the inherited stock of farm buildings. The former was rapid, since the decisions imposed by the times were abrupt and obvious, but the second was gradual and cumulative. Hall, in his agricultural tour just before the First World War, did not comment explicitly on the lack of new construction, for by his time men had come to take this for granted. But he found the farmsteads of the Hanoverians and Victorians in fair order. In some areas, buildings were good, in some areas bad, depending mainly on the type of material used. Farmsteads in stone districts naturally showed less wear and tear than those in districts which used clay, flints with mortar or bricks.[5] But as the years passed, the cumulative effect of human neglect and the steadily destructive power of nature began to turn the steadings which had served the most advanced farming system of its day into a collection of industrial slums.

Gradually, tirelessly, the rain seeped through roofs of decaying thatch or slipping slates, through holes where the wind had torn away tiles that were not replaced, and rotted the supporting timbers. Water from choked or falling guttering crumbled away walls and undermined foundations. Unpainted woodwork failed to hold window panes or door hinges. There was no end to it. Year by year, the patient processes of decay and disintegration probed for weaknesses in the unmaintained buildings. Year by year, they found less resistance and the slow, pervading degeneration they wrought became more obvious, less redeemable. As early as 1918 it was noted that many farmsteads in Berkshire had deteriorated too far for repair at economic cost,[6] and in the following decades the inefficiency of farm buildings became an accepted weakness in the rural economy. In 1939, a former Minister of Agriculture described their general condition as 'dreadful' It was difficult, he added, to 'exaggerate the extent of their dilapidation or the handicap it constitutes to good husbandry'.[7] Detailed local studies in this period provided a painful commentary on his generalisations.

Thus in the 1930s, when milk was the main source of the farmer's income, a survey of cowhouses in the Midlands reported that nearly a quarter of those visited needed complete reconstruction, and nearly a third substantial alteration if they were to be judged fit to produce clean milk.[8] Again, in East Anglia, once one of the most advanced and prosperous farming areas in the world, another study in the same decade showed that the buildings of 46 per cent of the farms investigated were inadequate or inconvenient, of 25 per cent in poor repair, and of 16 per cent inadequate or inconvenient *and* in poor repair.[9] And as it was in this area of large-scale arable farming, so it was among the small livestock farms of Carmarthen. Here most of the farms had most of the buildings they needed. But the buildings were old-fashioned and in poor condition. 'The cowsheds are very inadequate, the most prevalent faults being insufficient light and ventilation. . . . Stables are in many cases badly-constructed. . . . Many of the pigsties are small and so badly built that it is very difficult to keep them even moderately clean. . . . Another serious defect is the almost entire absence of any adequate accommodation for farmyard manure.'[10] Here as elsewhere, any general attempt at improvement had ceased and farmers were living patiently on their structural capital.

The agricultural costs of this pervading farmstead inefficiency were varied, considerable and obvious. Stored produce, manure, equipment, labour, livestock health and performance, there were few farming resources on which it did not levy toll. The more subtle personal costs were described in the 1920s by a Cambridgeshire farmer who considered his sodden morass of a yard, his century-old sheds and his dark, dank barn rendered just habitable for unhappy pigs by the addition of windows and half-doors, and reflected that his holding was typical of many thousands in England. 'We sometimes forget', he wrote, 'the large part of the life of the farm worker and farmer which is spent "somewhere round the yards". Much of this work is done in places which are dark, damp and draughty. . . . Poor as some of our urban factories may be, one would have to go down to the sweatshops of the East End of London to find anything as inefficient and uncomfortable as old-fashioned farm buildings. Farming with bad buildings is such a squalid job, that until this question is tackled, agriculture is bound to be a backward industry.' But the times offered little hope that it would be tackled and he concluded sadly that farming had got into a vicious circle. 'We dare not build because the industry will not stand it, and the industry gets worse because of the badness of the buildings'.[11]

IMPROVERS AND IMPROVEMENTS

Nevertheless, the pressures on the farmstead of the changing needs of the farm continued. New forms of enterprise, new equipment and techniques and, above all, the necessity of housing and feeding an increasing head of livestock, made direct and indirect demands on steadings designed for obsolete systems of farming.[12] Frequently, these pressures were ignored. It was cheaper to suffer loss from wastage, cheaper to accept the limitations imposed by an obsolete framework, than to rebuild. But there was a good deal of piecemeal, individual adaptation of old farmsteads to new purposes. The process is poorly documented, for it was essentially a matter of personal enterprise, particular farms and limited objectives—the conversion of an old building to a new purpose on one farm, the remodelling of a range of buildings on another. It was also inherently inefficient. For one thing, the proud and confident men of the Agricultural Revolution had assumed the permanence of the farming economy for which they planned and their steadings made little provision for the possibility of future change or expansion. For another, some of the older buildings were too unsound, some too solidly constructed, to allow easy or effective adaptation. But the times allowed no option. The farming community did its best with such resources as were available to it and sought no more than immediate answers to immediate problems. In this period, therefore, the inclusion in the textbooks of sections on modernising individual buildings or remodelling farmsteads became standard practice.[13]

Another sign of the times was the growing use of second-hand materials to meet the pressing need for economy. The first reference to the value of railway sleepers for walls for yards or sheds occurred as early as 1896; Nissen huts appeared on farms after the First World War; and in the next decade converted goods vans and railway carriages were common features of the agricultural landscape and an enterprising man could even find a profitable place in the farmstead for the funnels of an obsolete cruiser.[14] In these years, under relentless economic pressure, the farmer developed his current taste for structural improvisation with other people's discards into a recognised theme in the agricultural tradition.

Inevitably such conditions destroyed any hope that the farm-buildings designer would establish himself as a recognised ally of the farmer alongside the soil chemist, the veterinary surgeon, the agricultural engineer, the plant breeder and the other professionals who were by now accepted members of the agricultural system. The days of general development were past and there was no place for such men in a world of patchwork and slow degeneration. Neither landowner nor farmer needed outside assistance in meeting the routine problems of minimum maintenance and minor improvements. In particular, they no longer needed the steady supply of textbooks on which their early Victorian predecessors had relied for new ideas and up-to-date information—in the first thirty years of this period six such books appeared, in the last thirty only three. Almost alone among the various branches of agricultural technology, the planning of farm buildings remained entirely a matter for the local general practitioner.

Traditionally, this general practitioner was the land agent who administered the estate on behalf of the owner and employed either the staff of his estate yard or a local contractor for building work on the farms for which he was responsible. But the changes wrought by the depression brought into being a new and important figure in the history of farmstead development. This was the pioneering farmer. Of course, the views and needs of farmers had always affected building design, but from

Hanoverian times onwards, they had only done so indirectly, via the landlord who made the final decisions. Under the increasing economic pressures of the time, however, landowners were now increasingly prepared to sell land to farmers, thus creating a growing class of owner-occupiers. At the end of the nineteenth century, such men were rare. By the time of the First World War they occupied some 10 per cent of the agricultural land of the country, by the time of the Second some 30 per cent. As owners, they carried the responsibilities for the fixed equipment of their farms which had formerly been undertaken by their landlords. But they also enjoyed full managerial independence.[15]

The impoverished landowner might not be able or willing to raise the capital for such substantial investments as buildings—the Berkshire farmer who could not farm his hungry Down fields properly because his landlord could not provide the upland yards where bullocks could tread straw into manure typified the tenant whose farming was handicapped by his owner's inability to fulfil his traditional functions.[16] More particularly, in uncertain times when, in the words of a textbook on farm buildings, 'rotations once regarded as almost as fixed as the stars have passed away and in their place is little that can be regarded as permanent',[17] he would seldom be prepared to finance buildings which might meet the needs of the particular tenant then in occupation of the farm but not those of his unknown successor. The complaints in 1916 of the Oxfordshire land agents who had invested in dairy buildings at the insistence of their tenants only to find that the tenants who followed them did not continue in the milk business illustrated this general problem.[18] But the owner-occupier cared for none of these things. He could build, demolish, improvise or adapt as his interests suggested and his resources allowed. He could also, if he wished, innovate or experiment. He had nobody to consider but himself.

Admittedly, few owner-occupiers were able to take much advantage from this theoretical freedom. The burden of the depression was too great—'the better you farm, the more you spend, and the more you spend, the more you lose' was a familiar saying of the time. But to a minority of enterprising men, the tenurial changes offered unprecedented opportunity. A generation later, in a famous phrase, Sir George Stapledon proclaimed the need for 'mad farmers', by which he meant farmers capable of abandoning tradition and enthusiastically introducing new systems, unproven but promising techniques, anything which appeared remotely hopeful of success, before conventional wisdom had time to prove its impossibility. Now, for the first time, such men could apply their peculiar talents to the buildings on their farms. Farmstead development had gained a new and valuable source of ideas.

BARN AND GRAINSTORE

Throughout this period, the barn continued to dominate the farmstead. But it was now little more than an historical relic. There was less corn to be harvested; the decreased crop was no longer threshed indoors but ricked in the open and threshed by portable machines moved and driven by traction-engines; and by the 1890s the adaptation of these obsolete buildings to new purposes had become a standard problem for the landowner and the farmer.[19] Some were converted to implement houses or various forms of livestock buildings, some continued a reduced form of their original function as stores for bagged grain and straw, others degenerated into dignified dumps for anything that could not conveniently be housed elsewhere. Some, more symbolically, became fodder-stores and mixing-rooms from which the livestock which had replaced the corn enterprise were supplied with their concentrate rations. But nearly all of them shared a common neglect, for their design and construction, in particular their huge roof surfaces, made them the most expensive and least remunerative buildings on the farm to maintain. They survived not because the farmer needed them but because they were the most substantial structures he had inherited.

At the end of this period, however, a few barns recovered something of their ancient purpose. For in 1928 a new machine appeared in the English cornfields. This was the combine-harvester, a fusion of the reaper and the threshing machine which cut and thrashed the corn in one mobile operation, excreting the straw behind it on the land it stripped. It offered considerable savings in the labour and cost of harvesting. But it offered them at a capital cost which only substantial corn-growers could afford, and by 1939 there were no more than 150 'combines' in the country. Even so, the effects on the farmstead of this new harvesting technique were already visible.

For the combine brought problems as well as economies. It delivers the crop as grain, not as sheaves of unthreshed corn, and therefore eliminates the rick from the routine harvest. But it does not eliminate the needs met by the rick, which is essentially a form of aerated store that both protects the corn it houses and allows the wind and atmosphere to dry it. The combine produces a sudden mass of grain which always needs storage and generally needs drying as well to prevent heating and the development of moulds. The Norfolk farmer who in 1931 invested in two combines and in 1932 found himself forced to further expenditure on a grain-drying installation was only one of the first of those who turned to the engineer for new and complicated equipment to meet the new needs—drying plants of various types and sizes to rid the grain of its surplus moisture, bins to hold it, and conveyors to move it from place to place in the plant.[20] The combine, true to its inorganic origins, had sired a sort of mechanical rick.

Since the new grain-drying and storage plants necessarily served large arable farms, there was often no need to provide them with new housing, for the old barns commonly stood empty or half-used. So part of the harvest routine returned to its ancient home and the dryer and its associated bins stood where the Hanoverians had installed their threshing machines and forgotten generations of flailers had toiled in dusty discomfort. But we must beware of any sentimental assumption of continuity in these changes. It was mere structural accident that a building designed for the processes of one age happened to be available and suitable for the processes of another.

Page 175 (above) Some of the history of this Wiltshire farm can be reconstructed from its buildings. It probably began after some Hanoverian enclosure as a meat-and-corn stead-ng with two yards, a long, low shelter for stock on the right, with a granary at the end of t and stables facing the house. In the later nineteenth century the shelter became a cow-shed and a dairy was built at the back of the farmhouse. The Dutch barns and the corru-gated iron implement shed were added in the earlier twentieth century. The pigsties on he right were built between the wars when imported feedstuffs were cheap; (below) the development of a Berkshire farmstead. The barn and flanking ranges of buildings round three sides of an open yard illustrate the basic design of the Hanoverian and early Victorian farmstead. The buildings with corrugated-iron roofing were probably added early in the nineteenth century; those with asbestos-cement roofing after World War II

CHANGE IN THE DAIRY FARMSTEAD

It was, however, a sign of the times that the greatest single cause of change in the farmstead in this period was not connected with grain production. It was the expansion of the liquid-milk industry first made possible by the railways and later encouraged by the development of road transport. One sign of its triumph was the increase in the number of dairy cows in England and Wales from under two million in the early 1880s to over three million in the late 1930s. Another was the steady decline of the ancient farmhouse trades of butter-making and cheese-making, the result of competition from the new form of dairy enterprise as well as from home and overseas factories. By 1914, butter-making on the farm survived in only a few areas where communications did not allow the marketing of liquid milk,[21] by 1939 barely a thousand farms continued cheese production.[22] A third reason was the end of the dairy farmer's urban rival. The old system died slowly and as late as 1930 there were just over a thousand cows in inner London, including a herd of eighty-five head in Bermondsey, and nearly five thousand in 280 cowhouses in Liverpool, where the stocking rate in terms of cows per acre was higher than that of the dairy county of Somerset.[23] But its days were numbered and in the next age the town cowhouse was to become first a curiosity, then a memory.

More cows meant more cowhouses on more farms, but there was no radical change in the design inherited from the mid-Victorians. There was, however, a good deal of improvement in detail, mainly as the result of the steady pressure of a new set of influences on the planning of dairy farmsteads. Rules and regulations had come and with them a new figure on the agricultural landscape, the inspector, 'the man from the council', who enforced them.

The increasing importance of milk as an item in urban diet was welcomed by reformers as well as producers. But the legislators of an age in which Disraeli took '*Sanitas sanitatum, omnia*

L

sanitas' as the text as one of his most famous speeches were not likely to overlook the dangers inherent in the increased consumption of a highly perishable commodity peculiarly susceptible to contamination. Consequently, a series of measures, beginning with the Dairies, Cowsheds and Milkshops Order of 1885, made local authorities responsible for issuing by-laws regulating the design and construction of dairy buildings to secure 'the health and good condition of the cattle therein, the cleanliness of milk-vessels therein and the protection of the milk therein against infection'. The phrasing was general, the application particular and detailed, and over the years the various local authorities gradually developed codes and precedents to determine the standards of lighting, ventilation, drainage and water-supply acceptable in their jurisdiction.

The dairy presented a general problem, for most farmers naturally continued to use the dairy at the back of the farmhouse where their mothers had once made butter and cheese. Such dairies were commonly some distance from the cowhouse and the milk was too often exposed to contamination from the yards across which it was carried in pails. But it took many regulations, many arguments and many years to end this old tradition and establish the new type of dairy adjacent to the cowhouse it served. The change is difficult to follow in detail, but it was apparently the replacement of the older regulations by the more demanding Milk and Dairies Order of 1926 that finally established the familiar dairy with its corrugated cooler, its washing troughs and its steam-sterilising chest, as a necessary part of the cowhouse on the better milk-producing farm.[24]

In the cowhouse itself the new authorities required 'proper and necessary' standards of ventilation, window-lighting and air space per beast in the cowhouse. They preferred concrete floors to cobble or earthen floors, proper dung-channels to hopeful slopes, external to internal drain inlets. Taken separately, none of their demands were revolutionary—indeed, they asked no more than accepted good practice which, in many cases, made possible easier working as well as a higher standard of hygiene. None involved substantial structural

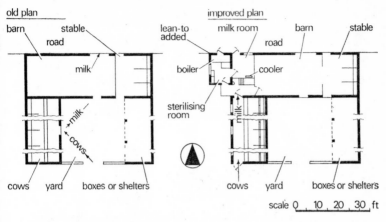

17 Typical inter-war example of the improvement of a milk production system by the addition of a dairy (see p 178). (Based on *The construction of cowhouses*, HMSO, 1929, p 19)

change. None, except the gradual insistence that the cattle in double-range houses should stand tail to tail instead of head to head to avoid cross-infection, even necessitated major changes in internal rearrangement. Taken together, however, they created a new form of an old building. In 1924, for instance, a visitor to the dairying county of Cheshire commented on the difference between the older houses, in which the stalls stood across the width of the building, and those constructed in the last twenty years, in which they stood along the length of the house, thus simplifying the feeding routine and allowing better supervision of the herd in addition to improving lighting and ventilation.[25] Much of the credit for such improvements must go to the by-laws and those who administered them. It is no accident that two of the farm-buildings textbooks of this period include appendices which quote the model regulations in full.[26]

These improvements in the milking environment were soon accompanied by an improvement in milking technique. In the early 1900s, nearly a century of inventions, patents and peculiarities finally produced a practicable form of milking machine, which for the first time enabled one man to milk more than one cow simultaneously.[27] The benefit was considerable, the ac-

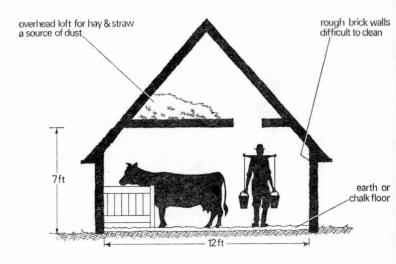

overhead loft for hay & straw
a source of dust

rough brick walls
difficult to clean

7ft

earth or
chalk floor

12ft

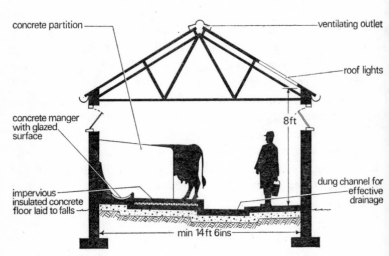

concrete partition

ventilating outlet

roof lights

concrete manger
with glazed
surface

8ft

impervious
insulated concrete
floor laid to falls

dung channel for
effective
drainage

min 14ft 6ins

18   The development of the cowhouse: (above) a typical mid-Victorian
cowhouse; (*below*) a typical cowhouse of the 1930s

ceptance slow and cautious. In 1919, an official committee reported that the machines gave good performance but that many farmers preferred hand-labour if it was available.[28] The proviso was important. The agricultural labour force was shrinking and under sheer demographic pressure the vacuum pump and pipes, the teat-cups and milk containers of the 'bucket' type of milking machine, gradually established themselves in the cowhouse. By 1939, some 8 per cent of herds and 15 per cent of cows were milked mechanically.[29]

The new machines greatly decreased the labour of milking in the cowhouse. But they did not remedy the inherent economic weaknesses of the cowhouse system. For a building in which each cow has a substantial stall of her own and men bring food and litter to her and take milk and manure away from her is necessarily expensive in both capital and labour. Economic pressures made a new system desirable, technical development made it possible; and the later years of the period saw the first break with the inherited traditions of the cowhouse.

The agent of this change was the bucket plant's more sophisticated successor, the 'releaser' type of milking machine, which appeared on the market in the early 1920s. For the bucket plant was literally a milking machine and only a milking machine. It did no more than transfer the milk from the udder to the bucket. But the releaser plant also carried the milk from the udder to the dairy in an overhead pipeline. It could not as yet operate satisfactorily in a building as large as a cowhouse, for the distance it could carry milk was limited. But its scope was sufficient to make it the mechanical basis of a new and revolutionary type of dairy building.

The possibilities it offered were first grasped by A. J. Hosier, a Wiltshire farmer faced with the problem of establishing a large dairy enterprise on a thousand acres of chalk and with no adequate buildings. Hand-milking of a herd the size he planned was out of the question. So was the cost of building the necessary cowsheds. With radical simplicity, therefore, he distinguished between the housing function and the milking-room function of the cowhouse. His cows, he decided, needed winter housing neither for their own sake nor, since his well-drained soil could stand concentrated treading in the winter months, for the sake of the land. But they still needed milking and it was cheaper to take a milking-point to a large number of cows than to bring a large number of cows to the milking-point. So in 1922 he constructed from bits and pieces of discarded machines a releaser plant on wheels, complete with a light roof and portable dairy equipment, which a tractor could tow to the cows in the fields.

In so doing, he secured advantages denied to those who followed the older tradition. For in the cowhouse the farmer with a bucket plant continued to milk each cow in her stall. His machine enabled him to milk several cows at once but it did not enable him to reduce the number of stalls his herd required. But Hosier needed only a few stalls. At milking-time, the cows filed through them one after the other, each cow remaining in them only long enough to be milked and then making room for her successor. So each of his stalls served eight, ten, or twelve cows. The milking machine reduced the labour costs of all who used it. But Hosier was the first for whom it also reduced capital costs.[30]

Neither Hosier's invention nor the system of open-air dairying which it made possible commended itself to local tradition. But both were successful and in 1927 Hosier was able to form a small company for the commercial manufacture of the portable 'bails' he had invented. Nevertheless, these bails were no more than the fore-runners of a more general technical change, for they could only be used in certain exceptional areas where the soil would not suffer excessively from the hooves of out-wintered cattle. This change began in 1932, when Hosier decided to establish a permanent milking-point on his farm and so created the prototype of the specialised dairy building we now call 'a milking-parlour'.[31] (See illustration p 140, bottom.)

Physically, this is best described as a bail in a building—a set of stalls to hold the cows while they are being milked, a releaser plant to milk them and a dairy to process their milk, with a floor beneath them, walls around them and a roof over them. Economically, it provided the dairy farmer with a new and efficient means of fulfilling one of the main functions of the traditional cowhouse. But it was cheaper to build, since a farmer with a parlour could milk as many cows as his neighbour with a cowhouse several times the parlour's size. It was also cheaper to run, because the releaser plant mechanised more operations than the bucket plant. But technically it owed its importance neither to its origins nor to its competitive advantages but to its own peculiar characteristics. For essentially the parlour is a 'housed mechanical process', one of the most unequivocal and successful examples of a farm building planned around a machine and in accordance with the routines it dictated. Its development heralded the revival in new form of the tradition created by the engineers of the steam age a century earlier.[32]

But this was for the future. The immediate impact of the parlour on the dairy farmstead was limited to areas where cows required no winter housing—or, more accurately, to such few farmers in such areas who were either starting a dairy enterprise or were prepared to abandon their existing cowhouses and invest in parlours. But in most of the country, where the needs of stock and soil combined to make the winter housing of the dairy herd necessary, the single-purpose parlour, which offered an improved method of milking, presented no real challenge to the dual-purpose cowhouse in which the farmer could house as well as milk his herd.

Even in these areas, however, economic pressures were already suggesting the shape of things to come. In 1926 an enterprising Northamptonshire farmer named W. S. Abbot converted an old barn into a cowhouse but, wishing to economise, built only sufficient stalls for milking his cows in batches, as in a bail or a parlour. In the winter, he housed them in one of the strawed yards traditionally occupied by fattening bullocks. Economically, this farmstead adaptation reflected the growth of the dairy herd at the expense of the grain and meat enterprises. Technically, it unknowingly foreshadowed the answer to a problem which had not yet arisen. The innovation attracted little attention in its own time, but in the next generation a substantial and increasing proportion of the national milk supply was to come from cows milked in parlours and housed in yards.[33]

The expansion of the national dairy herd created problems of feeding as well as problems of housing. Pasture provided grazing in the summer months, and the merchant provided concentrates all the year round. But the supply of bulk fodder for the winter months was a more difficult matter. Traditionally, the farmer relied for this on his hay and his roots. Now, however, the changing times were emphasising the disadvantages of both crops. On the one hand, the dairy farmer needed a supply of hay reliable in both quantity and quality if he was to get the best out of his herd. But hay-making, however delightful in literary retrospect, is inevitably a chancey process when cutting, drying and stacking are all at the mercy of a singularly unpredictable climate. On the other hand, he wanted his fodder cheap. But the root crops were the most costly part of the intensive ploughland system on which the depression had fallen so heavily and the rate of decline of the root acreage was even greater than that of the other arable crops.

Here, again, however, a combination of agricultural need and technical development produced an alternative to the inherited systems. This was silage-making, a process evolved on the Continent in the middle years of the nineteenth century.[34] Essentially, this is a crude form of canning, the cut grass or other green crop being stored undried in an airtight pit or structural container, which gives it an independence of the weather denied to hay-making. It therefore offered the farmer a way of producing a new form of bulk fodder less hazardous than hay and cheaper than roots. But it offered these benefits only to those who understood the problems involved, and the manner of its introduction to Great Britain provides an instructive commentary on the implications of technological change in this period.

The story began conventionally enough in the 1880s when the first campaign to introduce silage into the country maintained the familiar procedures of the Agricultural Revolution. Its sponsors were the traditional leaders of the farming industry, notably the Duke of Bedford and Lord Walsingham, its technical centres their estates and the farms of their more substantial tenants, its literature mainly surveys of practice and reports of individual experiences. But behind the façade of the old order the shape of things to come was already apparent.

For one thing, the British farmer was accustomed to develop his own improvements in his own way with little help from foreigners. But this time he necessarily relied for much of his original information on Continental sources. More strikingly, interest in the new possibilities produced in 1883 the first book to offer the home farmer the lessons of American research and development.[35] The days of the old insularity were numbered and one of the major sources of new technical knowledge made its first tentative appearance on the historical scene. For another, the private-enterprise system of communication on which the industry relied for the spread of new ideas and information could not meet the sudden demand for advice on this complicated innovation and the balance was redressed, prophetically, by the administrative resources of the State. The two substantial reports issued in this decade which recorded the findings of a comprehensive survey of all the silos in the kingdom by the Agricultural Department of the Privy Council and the proceedings of a Royal Commission into silage helped to make the early practice of silage-making one of the best-documented of all farmstead developments. They also marked the first modern appearance of the government in its now familiar role of agricultural investigator and advisor.[36]

To contemporaries, however, all this was merely part of the triumphant progress of the new system. The interest it aroused was considerable, extensive and fashionable—in 1884, for instance, the Prince of Wales publicly commended silage at an agricultural meeting[37]—and within a few years an astonishing variety of assorted silos, over a thousand in all, had appeared on British farms.

There was, of course, no standardised design for such a novel type of building and each man built as he thought fit. Some of these silos were below ground, either as lined pits or in the simpler form of mere 'holes to bury hay stacks in'. Some were above ground as clamps or towers, some partly above and partly below ground. Others were formed within existing buildings, such as 'barns whose occupation is to a great extent gone',[38] some were unprecedented types of structure specially designed for the new purposes. Some were equipped with hydraulic presses and other mechanical gadgets for the necessary consolidation of the material, and some relied on weights or treading by horses. It was all very picturesque, but it was not the way of the coming times. Gradually it became obvious that the results of these varied activities were not sufficiently attractive to win farmers from the familiar routines of the hayfield and by the end of the century only the occasional enthusiast continued to make silage. In 1912, for instance, it was noted that even in Westmorland, one of the counties where climate most strongly favours silage, none of the fifty-seven silos built a generation before were still in use.[39]

There were various reasons for this failure. The technique was new, many mistakes were made and there was no general advisory service to provide guidance on right and wrong methods. More fundamentally, there was insufficient technical knowledge of the type that can only be obtained by research, for the men of the time did not realise that the processes which produced the 'sweet silage' they so prized also caused substantial losses in digestibility, particularly in the digestibility of protein.[40] The field was yielding to the laboratory as a source of agricultural knowledge and the traditional combination of aristocratic patronage and the pooling of empirical observations was no substitute for recommendations based on prolonged scientific study.

The new century saw a new attack on the problem which was symbolised by the erection in 1901 of a new kind of silo on a new kind of farm. The former was a wooden tower silo of American type, the first product of American technology to establish itself in the English farmstead. The latter was the experimental farm of Wye College, for it was now clear that the future of silage lay largely in the hands of the research-workers.[41] As the years passed, scientific understanding of the complex problems of this method of crop conservation increased. So did the number of towers in the farmlands, for they soon proved their efficiency. But they were too expensive for general use and never spread beyond the minority of the larger and more advanced farms, notably in the eastern counties, where farmers developed special mixtures of arable crops, such as oats and vetches, to replace their increasingly uneconomic roots.[42]

Indeed, it is doubtful if the number of silos in the country in the 1930s was any greater than that in the 1880s. At first sight, therefore, silage in this period had done little more than establish itself as a possible means of greencrop conservation. But this is a superficial assessment. In sounder analysis, the farmer had mastered a new system whose value was to be made manifest in the next generation. But he had not done this on his own. He owed his success to the scientists who had learnt the principles of silage-making in their laboratories and field-stations and to the engineers who designed the towers to hold the new material and the equipment to handle it.

The point is of more than specialised importance, for the story of silage in this half-century epitomises the weaknesses of the old system for securing agricultural innovation and the reasons for the development of more sophisticated procedures. The improvised Victorian silos represented one of the last technical developments pioneered by the traditional leaders of agriculture, the towers of the twentieth century one of the first research-based technologies to affect the design and construction of the farmstead.

GRASS DRYING

The importance of the scientist and the engineer was even more obvious in the development of another method of grass conservation which made its appearance on the farm at the very end of this period. Farmers had long known from observation that young grass was a peculiarly rich feed. They also knew, however, that the only means open to them of ensuring a steady supply of young grass, intensive grazing or equally intensive cutting and feeding, were impracticable under normal conditions of management. But the scientists who investigated this problem in the 1920s showed that grass of this type could be preserved with little loss of feeding value by artificial drying and in due course the engineers produced equipment, housed in simple industrial-type sheds, which dried young grass, cut continuously during the growing season, into a convenient and stable form of fodder. The first of these grass driers started work in 1933 and by the outbreak of war over eighty of them were in operation on English and Welsh farms, not merely conserving grass at its most valuable stage of development but converting it from a bulky to a concentrate feed. Driers were too expensive, and the system of grassland-management required to supply them too exacting for the new technique to enter into general practice. But it did allow enterprising farmers to produce their own concentrates and sell the surplus of their industrially-processed grass to other farmers, thus turning a forage crop into a cash crop. The grass-drying farmer was, in fact, a part-time manufacturer.[43]

BUILDINGS FOR BEEF PRODUCTION

The depression favoured the dairy cow and therefore encouraged the buildings and technologies that her particular line of production required. But it dealt harshly with her beef-producing cousins which had fattened so contentedly in the yards and boxes of the mid-Victorians. They formed part of the failing arable system and their meat could not compete in price with the refrigerated products of overseas ranches. From the time of the First World War onwards there was no increase of beef cattle on British farms and even this static level was only maintained by farming habits which took little account of costings. By the 1930s, the intensive box system had gone down into history and the fattening of yarded bullocks ranked high among the more gentlemanly ways of losing money. Drink, it was admitted, might be simpler, horses quicker and women pleasanter, but none was so reliable or so respectable as the good old bullock in the good old yard.

So the farmers of the early twentieth century continued to fatten bullocks in the yards built by their nineteenth-century predecessors. Occasionally they improved them, notably by roofing open yards to preserve the manurial values whose continuing importance is amusingly illustrated by an unexpectedly personal passage in an otherwise detached textbook—'I have seen manure four to five feet thick cut out of the centre of a covered yard by a trussing knife, splendid stuff, resembling in section streaky bacon, for which hungry land would be grateful as a hungry man for the other.'[44] But generally they could not even afford to reach such standards of approved Victorian practice and they took, and left, the yards as they found them— the buildings of one of the better Berkshire estates in 1918 'were almost invariably easily identified by their covered yards'.[45] The unhappy, unprofitable bullocks in a dilapidated yard bottomed with a soggy morass of wasting manure so typical of these times proclaimed the failure of a major Victorian enterprise.[46]

MORE PIGS, NEW PIGGERIES

The pig was more fortunate, for the new age brought him cheap food as well as competition from overseas. Indeed, it is in terms of fodder that the development of the pig enterprise in this period is most convincingly analysed. The end of butter and cheese manufacture on the farm deprived the pig of the waste products which had secured him his traditional place on the dairy farm.[47] But the coming of cheap grain and cheap imported concentrates encouraged new types of pig farming which made necessary new types of piggery. In the first decade of the twentieth century, the pig population continued at its old level and textbooks still recommended the Victorian pen-and-run system of housing derived from the traditional cottager's pigsty.[48] By the 1930s, the number of pigs had increased by half, they were concentrated in larger numbers on fewer farms and technical writers were talking of pig buildings in terms of 'plant' and detailing new and sophisticated designs based on overseas models.[49]

But there was no wholesale revolution. By the end of this period, only one of the three main groups of pig producer made any general use of the new types of building. The smallholders and 'cottage garden men', whose pigs were a domestic asset rather than a source of cash income, were content with the cheap and simple pigsty.[50] The general farmers who kept pigs in various degrees of economic intensity, sometimes as major enterprises, sometimes as mere sidelines to turn tail corn and chat potatoes into meat and manure, took a more commercial line. But they were well aware of the celebrated 'pig cycle' of alternate booms and slumps which affected prices with such painful regularity and were seldom prepared to sink capital in specialised buildings. On the contrary, they exploited the pig's domestic adaptability and improvised pig housing from any form of cover that happened to be available. Some, indeed, went further. They revived the old tradition of 'the open air pig' and reared their herds in woodlands, providing them only with huts or rough shelters.[51] Thus, a survey of pig housing in the 1930s found that pigs were farrowed in anything from huts in the field via dog kennels, railway carriages and goods vans to artificially warmed pens, and fattened in converted dwelling houses, poultry houses, loose boxes, implement sheds, cowsheds, cottagers' pigsties, barns, yards, malthouses and even a disused railway-engine shed.[52] But the more specialist producers, including a number working on factory lines with pigs as their processing plant and purchased fodder as their raw material, sought higher standards of efficiency in their buildings, particularly in their fattening houses. It was, however, typical of the empirical times that they neither made nor sponsored any general attempt to identify the type of environment which best suited the fattening pig and to design a building to provide it. Instead, they copied the most successful type of house available.

This was the 'Danish' or 'Scandinavian' house, which first

appeared in Great Britain in the early 1930s, and soon became the standard piggery on advanced farms.[53] The principle on which this totally enclosed house was designed was sound, for it strove to keep the pigs warm by conserving their body heat and thus reducing the feed bill which was the main item in their production cost. So was its internal design, for it allowed the pigs separate living and dunging areas and the pigmen a convenient central feeding passage. Yet the performance of these houses in Great Britain varied wildly. At one extreme they allowed specialists to fatten pigs on a scale and with an efficiency never before seen. For example, they housed the pigs of R. P. Chester, the industrialist who converted a thousand acres of semi-derelict land in Hampshire into the largest pig enterprise in the country, complete with a substantial office and laboratory.[54] At the other, they proved less effective than the familiar improvised housing on general farms. The basic reason for this discrepancy provided a further illustration of the growing inadequacy of the practical tradition in the new technical times.

For the 'Danish' houses erected in Great Britain were not copies of their Scandinavian originals. They were adaptations to one climate of a type of building developed for another climate. Such adaptation was obviously desirable. It was the manner of the adaptation which was at fault. There was little attempt to devise a building which would reproduce in Great Britain the environment which their prototypes provided in their homeland. But there was a great deal of empirical guess-work on the degree to which the unfamiliar overhead lofts and the expensive degree of insulation of the true Danish houses could be reduced. Some farmers chose wisely. Many chose unwisely and in the years ahead a section on methods of improving conditions in Danish-type houses by decreasing heat loss was to become a commonplace of farm-building textbooks.[55] But the next age would do more than offer remedies for such defects. It would also provide for the first time recommendations and specifications based on something firmer than personal opinion.

The development of poultry housing in these years followed the general pattern of pig housing. For poultry, like pigs, benefitted from the new supply of cheap concentrates and offered alternative hopes of profit to farmers whose traditional lines were no longer paying.

For most of this period, however, poultry remained no more than a casual sideline of the mixed-farming system, by custom the responsibility of the farmer's wife who relied on eggs for pin-money. But between the wars a minor agricultural revolution created a new and expanded form of poultry industry, based on egg production. The number of hens in the country doubled; the old dual-purpose type of bird was largely replaced by more specialised egg-producing breeds; the average egg production per bird rose rapidly; and in the last quarter of this period the barnyard flocks found themselves competing increasingly not only with a substantial poultry enterprise developed on many general farms but, also, more prophetically, with the intensive systems of the specialist producers.

Traditional methods survived on many farms where a few dozen hens and a proud cock sheltered in simple timber huts fitted with perches or, like the birds of the Carmarthen smallholders which roosted in the cartsheds,[56] found what homes they could in the buildings of the farmstead. But on others long lines of unfamiliar structures appeared in fields once dedicated to corn and cattle. Sometimes these were movable pens with attached runs, shifted regularly by hand or tractor,[57] sometimes small sheds, sometimes substantial timber houses, open-fronted in the southern counties, totally enclosed like the 'Lancashire cabin' in the harsher north, each as large as a conventional cowhouse and fitted with 'scratching quarters, nests and all utensils for feeding, confinement of broody hens, etc'.[58] On many of these farms, however, the fields contributed little but space for exercise and sunlight to the thousands of birds concentrated on them. The intensive poultryman, like the intensive pigman, was buying his feed from the merchant and developing methods of production which had as much in common with the factory as with the traditional type of farm.

An even more radical break with tradition was now on the way. For the discovery that cod-liver oil could provide birds with the vitamin D for which they were otherwise dependent on the action on their bodies of direct sunlight enabled farmers for the first time to keep poultry permanently indoors. All that was needed for egg production, therefore, was a building, hens and food. There was no longer any need for fields. Soon even the limiting factor of floor space was to be reduced. For the early total confinement houses, like their less intensive predecessors, allowed the birds to run loose on the floor. But in the middle 1920s experiment with cage systems to control such anti-social habits as feather-pecking and cannibalism produced the battery system of three, four or even five tiers of hens in types of individual cage which allowed easy feeding, egg collection, egg recording and manure removal. Science and technology had devised a method of maintaining large numbers of birds in buildings independent of the farm.[59]

The immediate importance of the battery system was small, but the ultimate importance of the principles it incorporated was immense. It was a major step in the intensification of livestock husbandry, and typically, it raised in the countryside a problem hitherto confined to the cattle enterprises of the towns. It is no accident that one of the questions discussed in the first book published on this system was the possibility of selling poultry manure.[60] Livestock enterprises had long been able to exceed the productive capacity of the particular farm which carried them. This was first evidence that new systems of management incorporated in new systems of housing would also allow them to exceed its absorbtive capacity.

MECHANISATION IN FIELD AND STEADING

So the number of livestock on the farm increased. But the number of men steadily decreased as farm workers left their

M

impoverished industry for better prospects elsewhere. At the end of this period there were as many farmers as at the beginning, but the labour force they employed had fallen by half; and there were limits to the possible economies from lowered standards and less exacting systems of farming. So the farmer turned increasingly to forms of prime-mover cheaper and more readily available than human beings.

The most obvious change came in the fields. At first the farmer made greater use of four-legged horsepower and the number of horses used solely for agricultural purposes rose from 844,000 in 1881 to its peak of 937,000 in 1911 as the ancient combination of sickle, scythe or rake and human muscles finally yielded to the horsedrawn reaper and binder, the horsedrawn mower, swath-turner and side-delivery rake. Then he began to replace the horse by the more powerful and convenient tractor and the throb of the internal-combustion engine took its place among the normal sounds of the countryside. By 1939, there were still eleven horses to every tractor but the latter produced two-thirds of the total mobile power of the farm.[61]

The effects on the farmstead of such mechanisation were slight. The new implements, like their predecessors, required only simple shelter and the additional horses only more stables of a long-established pattern, while the tractor was content with 'a disused coachhouse or similar building',[62] preferably with a concrete floor to ease the task of maintenance and repair, and a small fuel store. All this was a matter of minor modifications and adjustment. But meanwhile an equally important though less spectacular revolution was developing behind the walls of the farmstead. The farmer was replacing human power by mechanical power in the buildings as well as in the fields.

The first agent of this revolution was the internal-combustion engine which lightened many farmstead chores long before it was harnessed to plough, drill or reaper. Gas-engines were used on farms in the 1880s, but were soon superseded by the 'petroleum engine' which made its earliest agricultural appearance at the Royal Show in 1888 and was recognised in the following decade as a 'highly useful means of driving farm machinery' and a serious rival to the steam-engine which had hitherto provided the only general alternative to manpower for indoor work.[63] In the next generation the progress of this new prime-mover was rapid. In 1908, it has been estimated, static petrol and oil engines provided the farming industry with 46,000hp; in 1913 with 108,000hp; in 1925 with 370,000hp and in 1939 with 540,000hp.[64] Only in the middle 1930s did the mobile horse-power of the farmer's tractor fleet exceed that of the stationary engines which worked in his farmstead.

The nineteenth century had provided the farmer with means of producing power, first the steam-engine, then the internal-combustion engine which gradually replaced it. The twentieth century, more radical, provided him with readymade power, manufactured centrally, distributed by wires and available at the flick of a switch. As far back as 1908 an enterprising engineer had proclaimed the agricultural possibilities of clean and quiet electrical power.[65] But such hopes were mere dreams until the general spread of powerlines into the countryside, and it was only at the end of this period that the farmer made any sub-stantial use of electricity except for lighting. In the 1930s, how-ever, the increase of electrical equipment exhibited at agricul-tural shows,[66] the conversion of the last horse-threshers in Nor-thumberland to electric drive[67] and the appearance of a section on electricity in a major agricultural annual[68] marked the ac-ceptance of the new power as a normal tool of the farming trade. The farmstead improver had acquired an ally, the internal-combustion engine a rival.

By the end of this period, therefore, static mechanical power, sometimes aided by stationary tractors, ground and mixed fodder, milked cows and pumped water in a substantial and increasing proportion of farmsteads. Yet it is more accurate to call this development the use of machinery than true mechanisa-tion. For, in general, the new prime-movers entered the farmstead on the farmstead's terms. They fitted themselves into existing buildings and took their place in existing routines. They were improved substitutes for earlier forms of power, for the power of men and horses, water and steam, and not means of creating new operational patterns. They saved the farmer time and energy but they brought few major changes to the processes they powered or the design of building that housed them. The appearance of the farmstead was no guide to the amount of mechanical power used in it.

Nevertheless, there were limited but prophetic exceptions to this generalisation, for the implications of the pervading and versatile mechanical power now freely available to the farmer for the first time were already becoming visible among the run-down steadings of the depression times. New mechanical processes made possible by the new forms of energy were beginning to create new types of farm building. In the 1930s, the milking-parlour provided an actual, the grain-drying installation a potential, example of this development. Their numbers were small. So was their immediate importance. But they represented the shape of things to come. In the next age, much of the old promise of the engineer of the steam age was to be fulfilled by his successor of the oil and electric age.

THE OASTHOUSE

The effects of such technical changes were interestingly summarised in the development of the oasthouse in this period. At its beginning, the familiar square or, more commonly, round kiln with its timber cowl which proclaimed its dependence on natural draught was in universal use. But the coming of fans, which were introduced early in the century and became general after experiments in the 1920s had made it possible to specify the degree of forced draught required, ended the necessity for such cowls, which were replaced in new buildings by cheaper louvres. Then, in the next decade, oil fuel began to oust coal even as coal had once ousted charcoal. The engineer and the scientist had enabled the hop-grower to exploit new methods, new resources. The oasthouse was very different from most types of building found on the farm, but its changing equipment and design in these years told the same general story.[69]

BUILDING MATERIALS

In these years the farmer became as dependent on the general economic system for the means of building and maintaining his farmstead as for his means of powering it. On the one hand, the old tradition of local self-sufficiency passed finally into history. Such time-honoured materials as 'clay lump' in Norfolk, 'clunch' in Cambridgeshire and sarsen stone in Wiltshire became mere survivals and homegrown timber could not compete with imported softwood.[70] On the other, the bricks, tiles and slates of the earlier nineteenth century were reinforced and in part supplanted by new and more sophisticated products peculiarly suited to the changed conditions. For the farmer was no longer interested in substantial new construction. He wanted cheap adaptations, cheap improvisation and cheap repairs.

In particular, he came to rely increasingly on two industrial products which, as we have seen, had appeared on the farm in mid-Victorian times and were now to establish themselves as standard materials. Both were cheap to buy. Both were simple to use, for they required little skilled labour and could be handled by normal farm staff. Both were convenient for small jobs, for the immediate repairs, first-aid and patchwork with which he strove to 'minimise the effects of a certain amount of unavoidable neglect'.[71] Between them, they changed the appearance of British farmsteads.

The first of these was cement for the concreting which in this period became one of the recognised farm crafts. Few farmers were as fortunate as Geoffrey Garratt, whose farm lay only a mile from a cement works. But many found as he did that 'it is extraordinary what good work can be done by direct labour and a little courage'[72] and in the twentieth century advice on making concrete became a normal feature of the farm-buildings textbook. But the farmer could only use cement as an ingredient of the mass concrete suitable for such literally basic purposes as foundations, yard bottoms or floors, in particular floors for the

cowhouses in which sanitary inspectors were increasingly demanding impervious, easily-cleaned surfaces and properly
formed and laid dung-channels. For its more sophisticated
applications he was dependent on the factory.

In 1911, for instance, a land agent had suggested the agricultural use of the new reinforced concrete in which steel rods
overcome the material's weakness in tension and so allow it to
be formed into beams, posts and other structural members.
Paying formal tribute to the lingering tradition of self-sufficiency, he considered the possible manufacture of such components in estate yards but concluded, inevitably, that the
technical difficulties were too great.[73] His interest was premature, but his verdict was sound. When reinforced concrete units
eventually came to the farm a generation later, they came prefabricated from the factory. The same point arose in more
immediately practical fashion in the years between the wars,
when farmers began building walls of solid concrete or, more
promisingly, of concrete blocks.[74] Technically, the latter were
preferable. Yet the change marked another break with the
older order of dependence on local resources. It was possible to
make concrete blocks on the farm. But it was generally wiser to
buy them readymade from the factory, where the manufacturing process was more precise and more reliable. The help which
cement could offer the farmer anxious to help himself was
considerable in scope but limited in kind.

The second do-it-yourself material was corrugated-iron
sheeting, which rapidly became the most conspicuous of all
farm-building materials. It appeared on the roofs of new buildings, it replaced tiles, slates or thatch on old buildings, it was
thrust under thatch or nailed to boards to give decaying barns a
few more years of life, and it provided walls as well as roofs for
sheds and yards. Its weaknesses, notably its poor insulating
properties and its need for protection from rust, were obvious.
But they were not so obvious as its virtues of low cost and general
utility, and there were soon few farms without corrugated iron
somewhere or other in the buildings.[75]

Only at the end of this period was its dominance challenged

by a new and equally convenient form of sheeting which offered better insulating properties and required no maintenance. This was asbestos-cement sheeting, which by the early 1930s was 'assuming very great importance in agricultural work'[76] and by the end of the decade was taken for granted as the normal roofing for new buildings.[77] Indeed, the new white roofing would eventually in large measure replace corrugated iron, even as corrugated iron had replaced the older materials.[78] But this lay in the future. The farmer of the depression times relied on mass concrete and corrugated iron to keep his obsolescent and decaying buildings operational.

PREFABRICATION

The industrial system which provided the farmer with these materials for existing and maintaining his buildings also provided him with an increasing range of fittings with which to equip them—rainwater goods of cast iron, galvanised iron and asbestos-cement, troughs of iron and glazed earthenware, automatic drinking bowls for cattle, metal window casements, sliding doors, cowls and louvre ventilators, overhead tracks for removing manure from cowhouses. Year by year, the list of such fittings lengthened and the trade catalogues grew in size. Few of the items listed were new in principle. It was their scope and variety which had changed. But they were only part of a more radical change. For the trade which produced prefabricated fittings now began to produce prefabricated buildings as component parts made in the factory for assembly on the farm.

The earliest prefabricated buildings were the proprietary portable silos and the more ambitious readymade iron farmstead which appeared in the 1880s.[79] But the manufacture of the former ceased when the system for which they were designed was abandoned and the latter was no more than a curiosity. For the future of this system of construction depended on the sale of a standardised product to a large and continuing market. Characteristically, it was first successfully applied to one of the commonest and simplest structures on the farm, the Dutch barn, which in this period provided a classic case of industrial response to agricultural opportunity.

For when the depression reinforced the general need to protect corn and hay with the particular need to reduce costs, above all labour costs, industrially-produced barns of steel members and corrugated-iron sheeting began to establish themselves as normal features of the farming landscape.[80] By Edwardian times, they were 'rapidly making thatching a lost art' and in the next generation they were classed among the few types of building which landowners and farmers regarded as a reasonable investment.[81]

So the farmer who had once built his own buildings from such materials as his village offered was now able to buy not merely materials but readymade buildings. All he had to do was to 'excavate and prepare concrete foundations' for his new barn.[82] Everything else was done for him by the suppliers and their mobile gang of erectors. A new and prophetic type of factory product had come to the farm.

PAST AND FUTURE

Technologically, therefore, this was a decisive period. On the one hand, it saw the end of many historical traditions hitherto preserved by the farmstead. In these years natural water supplies ceased to determine the siting of farmsteads,[83] the dovecote finally lost its lingering agricultural importance,[84] farm cider, like farm butter and farm cheese, was replaced by factory produce[85] and such local building materials as were still used and such longhouses as were still inhabited[86] became interesting survivals. On the other, it saw the establishment of a new agricultural system typified by the appearance in the textbooks of references to the fertiliser store for purchased 'bag-manure',[87] the cake store for purchased concentrate fodder,[88] the loading bay for the handling of the growing volume of materials the farmer bought and sold[89], and by the office from which he administered his increasingly complicated business.[90] It also offered a preview of the future. Intensive systems of housing pigs and poultry, farmstead mechanisation, milking-parlours and grain-drying installations, prefabrication, a new constructional pattern of concrete floors, walls of concrete blocks and roofs of asbestos-cement sheeting supported on steel and reinforced concrete members, were novelties in this age, conventional practice in the next. More subtly, it raised the radical question of the assumptions on which farm buildings should be designed. This period saw the appearance of the idea that the rate of agricultural change might make necessary buildings planned either for a limited life or for easy adaptation to different needs.[91]

Yet all these varied developments tell the same story. They all prepare us for the changes of our own generation. For they illustrate the growing integration of agriculture into the science-based industrial economy around it which is the fundamental theme of farming history in the twentieth century.

NOTES

1. Drummond, J. C. and Wilbraham, A. *The Englishman's food*, 1957, p 322
2. Ojala, E. M. *Agriculture and economic progress*, 1952, p 208
3. For the changing level of rents in this period see Orwin, C. S. and Whetham, E. H. *History of British Agriculture, 1896–1914*, 1967, Chart III. Figures of expenditure under various Acts encouraging capital investment suggest that the national outlay on farm buildings improvement decreased by about three quarters between 1873–82 and 1903–12 (ibid, p 196). The figures for expenditure on improvements, mainly on buildings, on two Cambridgeshire estates in this period are probably typical of changes in the more hard-hit arable areas. Up to 1880, about 50 per cent of the rent revenue was spent on improvements. For the next forty years, the figure was 20 per cent. In the 1920s it increased to 40 per cent. But the average rent per acre was that of the 1880s and by this time the purchasing power of this income was greatly reduced. (McGregor, J. J. 'The economic history of two rural estates in Cambridgeshire, 1870–1934', *Journal of the Royal Agricultural Society of England*, vol 98, 1937, pp 148–9.) Changes in the predominately livestock areas of the

north and west were not so extreme as in the arable counties of East Anglia. But they showed the same general tendencies.

4. These smallholdings were created and administered by the county councils under the supervision of the Board of Agriculture, later the Ministry of Agriculture and Fisheries. By the end of this period some 30,000 such holdings had been established, their average size being 15 acres. A number of these were horticultural holdings or specialised poultry holdings, but others were small mixed farms usually equipped with small editions of the types of farmstead found on larger farms but sometimes with the more technically interesting all-under-one-roof farmstead. Owing to the small size of the enterprises they served, however, such developments had little influence on general farmstead design. (Taylor, S. *Modern homesteads*, 1905, pp 60–4; Potter, T. *Buildings for smallholdings*, 1909; Maule, H. P. G. 'Farm buildings for smallholdings', *Journal of the Ministry of Agriculture*, vol 29, no 2, May 1922, pp 113–18; no 3, June 1922, pp 230–4; and no 12, March 1923, pp 1099–1104.)

5. Hall, A. D. *A pilgrimage of British farming*, 1914, pp 80, 98, 116, 119, 129

6. Orr, J. *Agriculture in Berkshire*, 1918, p 102

7. Addison, Lord. *A policy for British agriculture*, 1939, p 61

8. Dixey, R. N. 'The condition of cowsheds', *The Farm Economist*, vol 2, January 1936, p 3

9. Carslaw, R. M. and Graves, P. F. 'The condition of farm buildings', *The Farm Economist*, vol 2, January 1937, pp 101–2

10. Thomas, E. *The economics of smallholdings*, 1927, pp 55–7

11. Garratt, G. T. *Hundred acre farm*, 1928, pp x, 29, 30

12. In this period only one type of livestock decreased its demands on the farmstead. References to sheephouses continued to appear for form's sake in textbooks, but sheephousing was no longer practised. A long, hard winter in the 1880s raised the question of shelter for the flock. (Moore, H. F. 'The winter of 1885–6', *Journal of the Royal Agricultural Society of England*, vol 22, 2nd ser, 1886, pp 377–442.) But it was not followed by any general revival of interest in housing systems.

13. Malden, W. J. *Farm buildings*, 1896, pp 108–9; Taylor, S. *Modern homesteads*, 1905, pp 52–4; Lawrence, C. P. *Economic farm buildings*, 1919, pp 21–30; McHardy, D. N. *Modern farm buildings*, 1932, pp 182–8. Lawrence, p 21, described additions and alterations as 'the work which most often claims the attention of the agent'.

14. Malden, W. J. *Farm buildings*, 1896, p 111; advertisement by the Government Surplus Property Disposal Board of Nissen huts 'suitable for housing, storage or workshops, as accommodation for

pigs or sheep' in *Journal of Ministry of Agriculture*, vol 26, no 12, March 1920, p 1181; Price, W. T. and Ling, W. A. *Advisory Report on pighousing*, 1936, pp 19–24. For the use of a warship's funnels as silos, see footnote 42.

15. In 1919, C. P. Lawrence assumed that farm buildings were solely a matter for land agents. (*Economic farm buildings*, p viii.) In 1935, when owner-occupiers were more numerous, E. Gunn addressed his book to 'farmers, land agents and architects', though he implied regretfully that architects were seldom employed on farm buildings. (*Farm buildings*, subtitle, p 60.)

16. Orr, J. *Agriculture in Berkshire*, 1918, p 103

17. Malden, W. J. *Farm buildings*, 1896, p 13

18. Orr, J. *Agriculture in Oxfordshire*, 1916, p 113

19. Clarke, A. D. *Modern farm buildings*, 1899, pp 38–40

20. Robinson, H. G. 'Messrs S. E. and J. F. Alley's mechanised farming', *Journal of the Royal Agricultural Society of England*, vol 93, 1932, p 163. He was not, however, the very first to do so. The first grain drier in the country to meet the need created by the combine was built in 1929. (Cover, W. 'Electricity for grain drying', *Farm Mechanisation*, vol 1, no 4, January-February 1947, p 146.) The dependence of the combine on the drier was recognised very early. When Hosier bought his first combine in 1935, he took care that his drier was installed before harvest time. (Hosier, A. J. and Hosier, F. H. *Hosier's farming system*, 1951, pp 41, 189.)

21. Ernle, Lord. *English farming, past and present*, 1941, p 389

22. Cheke, V. *The story of cheesemaking in Britain*, 1959, p 272

23. *Man and his cattle*, issued by the Ministry of Agriculture, Fisheries and Food, 1967, pp 14–5. By 1938, however, there were only 151 cows in built-up London and the number of cows and cowhouses in Liverpool had dropped by a quarter. (Personal communication from the Public Relations Officer of the Milk Marketing Board; *Man and his cattle*, issued by the Ministry of Agriculture, Fisheries and Food, 1967, p 15.)

24. The 1923 edition of the bulletin on *The construction of cowhouses* issued by the Ministry of Agriculture and Fisheries made no reference to the dairy. The 1929 edition, however, gave detailed guidance on dairy design and construction, including suggestions on remodelling existing buildings to allow the addition of a dairy at one end of the cowhouse (pp 18–22). The improvement of the dairy was essentially a matter of the better application of existing resources. The familiar corrugated cooler, for instance, had been in use since the beginning of this period. (Fussell, G. E. *The English dairy farmer*, 1966, pp 178–9.)

25. Young, T. J. 'Agriculture in the county of Cheshire', *Journal of the Royal Agricultural Society of England*, vol 85, 1924, p 163

26. Clarke, A. D. *Modern farm buildings*, 1899; Laurence, C. P. *Economic farm buildings*, 1919

27. For the history of the milking machine see Hall, H. S. 'The mechanisation of milk production', *British Agricultural Bulletin*, vol 4, no 14, June 1951, pp 75–9 and Fussell, G. E. *The farmer's tools*, 1952, pp 194–8

28. *Final report of the Committee on the production and distribution of milk*, 1919, HMSO, Cmd, 483, p 60

29. Bridges, A. 'The economics of machine milking', *Agriculture*, vol 46, April 1939, p 64

30. Orwin, C. S. *A pioneer of progress in farm management*, 1931, pp 10–11, 17–18; Hosier, A. J. and Hosier, F. H. *Hosier's farming system*, 1951, pp 10–11, 14–21

31. The term was first used in the last years of this period. R. M. Currie in 1938 included the 'so-called parlour' on his list of milking systems. ('The production of higher grades of milk', *Journal of the Farmers Club*, February 1938, p 8.) Mr Brooke's reference in Chap 2 of *Middlemarch*, first published in 1872, to 'making a parlour of your cowhouse' was purely coincidental.

32. Appropriately, a textbook of the time noted that the 'fullest present development' of the milking-parlour was devised by one of the major milking-machine firms. (Gunn, E. *Farm buildings*, 1935, p 30.)

33. Bridges, A. *The flexibility of farming*, 1933, p 30. A few dairy cattle were housed in straw yards in the 1930s. (Mansfield, W. S. 'Cambridge University Farm', vol 97, 1936, p 107.) But even in East Anglia, where straw was plentiful and suitable yards common, the practice was rare.

34. Jenkins, H. M. 'Report on the practice of ensilage', *Journal of the Royal Agricultural Society of England*, 2nd ser, vol 20, 1884, pp 132–7; *Silos for preserving British fodder crops* by the sub-editor of *The Field*, 1884, pp 1–18

35. *Ensilage in America*, written by Thorold Rogers, the economic historian. It included on p 86 a remarkable prophecy of general as well as particular application by Dr George Thurber of the *American Agriculturist*. 'Much is yet to be done in *americanising* the whole matter (of silage)', he wrote, 'and we have no doubt that the experiments now being made will greatly simplify not only the building of the silo but every other step in this method.' The general point was appreciated by a contemporary who noted 'the cool effectiveness, as was to be expected' of an American pighousing system. (*The

Builder, vol 46, no 2140, 9 February 1884, p 218.) This was not, however, the first reference to the practical ingenuity of American farmers. A writer in the same journal had mentioned 'novelties' in American farm building design twenty years earlier (vol 20, no 992, 2 February 1862, p 92.)

36. *Return of the replies to questions relating to silos and ensilage.* Privy Council Office, 1885; *Report of the Private Ensilage Commissioners, 1886.* The contrast between the official professionalism of these papers and the casual amateurism of the old Board of Agriculture publications in George III's time illustrates very strikingly the effects of the mid-Victorian reform of the Civil Service.

37. Haydn's *Dictionary of Dates,* 1885, p 301

38. Jenkins, H. M. 'Report on the practice of ensilage', *Journal of the Royal Agricultural Society of England,* 2nd ser, vol 20, 1885, p 232

39. Garnett, F. W. *Westmorland agriculture,* 1912, p 209

40. Watson, S. J. and Smith, A. M. *Silage,* 1956, p 15–16

41. Largely but not entirely. Experiments with the Wye College silo showed a high loss in the feeding value of the crop stored. In 1910, George Jacques, a Norfolk farmer, imported a taller type of American silo and obtained better results which helped to establish the practice in the eastern counties. Hall, A. D. 'Can silage be substituted for roots?' *Journal of the Farmers Club,* March 1923, pp 20–1; Moore, S. *Silos and silage,* 1950, p 11

42. Watson, S. J. and Smith, A. M. *Silage,* 1956, pp 15–16. Few farmers could imitate the frugal ingenuity of the Bomford brothers of Worcestershire who in the late 1920s bought the four funnels of HMS *Diadem* from a naval scrapyard and used them as readymade silos. (Orwin, C. S. *Pioneers in power farming,* 1934, p 12.) Most of the steel and timber silos of this period have now disappeared but a number of concrete towers still survive.

43. Cheveley, S. W. *Grassdrying,* 1937, pp 11–16; Roberts, F. J. *Fodder Conservation,* 1939, pp 1–5

44. Clarke, A. D. *Modern farm buildings,* 1899, pp 92–3

45. Orr, J. *Agriculture in Berkshire,* 1918, p 103

46. The condition of such yards was a common cause of complaint in this period. 'With regard to the yards where the bullocks are kept and where the straw is trampled into manure, every one who knows a little about farming has lectured the farmers and landlords about the waste that goes on. . . . Those men will fare best who have the largest supplies of farmyard manure. Without exaggeration it may be said that the bullock yards where this is made and collected are absurdly arranged to serve the purpose. In most cases they seem to be constructed and situated rather as ponds or reservoirs to receive

the water from quite wide catchment areas.' (Orr, J. *Agriculture in Oxfordshire, 1916*, p 110.) Cf, 'A few days rain . . . and the open yards —nine-tenths of the yards in the eastern counties are wholly or partly uncovered—become ponds of sodden manure. . . . Farmers and farm workers mostly start young and get used to slipping about wet yards in six inches of mud. It is part of the regular routine.' (Garratt, G. T. *Hundred acre farm*, 1928, pp 22–3.)

47. As early as 1878 Jefferies noted the passing of the days when dairy farmers in Wiltshire kept pigs as a matter of course. 'Now the milk is sold, the sty is empty.' (*Field and farm*, ed Looker, S. J., 1957, p 136.)

48. Malden, W. J. *Farm buildings*, 1896, pp 76–80; Winder, T., *Handbook of farm buildings*, 1908, p 103. Clarke, A. D. *Farm buildings*, 1899, p 107 preferred boxes to pigsties.

49. McHardy, D. N. *Modern farm buildings*, 1932, p 153; Gunn, E. *Farm buildings*, 1935, pp 47–52

50. Anyone familiar, directly or indirectly, with the older rural society will recall the almost ceremonial importance of the cottage pig in the life and conversation of the village. Flora Thompson, describing an Oxfordshire hamlet in late Victorian and Edwardian times, referred to the lean-to pigsty at the back of each cottage. 'During its lifetime the pig was an important member of the family. . . . He was everybody's pride and everybody's business. . . . Men callers on Sunday afternoons came not to see the family, but the pig, and would lounge with its owner against the piggery door, scratching piggy's back and praising his points or turning up their noses in criticism.' (*Lark Rise to Candleford*, 1948, pp 21–2.) But the number of cottagers' pigs decreased as sanitary standards improved. The first sanitary inspector who visited Lark Rise about the turn of the century 'shook his head over the pigsties' (p 233). His successors were able to do more than shake their heads.

51. Lloyd, E. W. *Pigs and their management*, 1950, pp 134–7

52. Price, W. T. and Ling, W. A. *Advisory report on pighousing*, 1936, pp 19–24

53. The first descriptions of this type of house appeared in this country in 1931. (Stewart, W. A. 'Distinctive features of pig farming in Scandinavia', *Agriculture*, vol 38, no 7, October 1931, pp 689–93; *Pig keeping*, Ministry of Agriculture and Fisheries Bulletin no 32, 1931, pp 53–7, by the same author.) The first house of this type in this country was built shortly before these publications appeared. (Stewart, W. A., op cit, p 693.) Only five years later, there was 'probably greater agreement on the type of building suitable for fattening purposes than on any other point in pig housing. A

fattening house should be built on what is generally known as the Danish or Scandinavian plan'. (Rae, R. 'Systems of housing pigs', *Journal of the Royal Agricultural Society of England*, vol 97, 1936, p 132.)

54. Lloyd, E. W. *Pigs and their management*, 1950, pp 139–40

55. *Postwar building studies no 17. Farm buildings*, HMSO 1945, pp 119–20; *The housing of pigs*, Bulletin 160 of the Ministry of Agriculture and Fisheries, 1953, pp 37–8

56. Thomas, E. *The economics of small holdings*, 1927, p 57

57. The movable pen system was first applied to the commercial housing of the egg-laying flock in 1930. (Denham, H. J. 'Notable farming enterprises, IV. A commercial experiment in poultry farming', *Journal of the Royal Agricultural Society of England*, vol 94, 1933, pp 83–4)

58. Elkington, W. M. 'Poultry in agriculture', *Journal of the Royal Agricultural Society of England*, vol 90, 1929, p 147

59. Robinson, L. *Battery egg production* [1945], p 1–111; Blount, W. P. *Hen batteries*, 1951, pp 13–15. The battery system originated in the USA but seems to have developed independently in Great Britain. The first commercially manufactured batteries were produced in Britain in 1931. The first specific reference to American influence on cage design occurs in 1934. (Blount, W. P., op cit, pp 13, 17.)

60. Robinson, L. *Battery egg production* [1945], p 94. This book was published after the war but clearly refers to pre-war experience, since this intensive system was almost eliminated by wartime restrictions on feedstuffs.

61. Britton, D. K. and Keith, D. F. 'A note on the statistics of farm power supplies in Great Britain', *The Farm Economist*, vol 6, no 6, 1950, p 166

62. McHardy, D. N. *Modern farm buildings*, 1932, p 150

63. Pidgeon, D. 'Report on miscellaneous implements at Newcastle', *Journal of the Royal Agricultural Society of England*, vol 24, 2nd ser 1888, pp 210–12, including a reference to the 'enormous sales' of gas-engines on p 210; Pidgeon, D. 'Oil-engines in relation to agriculture', ibid, vol 3, 3rd ser, 1893, p 153; Malden, W. J., *Farm buildings*, 1896, p 158. By the turn of the century, the oil-engine was 'rapidly taking the place of the steam-engine as a provider of motive power in the homestead'. (Henderson, S. *The modern farmstead*, 1902, p 251.)

64. Britton, D. K. and Keith, D. F. 'A note on the statistics of farm power supplies in Great Britain', *The Farm Economist*, vol 6, no 6, 1950, p 166

65. Beauchamp, J. W. and Winder, T. *Handbook of farm buildings*, 1908, pp 155–71

66. Wright, S. J. 'Farm implements and machinery', *Journal of the Royal Agriculture Society of England*, vol 96, 1935, p 243

67. Pawson, H. C. *A survey of the agriculture of Northumberland*, 1961, p 37

68. Wright, S. J. 'Farm implements and machinery', *Journal of the Royal Agricultural Society of England*, vol 97, 1936, pp 229–32

69. Burgess, A. H. *Hops*, 1964, pp 11, 13, 16, 17, 205–11

70. By the end of the century, clay lump was 'rarely used' in Norfolk. (Haggard, R. *A farmer's year*, 1906, p 263.) A generation later, Geoffrey Garratt in Cambridgeshire followed local custom by bottoming his yards with another traditional local material, 'clunch' or hard chalk from the nearby hills, but without great success—'it can be had from the village pit for nothing, but like most things which cost nothing, it is worth little more'. (Garratt, G. T. *Hundred acre farm*, 1928, p 1.) Appropriately, his words contain what is probably the last current reference to the 'village pit' on which so many generations had relied for some of their basic building materials. Grigson refers to the use of sarsen stone in a new farm building in Wiltshire as late as 1923, but in the parish he describes with such perceptive detail this stone had not been used within living memory. (Grigson, G. *An English farmhouse*, 1948, pp 42.) Most textbooks of the period dismissed homegrown softwood as inferior and assumed that imported softwood would be used except for such rough work as homemade Dutch barns. (Henderson, R. *The modern homestead*, 1902, pp 43, 359; Winder, T. *Handbook of farm buildings*, 1908, p 131; Lawrence, C. P. *Economic farm buildings*, 1919, pp 5, 85; McHardy, D. N. *Modern farm buildings*, 1932, p 55.)

71. Clarke, A. D. *Modern farm buildings*, 1899, p 176

72. Garratt, G. T. *Hundred acre farm*, 1928, p xi

73. Orwin, C. S. 'An investigation into the value of ferro or reinforced concrete for farm and estate purposes', *Journal of the Royal Agricultural Society of England*, vol 72, 1911, pp 122–39

74. A query early in the century on the possible use of concrete blocks received an unenthusiastic answer. (*Journal of the Land Agents Society*, vol 3, 1904, pp 38, 101.) Lakeman, A. *Concrete cottages, small garages and farm buildings*, 1918, described farm buildings with walls of concrete blocks. But their use at that time was clearly exceptional.

75. Hall, C. P. 'The construction and arrangement of farm buildings', *Journal of the Royal Agricultural Society of England*, vol 7, 3rd ser, 1896, p 781; Douglas, L. M. 'Swine husbandry', *Journal of*

the Farmer's Club, January 1911, p 14; McHardy, D. N. *Modern farm buildings*, 1932, p 53. The life of this material could be prolonged by painting it. Few farmers, however, bothered to do so. They had no money to spare for jobs of this kind and in any case practical men doubted if such maintenance was economic. It was cheaper to let the sheeting rust away. (Taylor, S. *Modern homesteads*, 1905, p 49; Lawrence, C. P. *Economic farm buildings*, 1919, p 118.)

76. McHardy, D. N. *Modern farm buildings*, 1932, p 51

77. Thus, Colam R. 'Pighousing', *Agriculture*, vol 45, no 6, September 1938, p 553, assumed without comment that this type of roofing would be used.

78. In Leicestershire in the 1950s two surviving cruck barns were measured and described. One was roofed with corrugated-iron sheeting, one with asbestos-cement sheeting. (Webster, V. R. 'Cruck-framed buildings of Leicestershire', *Transactions of the Leicestershire Archaeological Society*, vol 30, 1954, p 55.)

79. Jenkins, H. M. 'Report on the practice of ensilage', *Journal of the Royal Agricultural Society of England*, vol 20, 2nd ser, 1884, p 207; Scott, J. *Farmbuildings*, 1884, p 43

80. There are numerous references to Dutch barns in the reports of the farm prize competition in the *Journal of the Royal Agricultural Society* in the earlier years of this period, eg vol 21, 2nd ser. 1885, pp 555, 561–3, 568; vol 1, 3rd ser, 1890, p 781; vol 2, 3rd ser, 1891, pp 554, 574. Clarke, A. D. *Farm buildings*, 1899, p 125, described them as 'increasing in popularity'. Some of these late Victorian Dutch barns were farm-made, but others were purchased pre-fabricated. 'Haybarns constructed entirely of iron are now very plentiful.' (Stephens, H. *The book of the farm*, 1889, p 442.)

81. Winder, T. *Handbook of farm buildings*, 1908, p 131; Lawrence, C. P. *Economic farm buildings*, 1919, p vi; McHardy, D. N. *Modern farm buildings*, 1932, p 161

82. McHardy, D. N. *Modern farm buildings*, 1932, p 161

83. The first textbook reference to the public watermains which enabled farm buildings to be sited independently of springs or streams appeared in 1908. (Winder, T. *Handbook of farm buildings*, p 5.) But, of course, the general value of local water-supplies continued. When the Hendersons in 1924 surveyed the Oxfordshire farm they were later to make famous, they noted among its assets 'a fine spring of water which supplied every field'. (Henderson, G. *The farming ladder*, 1956, p 15.) Shortly after the end of this period, a survey found that only just over a third of the farmsteads in England and Wales had a piped water supply and a quarter depended on wells. The remainder relied on roof water, streams etc, and, in

N

some cases, on neighbours. (*National farm survey of England and Wales*, 1941–3, HMSO 1946, p 61.)

84. In Nottinghamshire as late as the 1880s pigeons played 'a quite appreciable part in the economy of most farms' and manure from their cotes made 'quite an important addition to the general supply'. (Cooke, F. S. 'Report on prize competition in Nottinghamshire and Lincolnshire', *Journal of the Royal Agricultural Society of England*, vol 24, 2nd ser, 1888, p 534.)

85. By the time of the Second World War, there were still about a thousand farms making cider for sale. But they were the last of their line. 'Prior to the present century, most of the cider in this country was made on the farm from fruit grown in the farm orchard. . . . A complete change has occurred within the last fifty years. . . . Production has to a great extent been transferred from the farm to the factory.' (Barker, B. T. P. *Cider Apple Production*, Ministry of Agriculture and Fisheries Bulletin 104, 1937, p 2.)

86. In 1896 the report of a Royal Commission on rural conditions in Wales included descriptions of various longhouses which were still in use. But the number of such houses was falling rapidly, largely because of the requirements of sanitary legislation. (Peate, I. C. *The Welsh House*, 1944, pp 60, 66, 73.) The tradition, however, died hard. Some Welsh longhouses were still inhabited in the later 1950s. (Jope, E. M. and Threlfall, R. I. 'Excavation of a mediaeval settlement at Beere, North Tawton Devon', *Mediaeval Archaeology*, vol 2, 1958, p 122.) On Dartmoor, the cowhouse of one longhouse was in regular use till 1945 (Alcock, N. W. 'Houses in an East Devon parish', *Transactions of the Devonshire Association*, vol 94, 1962, p 228) and another till at least 1960. (Hoskins, W. G. 'Farmhouses and history', *History Today*, vol 10, no 5, May 1960, p 339.) In Cornwall, some survived into the present decade. (Dudley, D. and Minter, E. M. 'The mediaeval village of Garrow Tor, Bodmin Moor, Cornwall', *Mediaeval Archaeology*, vol 6–7, 1962–3, pp 281–2.)

87. Scott, J. *Farm buildings*, 1884, pp 116–17; Malden, W. J. *Farm buildings*, 1896, p 36. The first references to a fertiliser store date from 1850—see pp 142, 160—but this was exceptional. It was not until the later nineteenth century that the use of fertiliser became common practice.

88. Clarke, A. D. *Modern farm buildings*, 1899, p 45–6; Lawrence, C. P. *Economic farm buildings*, 1919, p 53; Gunn, E. *Farm buildings*, 1935, pp 11, 40–1

89. McHardy, D. N. *Modern farm buildings*, 1932, pp 172–3

90. Throughout this period, most farmers continued to do such office work as was necessary either at a desk in the living-room or on

the kitchen table, using the clock on the mantelpiece as a convenient filing-place. But the amount of office work judged necessary was increasing. Early in the period, textbooks recommended a farm office for accounts. These, however, were no more than desks in a small general-purpose storeroom. (Malden, W. J. *Farm buildings*, 1896, p 39; Clarke, A. D. *Modern farm buildings*, 1899, p 17.) A generation later, the control of the purchase and issue of concentrate feed on a large and advanced Cotswold farm required its own system of invoices and disposal sheets. (Skilbeck, D. 'Notable farming enterprises, Mr. Webster Cory's farms', *Journal of the Royal Agricultural Society of England*, vol 93, 1932, p 149.)

91. 'It used to be said that the mark of a good landlord was the erection of enduring rather than 'jerry' buildings, but an intelligent writer like Miss Jebb has seriously contended that the permanent character of buildings is a drawback, because it offers obstacles to speedy change dictated by an alteration in the methods of farming, and that buildings should be such that they could be readily "scrapped".' (Personal communication from L. L. Price quoted in Orr, J. *Agriculture in Oxfordshire*, 1916, p 149.) Miss Jebb's remarks, the source of which is not given, were the first reference to this question. The first textbook reference to 'free adaptability to possible future purposes' as an important factor in the design of farm buildings occurs in Gunn, E. *Farm buildings*, 1935, p 59

Chapter Nine

THE LAST AGE:

1939-60

THE FARMING REVOLUTION

In the first decade of this period, the pressure of overseas competition was abruptly replaced by desperate domestic need. War restored and peace continued the ancient challenge of hunger which two generations of Englishmen had all but forgotten. In response, farming revived, expanded, developed, repaying drastically increased investment by drastically increased production. In the second, the old competitive order gradually reestablished itself in modified form and the recreated farming system adapted itself to the changing economic times. But there was no return to pre-war conditions. Farming remained a prosperous, progressive and intensive industry.

Indeed, intensification was the dominant theme of these years. The total agricultural acreage changed little, for the reclamation of such minor areas of the waste as survived was counterbalanced by the loss of farmland to the builder and the engineer. But production increased steadily and by the end of the period it was some 60 per cent above the pre-war level.

One reason for this striking achievement was the conversion to ploughland of huge areas of less demanding, less productive permanent pasture. Another was the increase in all types of livestock and the adoption of more specialised systems of management. Throughout the post-war years, the number of farms carrying dairy cattle, pigs and poultry fell and the average size of herd or flock rose. But behind these was another reason on which in large measure their success depended. This

212

was a rapid and pervading technical revolution using new knowledge, new methods and new equipment. The farmer employed fewer men and ceased to use the horse as a source of power, but he spent a growing proportion of his resources on technical aids from the factory, from the laboratory and from the warehouse. The rise in production per acre, per beast and per man testified to their efficiency.

Nevertheless, none of this changed the basic character of the farming system. In the years after the war, as in the years before it, the farmer earned three-quarters of his income from his cattle, pigs, sheep, and poultry, only a quarter from the sale of his arable crops. Most of what was grown on the farm continued to reach the consumer as milk or meat. British agriculture remained essentially a livestock industry.

NEW NEEDS, OLD FARMSTEADS

Once more, therefore, old farmsteads faced new needs. The farmer wanted to store and process more crops, house more stock and protect more machinery and material from the weather. Moreover, he wanted to do many of those things in new ways, and with new equipment. Yet it was clear that the buildings he inherited from the past could not cope with the demands he now made on them. There were not enough of them; there were too many bad ones; and there were too many of the wrong kind.

The extent of their deficiency was only partly shown by an official survey undertaken during the war. This found that the buildings of no more than 39 per cent of English and Welsh holdings equipped with buildings could be classed as satisfactory. Of the remainder, 49 per cent were classed as fair, 12 per cent as bad.[1] But these figures referred only to the structural condition of the buildings, not to their agricultural value, and some which needed little repair were obsolete or otherwise unsuitable for the needs of the farm. Further, of course, the survey was only concerned with the buildings that were there. It was not concerned with the buildings which should have been there and therefore took no account of the inadequacy of existing steadings for contemporary needs. On this evidence, well below a third of British farms were at that time satisfactorily equipped with buildings.

So the nation faced in wartime the problem which Henry Williamson had faced in peacetime when he prepared his inventory of the buildings on the semi-derelict arable farm in Norfolk he planned to restore. 'Most of the walls were undermined by rat-runs. . . . The corn barn needed a buttress, the wall was cracked and leaning outwards. . . . Many of the rafters of the cartshed were rotten. . . . The roof of the granary . . . was broken in one place and three or four yards of the floor were sodden. . . . There were no drains to the yards, stable or cowhouses. . . .'[2] This was a fairly extreme case, for in the slump the corn areas had suffered worse than the livestock areas. But it was merely a difference in degree. Over all the country the same generality held. By depriving the farm's central workshop of maintenance and modernisation, the depression had limited the efficiency and intensity of agricultural development and left a bitter and restricting legacy to the next age.

IMPROVEMENT, NOT RECONSTRUCTION

Yet it was some time before the farming industry could even consider any general modernisation. In the 1940s, immediate needs were too pressing, available resources too few, to allow more than first-aid and the most urgent of minor improvements to the farmstead. In any case, expenditure of money and materials was rigidly controlled by the government. In the immediate post-war period, therefore, the general condition of farm buildings was little better than in pre-war years. For example, grain, feedstuffs and fertilisers are peculiarly liable to damage by damp. Yet in 1948 a survey of Exmoor, one of the most exposed areas in southern England, found that only half of the farms studied could provide those valuable materials with enough dry storage space.[3] Again, cleanliness and convenience are the two chief needs of the cowhouse. Yet in 1951 a survey of 2,500 representative dairy steadings showed that only two-thirds of them had piped water supply and only half had electric light.[4]

In the happier 1950s, conditions were more favourable. Building restrictions ended, farming was prosperous and agricultural development had made obvious the cost to the industry of inefficient buildings. Indeed, on many farms the inadequacy of the farmstead had become the main limiting factor to increased production or profits. Throughout this decade, therefore, investment in farm buildings increased and a steady flow of advisory publications reflected the growing need for technical guidance.[5] Few new farmsteads were built, for the days of substantial reclamation were past and it was seldom practicable to demolish even the most dilapidated of farmsteads and start all over again. But there was a general modernisation of existing farmsteads. At first this commonly took the form of minor or particular improvements, such as the erection of a Dutch barn, the gutting and re-equipment of a cowhouse and the addition of a dairy to serve it, the conversion of a stable to a milking parlour and bullock yards to dairy yards, or the installation of a grain-drying and storage plant in an old barn.[6] Towards the end of the period, however, when building restrictions were a mere memory and the speed and pressures of technological change were increasing, remodelling became more thorough and systematic. There was more demolition, more new buildings, less piecemeal adaptation. Even so, these years saw little comprehensive reconstruction and the familiar juxtaposition of new and old, good and bad, contemporary, traditional and frankly historical buildings continued. But the increasing proportion of new work was obvious to the most casual visitor to the countryside.

It was equally obvious in the statistics. Thus, a survey at the end of the period showed that the average farmstead, that characterless but informative abstraction, contained 2·5 buildings build since 1945, 2·4 built between 1918 and 1945 and 6·0 built before 1914.[7] In only fifteen years, half of them years of scarcity and restriction, the national stock of farm buildings was increased by over a quarter. The resultant improvement in efficiency cannot be measured but was probably at least as great. It was a remarkable achievement.

Physically, of course, this achievement was based on the traditional resources of the farming industry. But technically it owed much to the industry's use of new information from new sources, above all, information from the expanding research services.

Traditionally, farm buildings had been designed by practical men for practical men on the basis of practical experience. Experimental evidence played little part in their decisions and deviations from this sternly empirical approach were few and inconspicuous. But in these years for the first time the conclusions of the research worker became an accepted factor in the design of most types of farm building. The farmer and his technical allies began to depend increasingly for knowledge and ideas on the growing mass of reports from a growing number of research centres on the needs of stock, on the properties of materials, on types of equipment, on methods of organising and housing the varied activities of the farmstead.

Some of these reports came from the industrial research services. In particular, the farm shared in the benefits of general research into building methods and materials. But the majority came from specifically agricultural centres. A number were directly concerned with the performance of selected types of farm building. Most of them, however, were concerned with the processes around which farm buildings were designed, providing in increasing volume and with increasing precision data on the agricultural problems for which the designer sought structural solutions. He still needed his old skills, his old practical understanding. But he added a new and valuable type of evidence to his stock-in-trade. Once again, the technical literature illustrates the change. In 1945 it was still possible to compile a textbook by collating the views and experience of practical men. But the official committee which produced it lamented the lack of knowledge on such subjects as the health and comfort of livestock and urged research into farm buildings problems. The plea was heard. The next major textbook, published twenty years later, was largely based on the research findings of the intervening period.[8]

This was in itself a considerable revolution, but it was also part of another revolution which ended the insularity of farm buildings development in this country. For until this time the influence of foreign research and experience had been minimal. Now, however, many of the research reports which offered the British farmer directly or indirectly relevant information and advice came from the Continent, from Australia and New Zealand, above all from the USA. And with them came a mass of less academic accounts of the practices and ideas of farmers elsewhere, frequently collected and made available to the home farmer by the wandering agricultural scholars who in this period began to earn themselves a place in agricultural history.[9] The British farmer was now a beneficiary of an unorganised but effective international information service. The appearance in this country of the loose-housing system incorporating American experience, of the herringbone parlour originally developed in New Zealand, of slatted-floor yards based on Norwegian practice and broiler houses designed with the aid of data from American experimentation illustrated the use he made of this new resource.

The British farmer and his commercial allies, however, were no mere passive recipients of other people's ideas. The landlord of rented acres, necessarily concerned with the possible needs of future tenants, tended to prefer proven systems and types of building efficient for present purposes but adaptable to future uses. But the owner-occupier, who in this period increased his share of the national farmland from a third to a half, could afford to try more specialist systems and indulge his own particular views and hopes. With the aid of the builder and the engineer, he experimented with the new ideas, adapted them to his particular needs and produced others of his own. He also pioneered untried systems and evolved variations of methods developed for different circumstances in different countries. The full technical history of this highly active period, which added a dozen new processes and a score of new types of buildings to the farmstead, has yet to be written. But the available evidence suggests the emergence in these years of a general pattern of innovation and development.

A new idea appeared, derived perhaps from research, perhaps from overseas practice, perhaps from the brain of some thoughtful farmer; research workers studied it, enterprising farmers and manufacturers applied it with various modifications; and finally, with the aid of continuing research, it established itself in common practice. So the final process and the building which housed it came as the result of a number of efforts by a number of individuals and groups.[10]

In theory, it was possible to picture the creation of a new type of farm building in terms of an assembly-line along which scientists provided the basic data on the process to be housed, engineers and builders designed equipment to serve it and structures to cover it, and field investigators surveyed its performance under farm conditions, each group making their particular contribution while the farmer waited patiently for the finished product. In practice, farm and firm between them simplified the matter considerably. They welcomed research, but they did not wait for it. They applied what they knew when they could and the field investigator was commonly studying buildings erected long before final or perhaps even interim research findings had been published. The farmer, particularly the 'mad farmer' so rightly admired by Stapledon, and the manufacturer were necessary partners of the research worker in the business of farm buildings development.

OFFICIAL SUPPORT

Another partner in the process was less obvious, less personal. This was the government, which financed most of the relevant research work undertaken in Great Britain. But it also aided the farm buildings revival in more direct fashion. At first, official assistance was confined to technical information and advice. The issue in 1945 of a monumental textbook on farm buildings prepared by the Ministry of Agriculture and Fisheries[11] was followed a year later by the inclusion in the new official extension services of a number of general and specialist officials to advise landowners and farmers on their farm buildings problems. From this time onwards the farmer could call at will on officials whose business was the provision of technical information and advice on its application to particular cases. Later, the government turned financier as well as advisor, notably by providing grants towards the capital cost of most types of farm building under the Farm Improvement Scheme which came into operation in 1957. By the end of this period, the official leaflet behind the clock on the farmhouse mantelpiece, the cars parked beside the village hall where the local advisory official was holding a meeting on the design of piggeries or the choice of building materials, and the new grant-aided building in the farmstead were rural commonplace. 'The man from the Ministry' had taken his place among the farmer's allies.

A NEW PROBLEM

The growing mass of information on farm-building design and construction helped to solve many problems. But it also created a new one. Those who advised the farmer on his buildings, which included as the years passed a growing number of private and commercial advisors as well as Ministry officials, found increasing difficulty in keeping themselves adequately informed on current developments.

For gradually the increasing volume of publications surpassed the individual's reading capacity and the task became too great for even the specialist advisor. There was too much to read and it was too scattered in too many journals. In the early post-war period the number of research publications affecting farm-building design and construction was small. But the rate of increase was rapid. By 1955, they were appearing at the rate

of 180 a year, by 1960 at the rate of 400 a year. No figures are
available for general or advisory publications or for trade
literature, but the increase here was probably at least propor-
tional. Of course, only a fraction of this mass of documentation
was immediately relevant. But the amount which a properly
informed advisor could reasonably be expected to scan for
points of interest was considerable. The gap between existing
knowledge and general practice was, of course, an old one. But
hitherto it had been the landowner or farmer who for various
reasons failed to make the best use of available information.
Now it was the advisor who could not keep fully abreast of
publications and possibilities.

This difficulty was increased by professional fragmentation.
Before the war, the land agent and his estate staff or the local
builder had met most of the farmer's building needs. But in the
post-war years, as the volume and complication of farm buildings work increased, they were joined by architects, surveyors,
engineers, manufacturers of components and equipment,
general agriculturists, anybody with the necessary interest and
experience, some working as wholetime specialists, most spending only part of their time on farm-buildings problems. Such
men shared a common trade, but they did not share a common
profession or common information services.[12]

Various efforts were made to meet the needs thus created. In
1956 the first association of those concerned with farm buildings
was formed[13] and throughout this period a growing number of
conferences, demonstrations and publications strove to popu-
larise the information developed by research and practice.
Success was considerable but inadequate. The problem of communications was one of the legacies left by this generation to the
next.[14]

MECHANISATION

Research and advisory services were new factors in farm-
buildings design. So was mechanisation in the forms it now
took.

In this period the mechanisation of field work was completed.

This meant larger and more complex equipment and therefore bigger and better implement sheds, sometimes including an enclosed bay for housing the tractor. It also meant more farm workshops, ranging from a workbench and a few pieces of equipment in the tractor shed on small farms to a separate building complete with inspection pit and overhead joist for lifting tackle on large ones.[15] These needs could often be met by the adaptation of existing buildings, notably and appropriately disused stables. But the new need for storage for tractor fuel required a more obtrusive type of installation. By the end of this period British farms were using over a million tons of liquid fuel annually, most of it in tractors, and the greasy black tanks on piers which commonly stood by the side of the roadway on large farms reminded visitors that they were entering the premises of an increasingly industrialised enterprise.[16]

The mechanisation of work in the buildings was less complete but its effects on the farmstead were considerably greater. Of course, mechanical power was no stranger there. But in these years it increased so drastically in scale and scope that it began to dominate the buildings it had once served. Economically, this reflected a combination of the rising cost of human labour, the steady post-war decline in the number of workers employed and the growing importance of farmstead processes, particularly livestock processes, in the farming system. These, however, were familiar trends. Technically, it reflected a new development, the coming of cheap and convenient electric power which first reinforced, then in part replaced, the internal-combustion engine.

The workings of this change are shown in the figures. Between 1939 and 1960 the proportion of farms served by public electricity grew from 11 per cent to 80 per cent and the average consumption of electricity per farm increased fourfold.[17] In the same period the number of static internal-combustion engines in farmsteads rose from 120,000 to a maximum of 200,000 in 1952, and then declined to 171,000 but the number of electric motors rose steadily from 11,000 to 253,000. The farmer's appreciation of mechanical power was obvious. So was his preference for electricity.

The most obvious achievement of the new equipment was the final mechanisation of the static chores in the farmstead begun by the steam-engine in Hanoverian times. By the end of this period nearly all cows were milked, nearly all homegrown feed ground and mixed, and nearly all water pumped by machinery. But the new technical resource also brought less precedented benefits. It brought light and with it a pervading increase in efficiency and cleanliness. It brought localised heating of a type suitable for rearing piglets and chicks. Above all, it brought the means of controlling microclimate in livestock houses. Few innovations in this period were more important than the electric fan and the thermostat on which the pre-determined, man-made environments in the new piggeries and poultry houses depended.

Yet this revolution had its limitations. Its effect, of course, varied greatly from area to area, from farm to farm. It took, for instance sixty hill-farms in Wales to muster the total of thirty-four motors which an advanced farmer in Oxfordshire installed in the buildings of his 85-acre holding.[18] More fundamentally, it mechanised stationary work but failed to replace man as the prime mover in the transport and handling of materials which forms so large a proportion of farmstead routines.

Sometimes, it is true, whole processes could be comprehensively mechanised and neatly housed in such special-purpose installations as the milking-parlour and the grain-store, or in the more dramatic silo-to-trough cattle-feeding systems which appeared on the farm in the last years of this period. But this was exceptional. More commonly, permutations and combinations of fixed and mobile equipment, of conveyors, pumps and pipelines, of tractor-mounted scrapers and foreloaders, self-unloading trailers and portable augers, could do no more than increase the efficiency of existing systems of movement. They secured substantial reductions of the labour required, but the design of existing buildings and the scale of existing enterprises prevented the general adoption of industrial-type circulations. For example, the increasing volume of fertilisers, now one of the basic raw materials of the farmer's trade, was manhandled in sacks from lorry to farm-store for later and equally laborious loading on to the trailer which took it to the fields. Similarly, in the 1950s the amount of feeding-stuffs bought by the British farmer rose from 4 to 8 million tons, all of it consumed in or around the farmstead. Yet the sack remained the unit in which this mass of material was handled. Only at the very end of the period was any of it delivered in bulk to the farm ready for distribution in bulk in the farmstead.[19]

At the end of this period a speaker at a conference expressed amazement at the number of ways in which farm materials could be mechanically carried, scraped, dragged, blown, sucked or floated from one place to another. He might well have expressed equal amazement at the amount which was still moved by manual effort. The point was made more generally in the statistics. Between 1945 and 1958, it was calculated, production per agricultural manhour rose on average 6·4 per cent annually. But the increase in production per manhour spent on livestock, nearly all of it on work in buildings, rose only 3·6 per cent annually.[20] In the fields, horsepower was by this time almost totally mechanised. In the buildings, manpower was still an important prime-mover.

GRAIN STORAGE

The revival of farming included an increase in corn production and throughout these years the cereal acreage remained well above its pre-war level. But the most important change was technical, not statistical. In this period, the combine-harvester fulfilled the promise it had shown in the fields of its pioneers a generation earlier. In so doing it raised on a national scale the problems once confined to their farmsteads.

As the number of combines in the country rose from 3,200 in 1946 to 10,000 in 1950, 31,000 in 1946 and nearly 50,000 in 1960, the proportion of the harvest which waited for the threshing machine as sheaves neatly stacked in thatched rick or Dutch barn shrank, the proportion delivered as grain requiring storage, and therefore drying to make it ready for storage, rose rapidly. So the grain drying and storage installations which had first appeared on British farms in the 1930s increased in number and developed types of design suitable for a wider range of farms. At first dryer and bins were separate. Then smaller and cheaper systems, notably the 'ventilated bin' which dried grain in the structure in which it was stored and the self-explanatory 'on-floor system', were evolved. The on-floor system was designed to make use of existing buildings and a number of other types of plant, particularly those serving large arable farms, found convenient homes in old barns. But many were housed in appropriately factory-type buildings of appropriately factory-made materials.[21]

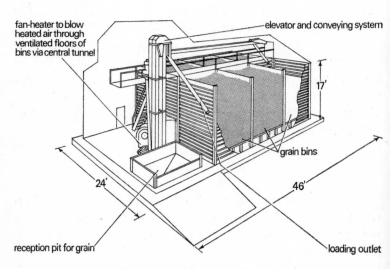

19 A modern grain drying and storage plant. In this example of a 'housed mechanical process' grain is conveyed mechanically to bins in which it is dried by heated air. Such plants are usually protected by simple structures of steel or reinforced concrete roofed with asbestos-cement sheeting

In 1946, there were about 1,000 such plants in the country. By 1960 there were over 16,000 and in many areas the once familiar cornstack had become as obsolete as the windmill or the flail, and the starkly industrial outlines of the farm grain store had replaced the barn as the dominant feature of the farmstead. Behind this general change lay a mass of detailed technical achievements in research and development centres at home and overseas. A similar combination was now preparing to bring further change to the corngrower's farmstead.

For in the 1950s research in this country made possible the introduction of a system, originally developed in France, of storing undried grain in airtight silos.[22] The method was limited to farms where the grain was fed to livestock, for grain thus stored is unsuitable for milling or for seed. Nevertheless, its economic advantages were obvious, particularly to the grower and feeder of barley, for an airtight silo did not cost much more than a conventional one but it ended the expensive necessity of drying equipment. Yet the first silos of the new type which appeared on British farms at the very end of this period illustrated more than a change in local methods. They were imported from the USA, and so symbolised the increasing integration of the British farmer into a technological order which paid little attention to frontiers.[23]

The point, of course, was not new. In 1954, for example, Pierce Worlidge of Biggins Farm, Dagenton, had reflected on the variety of resources which made possible the new grain dryer and bins that safeguarded his corn crop. 'The water that had threatened and often destroyed the grain harvests here for a thousand years and more was now no longer a danger . . . but only a nuisance to be thrust aside at some expense but nearly no trouble. The rubber plantations of Malaya, the softwood forests of Scandinavia, the aluminium ore of Canada and the oil fields of Kuwait would in future each play their part . . . in keeping wheat and barley from Dagenton fields dry and clean and sweet until it became a biscuit for a small boy or beer for an old man'.[24] He spoke in fiction but expressed fact, though not exhaustively, for he omitted from his list the contribution made by the research stations of a half-a-dozen countries. The tall towers of American steel which exploited to the farmer's advantage biological processes whose predictability had been established in English and French laboratories merely continued his

o

argument. Agriculturally, they proclaimed the coming of a new technique. Historically, they were just another example of a familiar line of development. In the nineteenth century, the British farmstead became part of a steam-age national economy. In the twentieth, it began to form part of the scientific, international order which succeeded it.

POTATO STORAGE

The same general tendencies were illustrated on a smaller scale by the development of indoor potato storage in this period. At its beginning, nearly all potatoes not sold off the farm at harvest wintered in the fields in clamps of straw and earth. By its end, nearly half were stored indoors. This change was made necessary by a combination of economic and technical pressures. Labour was becoming too expensive to use for building such temporary stores as clamps or for working in rain, cold and mud when it could be employed more efficiently under a roof; the supply of long, firm straw suitable for clamps was shrinking as the growing fleet of combines delivered only short, broken straw; and the new system allowed greater possibilities of mechanisation. But it was made possible by comprehensive research into the properties of potatoes in storage and the insulation, ventilation and structural strength required in buildings to house them, which began in 1946 and produced the first new-model potato store two years later.[25] The new stores, sometimes special-purpose buildings, sometimes existing buildings adapted to new purposes, provided potatoes with improved conditions for conservation, and the men who loaded and graded them with improved conditions for working. In so doing, they illustrated the growing ability of the research worker to specify the needs of farm materials and of the engineer and builder to meet them.[26]

HOP BUILDINGS

So did the buildings which served the hop-grower. In the hop areas, farmers still used the traditional cowled oasts, but they no longer built them. For the pre-war innovations of oil-firing, electric fans and roof louvres had now created an improved type of kiln which was now accepted practice. An equally conspicuous physical change was the appearance of large industrial-type sheds to house the hop-picking machines which came into general use after the war and by the end of this period picked three-quarters of the crop. As it was on the general farm, so it was, in microcosm, on the specialised hop farm. Major changes in the farmstead reflected major changes in methods of harvesting and handling crops.[27]

DAIRY BUILDINGS

The dairy farmer of this period inherited the specialised trade of liquid-milk production, farmhouse butter-making being now all but forgotten and farmhouse cheese-making surviving only on a decreasing handful of farms.[28] He also inherited an expanding market and an agreeable lack of competition, for the importation of fresh milk was not a practical proposition and even his minor rival in the towns had ceased business.[29] Nevertheless, throughout these years his systems of production were exposed to a variety of particular economic and technical pressures as well as to the general demands of the Milk and Dairies Regulations, administered since 1944 by the Ministry of Agriculture and Fisheries, which compelled a steady sequence of changes in his methods and his buildings.

The starting-point of these changes was the traditional cowhouse, in which cows were tied in individual stalls while men milked them and carried their milk to the dairy all through the year and brought them food and litter and removed their manure during the months of winter housing. The system had many advantages, but it was developed in the days when labour was cheap and farmers were prepared to pay men to spend most of their time on purely mechanical haulage chores. Consequently it continued unchallenged only as long as wages were low and men plentiful. But from the outbreak of war onwards

wages rose continuously and farmers sought increasingly to reduce the labour costs of their cowhouses. In particular, they
followed the example of the pre-war pioneers and introduced
milking machines, so that by the end of this period the hand-
milked herd was a curiosity. Many, too, introduced mechanical
equipment or trolleys for handling milk, fodder or manure, but
there were limits to the economies such methods could secure.
Over the years, more and more farmers abandoned their cowhouses for some form of the 'loose-housing' system in which
cows and machines did more work and men did less.

Essentially, this system provided two separate and specialised
areas, one where the cows lay and one where they were milked,
and relied on the cows' legs to solve the transport problems thus
created. Men no longer brought the job to the cows; the cows
went to the job. And since the jobs involved the whole herd
instead of individual cows in individual stalls, machinery could
deal wholesale with work formerly done retail by hand or
barrow. The principles of the new order in dairy housing were
simple. But its practice was varied and complicated.

Consider first the cow's lying area. The original break with
the individual stall of the cowhouse tradition came at the end of
the war, when farmers began to house their cows communally
in yards.[30] One of the main causes of this change was the desire
to reduce labour by replacing the daily manual chore of
mucking-out by a mechanical, annual clearance. This was
achieved and other benefits followed in its train. Loose-housed
cows were commonly cleaner than their cow-housed sisters and
suffered fewer injuries, while yards could be adapted to expanding herds more cheaply and conveniently than cowhouses.
But, as the years passed, new difficulties appeared. A fall in the
corn acreage, the combine-harvester which left more straw in
the fields than the reaper-and-binder, and the increased use of
short-strawed varieties of corn steadily reduced the supply of litter
on which the efficiency of the system depended, while inexorably
rising wages increased the cost of hauling it into the yards as
bedding and out again as trodden manure. Once more the farmer
sought means of adapting his system to changing circumstances.

One possibility was the slatted-floor yard, which dealt drastically with the litter problem. It required no litter at all, for the cattle trod their manure through the floor into a cellar from which it was removed in solid or liquid form. This system aroused considerable interest when reintroduced to Britain from Norway in 1955,[31] but results on dairy farms were inconclusive and, while the technical debate on its virtues and weaknesses continued, a new and startlingly simple alternative appeared. This was the cubicle system, which provides one of the most remarkable success stories of modern agriculture.

For cubicle housing combines the best features of the cow-house and the yard and adds certain advantages of its own. It provides the cows with individual stalls where they can lie and ruminate in peace, yet allows them freedom of movement and access to a common feeding area. Admittedly, the cubicles require bedding, but little litter or labour is needed since their design compels the cows to drop their dung in the passage behind them and not in their beds. The system pleases cows and cowmen alike and within a few years of its appearance in 1960 it housed a significant and increasing proportion of the national dairy herd. Seldom has a new type of farm building been adopted so rapidly, so widely and so painlessly.[32]

Changes in the milking-parlour were as drastic as those in the housing system. The early 'abreast' parlours, as the name implies, continued the tradition of the cowhouse in which the cows were milked side-by-side on a level floor. Consequently the cowman spent much of his time and more of his energy on continuous stooping as he attached and detached the teat cups. So the first major change in parlour design was the appearance shortly after the war of the 'tandem' parlour, in which cows stood at a higher level than the cowman who thus worked with the cow at convenient elbow-height. It was typical of the times that this difference in heights, once decided empirically, was later precisely determined by the first application of ergonomic research to farmstead problems.[33] It was equally typical that the improvement was no more than a temporary stage in parlour development.

For this original form of two-level parlour decreased the effort of milking but increased the amount of walking required, since the cows stood head-to-tail in the parlour with their udders a cow's length instead of a cow's breadth apart. But a New Zealand system, first introduced into this country in 1956, neatly economised both time and energy. It continued the two-level system but reduced the distance between udders by 'angle-parking' the cows at some 30° to the milker's pit with their heads pointing away from it, thus forming on plan the cow-pattern which earned it the now internationally famous name of the 'herringbone' parlour. It was a highly sophisticated installation, at first glance rather resembling the interior of a submarine. It was also highly efficient and enabled each man to operate more milking units and therefore milk more cows per hour than any other system so far devised.

So the herringbone parlour, like the cubicle, was the successful product of a lengthy process of evolution. Yet their manners of origin were radically different. The new housing systems were all introduced by farmers and many of the later improvements in them came from trial-and-error on commerical farms. But the development of the milking-parlour was necessarily a more complicated matter. In particular, it depended on the availability of the necessary special-purpose equipment. From the first, therefore, its future lay in the hands of 'the Trade'. Hosier, it is true, continued to improve the parlour he had originated, but he did so as engineer, not as farmer. Similarly, the herringbone parlour was invented by a New Zealand farmer named Sharp, but his system was adapted to British conditions mainly by commercial firms which devised, *inter alia*, the feeding and milk-recording equipment required in this country.[34] Technical development decreased the ability of the farmer to apply his own ideas but increased the efficiency with which others could do so.

Technological change and the manufacturing presence were equally obvious in the dairy. First came electricity, which gradually replaced coal as a means of raising steam for sterilising equipment, then chemicals which began to replace steam as a

abreast

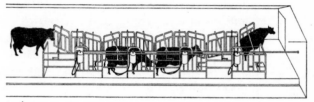

tandem

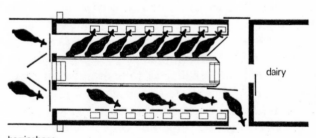

dairy

herringbone

20   The development of the milking-parlour (see pp 229–30)

means of sterilisation, then refrigeration equipment which began to replace water from pipe or well for cooling the milk, and finally the refrigerated tank which enabled the advanced and substantial milk producer to cool and store his milk in bulk instead of cooling it by the pailful and storing it in churns. But there were more parties to this last change than farmer and engineer. The bulk system certainly reduced labour and milk loss on the farm, but its capital cost was heavy and the savings with the smaller herds seldom sufficient to make the investment profitable. The main beneficiaries were the hauliers and processors of the milk and it was largely their attitudes which determined the rate of spread of this innovation.[35]

The effects of external developments on the buildings of the farmstead were illustrated in neater and more abrupt form by the story of the bullpen in these years. In the later 1930s efforts to raise the standard of breeding stock included the introduction of progeny-testing schemes which made it profitable to keep potentially valuable bulls on the farm until the milk yields of their daughters were known. By this time their strength and weight were considerable and, more important, their natural tendency to bad temper had increased with age. Clearly, some form of housing better for the bull and safer for the farmer and his men than the traditional stall in a cowhouse or box in a corner of the yard was required. The war allowed only home-made improvements. But the following years saw the general adoption of a fairly standardised form of pen and run which provided the bull with shelter and opportunity for exercise in the open air and incorporated various safety devices that made it unnecessary for the stockman to enter the building while the bull was loose. The most important single animal on the farm was at last honoured with a house specially planned for his particular needs. But he seldom enjoyed it for long, for the post-war development of artificial insemination made his general presence on the farm unnecessary. Between 1950 and 1960 the number of bulls on farms was nearly halved and many of the new bullpens were abandoned or used, not very conveniently, for some other purpose. The artificial insemination centre, not the farm, was the true beneficiary of the new improved bull-pen.[36]

All these changes affected the design of dairy buildings, but the growing intensification of agriculture also began to influence the duration of their use, for in the middle 1950s modernised forms of the forgotten practice of soilage were introduced to the country from America under the name of 'zero-grazing'. These systems were made possible by new field equipment, notably the forage-harvester and the self-unloading trailer which cut and carried the grass to the permanently yarded cattle. But they served the old principle of securing the better utilisation of pasture by taking grass to the cows instead of cows to the grass. In so doing, they also secured the better utilisation of the buildings which were occupied all the year round instead of lying empty during the grazing season. The managerial difficulties of zero-grazing, however, were considerable and the technique did not spread far or fast. But its appearance reflected the trends of the time. Under economic pressure, the farmer was seeking ways of making more intensive use of both land and buildings.[37]

THE HOUSING OF BEEF CATTLE

Methods of housing dairy cattle changed radically, methods of housing the less profitable beef cattle hardly at all. Economics ensured that fattening cattle were run in the fields or in such yards as were available, where they continued their traditional functions of turning bulky fodders into meat and straw into manure. In the 1950s the development by research workers of systems of fattening cattle entirely on barley and supplements enabled farms which did not produce bulk feeds to carry beef enterprises but did not inspire any general development in types of building. More intensive methods of housing were sometimes discussed but seldom practised. Characteristically, the only major structural innovation in these years was the limited but successful use of the slatted-floor system which required less labour and litter than the conventional yard; and this, as we have already seen, was originally reintroduced from Norway as a system for housing the dairy herd.

The necessity of feeding more cattle from fewer acres of pasture helped to produce the general revolution in grassland management, predicted and inspired by Stapledon, which was one of the most substantial achievements of this period. This revolution began with improvements in the production of grass but continued inevitably with improvements in its conservation. Equally inevitably, it brought further changes to the farmstead where the produce of the fields was stored and eaten. It was a sign of the international times that many of these changes reflected American developments or, more pointedly, incorporated American equipment.

In 1939, nearly all grass was conserved as hay. A little was made into silage, a little was dried, but silo and drier were alike exceptional. In 1960, most grass was still made into hay, though not all of it was now cured in the field. 'Barn hay drying', the practice of drying hay in buildings by a forced draught of cold or warmed air, which was introduced from America at the end of the war, had established itself in some of the rainier areas where a better quality end-product more than compensated for the higher cost of production.[38] Nevertheless, hay had acquired a rival. Grass-drying, it is true, was now hardly a competitor. In the decade after the war, when concentrate feeds were scarce, the number of grass-drying plants in their new sheds of reinforced concrete members and asbestos-cement sheeting rose from under three hundred to over twelve hundred. But expansion ceased in the early 1950s, when concentrates were again imported freely. Many plants went out of production and those which continued in operation became part of specialised enterprises which supplied the manufacturers of pig and poultry feed with high-grade meal.[39] On the other hand, the making of silage had now become common practice.

For the twentieth century had overcome many of the weaknesses which had prevented the development of silage in Victorian times. The scientist had provided greater understanding of the biological processes involved, the advisor had made such knowledge generally available, and in 1946 an enterprising farmer had invented the buckrake which, in conjunction with the tractor and its hydraulic lift, made possible the complete mechanisation of the peculiarly exacting chore of silage-making. Nevertheless, it was some time before the farmstead showed any very obvious signs of the establishment of this revived technique.

In the 1940s, a number of farmers built small and often temporary versions of the tall pre-war tower-silos, sometimes of prefabricated concrete panels, sometimes of timber or wire mesh and sisal paper. But the majority came to prefer pits or, more commonly, above-ground clamps walled with sleepers or concrete slabs which fitted conveniently into the loose-housing systems developed by the dairy farmer. These were cheap to build and simple to operate. They also allowed cattle to feed themselves from the silage face through light, movable barriers, thus ending the laborious necessity of cutting and carting a heavy and unpleasant material from silo to trough. This self-feeding technique, which originated in the USA and first appeared in Great Britain in the early 1950s,[40] was soon followed by a more tangible and conspicuous type of import. The tall towers began to return, and some of them came from America. Farmers on both sides of the Atlantic faced similar problems. But economic pressures and therefore technical responses developed earlier in the USA, and British farmers frequently found it convenient to begin this process of adjustment by adopting readymade American systems.

Economically, wages were rising and with them incentives to invest in labour-saving equipment, while the growing size of enterprise made possible capital expenditure on a scale hitherto unprofitable. Technically, the Americans had developed new types of tower silo, and a variety of mechanical equipment to load, unload and distribute their contents, thus achieving a degree of 'press button farming' never before seen in the cattle-yard. The forgotten prediction made by Dr George Thurber a lifetime earlier had finally and literally come true. The whole matter of silage had now been Americanised; and the British farmer was among those to take advantage of it.[41]

The first installations of this type appeared in Great Britain in the later 1950s. Most of them used imported equipment, including the expensive but efficient airtight silos made of glass-lined steel which, by preventing the entry of oxygen, eliminated one of the main causes of wastage.[42] These huge new towers dominated not only the farmstead but the farming scene around it and provided the travelling townsman with sudden and spectacular evidence of agricultural change. Nevertheless, they were the results, not the causes, of such change. Their importance lay in the part they played in a new and pervading system of farmstead mechanisation. Machines now handled grass in the buildings even as they cultivated and harvested it in the fields. The connection between the development of machinery and the progress of silage-making which contemporaries noted illustrated one of the pre-requisites of many changes in the farmstead of this period.[43]

PIG HOUSING

War and scarcity made necessity a dramatic increase in agricultural production. They also, however, made necessary an equally dramatic decrease in pig production, for the war prevented importation of the concentrated feedstuffs on which the pig industry had previously depended. In 1939 there were three and a half million pigs in England and Wales, in 1947 less than a million and a quarter. But once supplies became available again recovery was rapid. In 1951 the pig population reached nearly three million, in 1952 nearly four million, and for the rest of the decade it never fell below four and a half million.

The need for more piggeries was obvious. So was the need for bigger and better piggeries. For with the return of imported feedstuffs came the return of imported pig products. The home farmer met this competition by specialisation and intensification. As the years passed, a growing proportion of the national herd concentrated on a shrinking number of farms and the piggery became an increasingly important means of ensuring productive efficiency. In the depression times, the farmer had exploited the pig's ability to adapt itself to a wide variety of conditions. Now he exploited its ability to respond to the right kind of environment created by the right kind of housing.

He was also able to exploit the findings of the research workers who, in the years after the war, patiently produced a growing mass of evidence on the environmental needs of pigs. Their findings left plenty of scope for individual decisions and managerial skills, but the new knowledge ended the old dependence on tradition and informed guesswork. From now onwards the farmer could specify in reasonable detail the microclimate his pigs required and judge the work of the builder and the engineer by the efficiency with which their designs provided it. Thus was fulfilled the prophecy inherent in the recommendation of an official committee in 1945 that research should be undertaken into 'the influence of design and structure on housing environment and the effect of environment on pig health and comfort'.[44] Such research was undertaken and within a few years it revolutionised pig housing.

The change can be followed in the technical literature on fattening houses. The textbook which the committee sponsored could only quote those familiar pre-war types of piggery, the cottager's pigsty and the Danish house.[45] The first edition of its official successor in 1953 repeated the description of these two systems and added a variety of new designs produced by enterprising farmers and frequently called after them. Clearly, tradition and empiricism still ruled. But its second edition, published in 1962, illustrated the coming of the new scientific order. It began with definitions of such terms as thermal conductivity, saturation deficit and sensible heat and filled a third of its length with graph-illustrated sections on temperature and relative humidity, insulation, and ventilation before it described its first piggery.[46] Finally, in the following year, another manual bore precise documentary witness to the realisation of the committee's hopes. It supported its chapter on the environmental needs of the pig by references to twenty-five scientific papers, all of which had been published in the previous fifteen years.[47]

Nevertheless, the committee's order of priorities required reversal, for it was the effect of environment on the pig that determined the design and construction of its housing. In particular, research showed that pigs required higher and more constant temperatures than was previously believed. For farrowing sows and their litters this meant greater use of artificial heating, generally by infra-red lamps. For fatteners it meant the development of housing which conserved the pigs' natural heat, which in turn meant carefully-planned combinations of insulation and ventilation to maintain proper conditions in the building. It meant, in short, increased environmental control and therefore increasingly enclosed buildings. Piggeries which relied on deep straw to keep the pigs warm were replaced first by piggeries which relied on insulation and natural ventilation, and then by piggeries which relied on insulation and artificial ventilation. Once more the textbooks tell the story. In 1953 the first edition of the official bulletin on pig housing previously quoted described artificial ventilation by fans as experimental. Its second edition, only nine years later, took artificial ventilation for granted and unenthusiastically informed such farmers as were compelled by circumstances to use natural ventilation that they could expect 'fair results' if proper care was taken.[48]

It was typical of the changed times that the pig-farmer who had once devised his own buildings turned to the research worker and the engineer for improvements to ease the working of his new houses. The slatted-floor system which he began to adopt at the end of this period to reduce the labour of manure-handling came to him not from other farmers but from research centres in Norway and the USA. It was equally typical that within ten years of its first appearance in a piggery this technique had produced a research literature of over fifty papers.[49]

The general consequences of these changes were obvious to the most casual visitor to the countryside. He would still see sows and their litters housed in arks in the fields and occasional

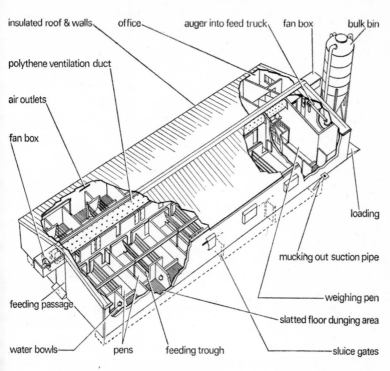

insulated roof & walls   office   auger into feed truck   fan box   bulk bin

polythene ventilation duct

air outlets

fan box

loading

mucking out suction pipe

weighing pen

slatted floor dunging area

feeding passage

water bowls   pens   feeding trough   sluice gates

21 A modern fattening house for 200 pigs. Note the degree of environmental control and the mechanisation of feeding. (Based on *Power Farming*, vol 35, no 4, October 1965, enclosure pp 3–4)

groups of pigs in yards in the farmstead. But he would no longer see pig fattening in sties or in Danish piggeries a few bays long on the mixed farms he passed. From time to time, however, he would pass long, vaguely industrial-type buildings in which the more specialised pig producer was raising and fattening pigs in environments specified by the scientist and created by the builder and the engineer.

POULTRY HOUSING

The general development of the poultry enterprise and therefore of poultry housing paralleled that of the pig enterprise and pig housing. There was a considerable, though less drastic decrease in numbers in the war years and a similar rapid recovery when feedstuffs became freely available, the same specialisation and increase in size of unit, and the same replacement of traditional types of housing by new and more intensive systems based on the new knowledge gained from research. There was also the same independence of the productive capacity of the land, for the poultry farmer, like the pig farmer, fed his stock on the processed products of other people's farms.

Yet there was one important difference. The pig farmer continued his familiar lines of production. The poultry farmer added to his business a major new line of production dependent upon the most intensive system of management yet seen on the farm. The achievement of the traditional poultry farmer, the egg producer, was considerable. In the 1930s, Great Britain imported a third of its eggs, in the later 1950s it was virtually self-supporting in eggs. But it was surpassed by that of a new type of poultryman, the broiler producer, who started business in 1953 and seven years later was marketing 100 million birds a year. So one of the themes of this period is the intensification of an inherited system, another the rise of a system intensive from its beginnings.

The background to these changes was the extensive 'range' system of light, fixed houses or movable folds standing in pasture fields which, in the later 1940s, housed nearly all the hens in the country. Such a system required little capital outlay and improved the fertility of the soil which the birds scratched and manured. But its labour costs were high and it suffered from the inherent weakness of low winter egg yields, for egg production is stimulated by light and the range birds were necessarily dependent on such light as nature saw fit to provide. When post-war economics emphasised the rewards of winter egg production and research made clear the importance of duration and periods as well as the extent of lighting, it became obvious that some system which allowed greater control of the factors affecting production was required.

One answer was the intensive cage battery system which

allowed a substantial control over environment in general and complete control over lighting in particular, with consequent increase of egg yields at a cost of greater capital investment. This method had established itself in Great Britain before the war but had barely survived the feedstuffs restrictions of the years of scarcity. Once supplies of concentrates returned, however, its expansion was rapid and by the end of the period it housed over a third of all the hens in the country.[50] But meanwhile another alternative had appeared. This was the deep-litter system which concentrated the birds in an enclosed building, thus enabling the farmer to exploit artificial lighting to maintain winter egg production, but allowing the hens free movement on a floor of straw bedding. Introduced from the USA in 1948, it spread rapidly and by 1960 housed another third of the national flock. With the aid of new buildings, therefore, the egg producer had intensified in little more than a decade two-thirds of a once extensive enterprise.[51]

So egg production achieved intensification and with it the mechanisation of henhouse operations which allowed a steady increase in the number of birds for which one man could be effectively responsible. But broiler production was born intensive. It depended for its success on securing the most efficient rate of growth from birds at their most efficient period of growth, which is the first three months of life, and it pressed into service nutritional, genetical and veterinary science, the skills of the builder and the engineer, and a standard of managerial ability seldom previously applied to the business of food production. All these resources were concentrated in the new broiler houses which so suddenly appeared in the farmlands to house the increasing multitude of young chickens which fattened with factory-type precision on a factory-type schedule for pre-planned delivery to the packing station.

Indeed, the whole development was to some extent pre-planned, for the broiler industry originated in the USA in the war years and its quick and profitable expansion was watched by enterprising Englishmen for some years before the end of feedstuffs rationing in 1953 enabled them to introduce it to Great

P

Britain. The advantages of such vicarious experience were re-flected in the phenomenal rate of expansion of the new trade which far exceeded that of any other line of farm production. Changes in the structure of the industry were equally rapid, for here as elsewhere economics favoured the big battalions. A number of the early broiler producers raised flocks of under a thousand birds but a few years later some of the groups that were formed to run co-operative packing stations demanded a minimum delivery of 10,000 per batch from prospective members. Broiler houses grew larger. They also grew more standardised and more efficient.

Essentially, these houses were means of providing a closely-specified environment, notably a temperature of 65° to 70° F, subdued lighting for predetermined periods, and clean air free from excessive moisture. This implied careful design, artificial heating, heavy insulation and the precise control of ventilation. At first, attempts were made to adapt existing buildings for the new purposes. It was soon clear, however, that specially-designed buildings were preferable and specialist firms began to produce prefabricated houses.[52] There were, of course, numerous differences in detail. But the basic design became increasingly standardised. For example, growing appreciation of the effects of light regimes on growth caused a steady increase in the proportion of windowless houses. In general, similar needs produced similar installations—parallel lines of long, low, widespread buildings, each housing mechanically-fed and mechanically-watered flocks whose average size increased in-exorably as the years passed. Typically, the most conspicuous objects in the broilerised farmstead were the tall hoppers with which houses were commonly equipped to receive the bulk deliveries of feedstuffs which the size of these enterprises made economic. A new, intensive and large-scale trade had produced a new and appropriate type of building.[53]

Yet the broiler house was not as revolutionary as it appeared to many men of the time. It certainly formed part of a new system of production, for successful broiler farming implied the development of an economic chain linking the hatchery, the

broiler house and the packing station with the retailer. It is no
accident that one of the pioneers of the broiler industry was also
the author of one of the first books published in Great Britain
on vertical integration in agriculture.[54] But technically it did no
more than present old and general trends in a new and particular form. The broiler-house system was not dependent on its
own farmland, for the producer bought the materials of his
trade, chicks, litter and feed, as well as his buildings; but neither
was the battery system for layers nor the urban cowhouses and
fattening-houses of an earlier age. It provided livestock with a
man-made environment; but in this it differed only in degree
from any other type of building which sought to influence
microclimate. Indeed, it hardly differed even in degree from
some contemporary piggeries. Nevertheless, the historical importance of the broiler house is considerable. For it made
manifest with spectacular efficiency the capabilities of the
advanced agricultural building and the part it could play in the
enterprise it served.[55]

SHEEP HOUSING

An interesting by-product of the general intensification of
agriculture was the beginning of a revival of sheep housing.
Traditionally, the hill farmer had wintered his ewe lambs on
lowland farms. But by the 1950s many of the lowland farmers
who had once received these lambs had turned milk-producer
and were unwilling to lease to other people's sheep the winter
grazings from which they expected the valuable 'early bite' of
spring grass for their own cows. So upland farmers began to
devise shelters, sometimes floored with wooden slats, which
would enable their lambs to winter on the hills. By the end of
this period this new form of housing was barely out of the
experimental stage. But its success was one of the factors which
encouraged the development of all types of sheep housing
which was so striking a feature of farm buildings development
in the next decade.[56]

THE FARM OFFICE

Clearly, the demands of the farm on the farmstead were growing. So were its demands on the farmer who, year by year, needed more technical knowledge, more records and more figures to assist him in his increasingly crucial managerial decisions. By the later 1950s, therefore, farm management had established itself among the major agricultural disciplines and the description of the farm office as 'the most important building on the farm' had found a place among familiar rural proverbs. Most farmers, it is true, continued to use the traditional desk in the front room, but on the larger and more intensive holdings neat new buildings or refurbished sections of old ones, through whose windows wall-graphs could be seen and a typewriter heard, became increasingly common. The formal acceptance by the farming community of contemporary business techniques and apparatus was symbolised shortly after the end of this period by the first appearance in a textbook on farm buildings of a section, complete with plans, on the farm office and its equipment.[57]

PREFABRICATION AND ADAPTABILITY

In this period the industrial system took final control of the construction of farm buildings. The most obvious sign of this was a comprehensive change in the materials of which they were built. Nearly all those used in new work now came from the factory; cement to make concrete for floors where earth would not suffice, steel and reinforced concrete, including prestressed concrete, for framing, concrete blocks for walls, asbestos-cement sheeting for cladding and, almost universally, for roofing instead of the corrugated iron which required maintenance, or the tiles and slates which required more complicated and expensive forms of roof-construction.[58] Less familiar products, too, were now beginning to make their appearance in the farmstead—aluminium sheeting, plastic rainwater goods and rooflights, and a variety of plastic or mineral insulating materials on which the efficiency of so many new livestock buildings depended. It was typical of the new order that the only old materials to retain a place in it were those which did so on its industrial terms.

Thus, bricks were no longer made in local brickyards. They were bought through the general trade from the big brickworks. Timber adapted itself more subtly to the new needs with the aid of industrial resources. Timber connectors decreased the weight and increased the scope of wooden members; waterproof glues made possible new forms of plywood and laminated components; and new preservatives prolonged its life and lowered its ultimate cost by ending the need for maintenance. It became, in fact, a sort of industrial product. But stone and thatch could not so transform themselves and, typically, the most memorable reference to thatch in this period was a frankly elegiac description of 'the strange intermingled crop' of ragwort and willowherb that grew on the roof of an abandoned stable.[59]

With these changes in the materials of building, however, went less immediately obvious but more basic changes in the methods of building. For traditionally farm buildings had been built with substantial walls that carried the weight of the roof. But new buildings were increasingly formed of a frame of reinforced concrete, steel or timber to which roofs and walls or side-cladding were added. The principle, of course, was not new. It was as old as the timber-framed barn and had been successfully exploited by the industrial age which made the framed Dutch barn the most common and conspicuous of all agricultural buildings. But its practice in this form and on this scale was revolutionary. So were its implications.

By this time the farmer had, of course, ceased to grow, dig or fell his own materials. Nevertheless, as long as he bought such small components as blocks, sheets and minor members he remained master of the size and shape of the buildings he erected. But the dimensions of prefabricated frames were determined by the sizes of the columns and trusses on which they depended and these were determined by the commercial and technical decisions of the firms which made them. Further, the type of framework the farmer chose frequently influenced his choice of the materials with which he clad it. In many cases, therefore, it was manifestly more convenient to buy whole buildings, frames, roofs and walls together, from the firms which supplied them, particularly if, as was usual, they were prepared to erect them as well. Again, there was nothing totally unfamiliar in all this. It was the scope and scale that were new. The work of the local builder continued. So did improvisation and self-help on the farm.[60] But an increasing proportion of the new buildings erected in these years came to the farm as sets of factory-made components.

The development and acceptance of prefabrication were rapid. In the post-war years, mass-production techniques were increasingly and successfully applied to the manufacture of sets of structural parts, generally based on some form of the frame system, from which the farmer could choose those which provided the particular building he required. This revolution was not, of course, either painless or complete. The design, transport and erection of factory-made buildings presented a variety of technical and physical problems, while no range of prefabricated buildings could hope to meet more than a majority of needs on a majority of farms. In particular, such standardised products could not always be conveniently fitted into the limited spaces available when farmsteads were remodelled. Nevertheless, by the end of this period the prefabricated framed building was widely accepted as 'a means of providing 90 per cent of our agricultural building needs'.[61] The farmer had long been accustomed to choose his building materials from catalogues. Now he was becoming accustomed to choose the buildings themselves from the same source.

This change reflected the general advantage inherent in any system of mass-production and the standardised assembly of standardised components. But the increased use of the framed building also reflected a particular agricultural advantage. Such a building was inherently easier to adapt to other purposes than the traditional type of structure. The insertion of new doors or new windows, the conversion of a four-sided house into a three-sided shelter, the addition or removal of a bay, all were simpler and cheaper in a building where the weight of the roof was supported on vertical members spaced some fifteen feet apart instead of on necessarily substantial walls.

The question of adaptable designs had been raised academically thirty years earlier.[62] But this was the first age in which it assumed general importance. For the farmers of the post-war years had lived through a series of technical revolutions which showed no signs of ending and many signs of accelerating. They were, indeed, the first agricultural generation to take rapid, drastic and continuing change as a normal and natural condition. They had spent much of their working lives fitting new technologies into old farmsteads and they strove to plan their new buildings in accordance with the lessons they had learnt.

The importance of this point was appreciated early in this period and the first post-war textbook on farm buildings listed adaptability high among design considerations.[63] In the following years many others said the same thing at greater length. Indeed, no discussion of farm buildings was complete without some reference to the problem. Certain types of building were inherently specialised. How could the less committed designs be planned to allow for future change?

In principle, there were three possible answers. At one extreme, the most obvious form of temporary building was one with a limited life which could be scrapped when its purpose ended and a new one built in its place. This implied, of course, a cheap building. Yet there was no generally acceptable type of construction between the architectural equivalent of stick-and-string suitable for only a few agricultural purposes and the conventional buildings of indefinite life which were too costly to abandon after only a few years' use. At the other extreme stood the multi-purpose building designed *ab initio* to be readily and cheaply convertible to a variety of possible jobs. But the difficulties of combining in one structure immediate efficiency for known purposes with possible future efficiency for a number of hypothetical purposes were considerable. Between these, however, stood the framed building which served present needs as efficiently as its heavy-walled predecessors yet offered a considerably greater degree of convertibility. In the 1950s, therefore, it was generally agreed that a framed building of wide enough span to allow relatively easy adaptation to a number of different purposes was the most practicable answer on most farms; and the components of such buildings came from the factory. Once again, the resources of the industrial age helped the farmer to control a problem which its pressures had created.

NOTES

1. *National farm survey of England and Wales, 1941–3*, HMSO, 1946, p 41

2. Williamson, H. *The Story of a Norfolk farm*, 1941, pp 86–7

3. Baker, V. 'Exmoor, an economic survey', *Bristol University, Selected papers in agricultural economics*, vol 2, 1949, p 69

4. 'Equipment and facilities on dairy farms', *Home Farmer*, vol 18, no 9, September 1951, pp 15–16; ibid, vol 18, no 10, October 1951, pp 14–16

5. The 1950s saw the publication of two new textbooks on farm buildings, of the first official bulletins on pighousing and on grain-drying and storage and of a new series of official leaflets on the fixed equipment of the farm, most of which concerned farm buildings.

6. This process of change is admirably typified in a novel of the period. 'At the Worlidges' new farm a revolution was being wrought; a quiet and gradual change, indeed, for capital was too short to allow everything to be done at once, but a revolution none the less. For a quarter of a century the buildings had been the rotting framework into whose corners the undemanding agriculture of old Amos Jackman had been thrust. It was a farming frame which had descended to him from his predecessors here and which he had been content not only to leave unchanged but also to leave to moulder and rot and fall away. . . . The superficial signs of the new order were a clean, concreted yard; new field gates well hung; unblocked drains; patched and weatherproof walls and roofs; and the dis-

embowelling of the cowsheds and stables to make freer, more spacious covered quarters for calves and yearlings and in-calvers.' (Trow-Smith, R. *Clay Village*, 1954, p 174.)

For a general description of such changes in an arable area in these years see Sayce, R. B. 'The farm buildings of Norfolk', *Agriculture*, vol 64, no 4, July 1957, p 169. Sections on the adaptation of old buildings to new purposes were included in all textbooks of the period as a matter of course. One of these books, subtitled 'conversions and improvements', was essentially a collection of case-studies of farmstead remodelling. (Benoy, W. G. *Farm buildings*, 1956.)

7. Charlick, R. H. *Farm buildings surveys*, *Wales*, 1965, p 6; *England*, 1967, p 6. (Figures kindly collated for England and Wales by the author.)

8. *Post-war building studies, no 17, Farm buildings*, HMSO, 1945, pp 7, 30; Weller, J. B. *Farm buildings*, 1965. The former quoted no research findings and listed only one research body among the thirteen organisations from which it received written evidence (p 202). The latter cited a mass of research findings and included a list under eight headings of 'The organisations that promote research' in a chapter entitled 'The need for research' (pp 25–8). A minor but striking instance of the same change was the discussion in another textbook of the 1960s of the ancient need of farmsteads for shelter with the aid of advice from an 'Index of exposure to driving rain' published by the Building Research Station. (Pasfield, D. H. *Farm building design and construction*, 1965, pp 7–9.)

9. A series of official missions immediately after the war to study agricultural developments on the Continent and in North America was followed by an increasing flow of individual and group visits by farmers and agriculturists to universities and interesting farming areas overseas, particularly those in the USA. Many of these visitors were concerned in one way or another with farm buildings and their reports added substantially to the literature of the subject. The influence of particular individuals or reports can seldom be assessed but the total effect of the publications and lectures of these agricultural travellers must have been considerable. The contribution to British farm buildings design of visitors sponsored by such bodies as the Kellogg and the Nuffield Foundations would make an interesting study in technical communications and their consequences.

10. The introduction of most of the major innovations in this period came within this general pattern. For a case-study of a minor but typical instance see Harvey, N. 'The Ruakura farrowing pen', *Agriculture*, vol 67, no 10, January 1961, pp 530–3

11. *Post-war Building Studies, no 17, Farm Buildings*, HMSO, 1945

12. The hopes expressed in the early days of post-war reconstruction that the architectural profession would, in general, play a large part in the design of farm buildings and, in particular, develop a specialised class of farm architect were not fulfilled. (*Post-war Building Studies, no 17, Farm Buildings*, HMSO, 1945, pp 32–3.) The only systematic study in these years of those responsible for designing farm buildings found that about a third of the buildings in the survey were designed by professionally qualified men, two-thirds of whom were land agents, one third architects. In addition, one building in six was planned with the help of an official advisor, who probably had qualifications in land agency or architecture. The remainder, about half, were designed by landowners, farmers and builders. (Ingersent, K. A. and Manning, P. *New housing for dairy cows in the East Midlands*, 1960, p 20.) At the end of this period an architect noted sadly that none of the winning designs in a milking parlour competition were by members of his profession. (Voelcker, J. 'Farm buildings competition', *Architect's Journal*, vol 133, 22 June 1961, p 917.)

13. The Farm Buildings Association. By 1960 it numbered some 500 members.

14. A curious illustration of the extent of this was the frequency of demands for research into particular problems without regard to existing research literature on the subject which was in many cases substantial. Significantly, these first became obvious in the middle 1950s, when the volume of published work was beginning to outstrip the individual advisor's ability to master its contents. Equally significantly, one of the first tasks of the first official group solely concerned with farm buildings research when it was established in 1957 was the compilation of a bibliography of relevant research literature.

15. The first book on farm workshops appeared in 1953 (Hine, H. J. *The farm workshop*). The increase of implement sheds was noted as a recent development in Oxfordshire in 1949. (Huthnance, S. L. 'Farming in Oxfordshire and Berkshire', *Journal of the Royal Agricultural Society of England*, vol 110, 1949, p 5.) The first formal study of implement housing was undertaken in 1952, the first official leaflet on the subject issued in 1955. (Denman, D. and Roberts, H. *The provision of implement accommodation*, 1959, p ii; *The implement shed and farm workshop*, HMSO, 1955.)

16. The first official advisory leaflet on this subject was issued in 1956. (*The tractor fuel store*, HMSO.)

17. In 1953 the British Electricity Authority launched a rural electrification programme which planned to increase the number of

farms connected to a public supply to 85 per cent by 1963. This figure was reached eighteen months ahead of schedule. (Abell, R. H. and Meadows, F. P. 'Rural electricity supply', *Proceedings of the Rural Electrification Conference*, 1962, pt 1, p 61.)

18. Slater, J. and Jones, M. 'A survey of Welsh hill farm mechanisation', *Journal of Agricultural Engineering Research*, vol 2, no 3, 1957, pp 222–34; Henderson, G. *Farmer's Progress*, 1950, p 95

19. 'Developments in handling grain and feed', *Agricultural Merchant*, vol 38, no 11, November 1958, p 54; 'Delivery of feed in bulk', ibid, vol 41, no 2, February 1961, p 59

20. Calverley, D. J. B. 'Mechanisation in livestock husbandry', *Journal of the Royal Agricultural Society of England*, vol 128, 1962, p 69

21. For the development of these types of plant see Mountfield, J., Oxley, T., Cashmore, W. and Williamson, W. *Storage and drying of grain in bulk. Bin ventilation (1945)*, 1946; *Grain drying and storage in the USA*, HMSO, 1952, which summarised the lessons of American experiences; *Grain drying and storage in Great Britain*, HMSO, 1952; Theophilus, T. *Economics of grain drying and storage*, 1955; Gammon, F. 'Grain drying survey', *Journal of the substitution of British Agricultural Engineers*, vol 13, no 13, 1957, pp 28–32; Mathieson, M. *The mechanisation of the grain harvest*, 1961; and also the various advisory bulletins and leaflets of the Ministry of Agriculture, Fisheries and Food and the publications of the National Institute of Agricultural Engineering, where much of the research was undertaken. For a detailed account of the development of one system of graindrying by an inventive farmer see Ensor, T. *Floor-drying of cereals*, 1967

22. The main causes of deterioration in stored grain are moulds, fungi and insects. This method turns these enemies of grain against themselves. The respiration of these organisms in sealed grain, aided to some extent by the respiration of the grain itself, replaces the oxygen in the atmosphere of the container by carbon dioxide which represses or kills them before they can do much damage.

23. British manufacturers first produced silos for the storage of damp grain in 1962 (Messers Hill, H., Whittenbury, R. and Lacey, J. *The use of concrete stave silos for storing high moisture grain, 1967*, p 7). See also Hyde, M. and Oxley, T. 'Experiments on the airtight storage of damp grain', *Annals of applied Biology*, vol 48, no 4, 1960, pp 687–9; the publications of the Pest Infestation Laboratory where much of the research was undertaken; and footnote 68 to Chapter 6.

24. Trow-Smith, R. *Clay village*, 1954, pp 172–3

25. Twiss, P. T. G. 'Electricity and potato storage', *Agriculture*, vol 68, no 5, August 1961, p 264

26. 'The first important growth in indoor storage came . . . about 1947. This pre-dated the publication of British research findings, but is perhaps less surprising when one considers that farmers were active from the start as innovators. The three-man mission to North America may be said to have begun the scientific study of the subject. . . . (This mission) to America found a bewildering range of stores, mostly of rather complicated construction. . . . It was a significant achievement on the part of the research teams to have shown that under British conditions the basic requirements were few and simple.' (Dawson, E. *Potato production in Yorkshire*, 1967, pp 24, 26.)

See also Burton, W. G. and Mann, G. 'Late storage of potatoes in England and Wales', *Agriculture*, vol 60, no 10, January 1954, pp 466–72; Bissett, G. B., Dawson, E. and Jones, R. B. *The economics of potato storage*, 1959; and the various advisory bulletins and leaflets of the Ministry of Agriculture, Fisheries and Food and the publications of Ditton Laboratory where much of the research was undertaken.

27. Darling, H. S. 'Hop growing in England, *Journal of the Royal Agricultural Society of England*, vol 122, p 91; Burgess, A. H. *Hops*, 1964, pp 17, 193

28. At the outbreak of the Second World War there were over a thousand farmhouse cheesemakers, in 1960 only one hundred. (Cheke, V. *The story of cheesemaking in Great Britain*, 1959, p 272; Personal Communication from P. D. Anderson, Milk Marketing Board.)

29. The date when the last cow was milked in the last cowhouse in the City of London is uncertain. David Carson of Swedenborg Square, Stepney, who was described in 1951 as 'London's last cowkeeper', had ceased production by September 1953. But it is possible that R. J. Jones & Sons of Black Lion Yard, Whitechapel, continued milking after the cows had disappeared from Swedenborg Square (*Home Farmer*, vol 18, no 6, June 1951, pp 11–13; personal communication from Mr J. L. Vosper, Express Dairy Group Services Ltd, London). J. Jorden of Lugard Rd, SE 15, probably the last cowkeeper in a fully built-up area of London, ceased milk production in 1966. (Williams, M. 'Milk and beef five miles from Trafalgar Square', *Farmers Weekly*, vol 62, no 16, 16 April 1965, p 50; personal communication from Mr Jorden.) Such other herds as survived in London had access to pasture and were therefore different types of enterprise from these totally enclosed herds. Milk production also continued in Liverpool. In 1966, there were four herds with access to pasture and three, containing in all fifty cows, totally enclosed herds in the city. (Personal communication from Mr G. A. Barley, Milk Marketing Board.)

30. The origins of the yarding system are obscure. It apparently began in East Anglia, where farmers increasing their dairy herds beyond the capacity of their cowhouses naturally considered the possibilities of their large and frequently understocked or empty bullock yards. Its origin was certainly spontaneous. Abbot's pre-war innovation (see p 183) was forgotten and little was known for some years of the parallel but unconnected developments in the USA. Indeed, the negligible use made at the time of American experience of this system was one of the earliest instances of the growing failure of the farm buildings designer to keep abreast of current literature.

31. Buckler, P. 'Slatted floors and other forms of bedding' *Journal of the Farmers Club*, 1961, pt 4, p 51. The first such slatted-floor yard in this country was built by a Devon farmer. ('Slats in practice', *Farmers Weekly*, vol 52, no 27, July 1960, p 112–13.)

32. The cubicle system was originated in Great Britain by a Cheshire farmer. Various forms of cubicle appeared independently about the same time in Germany and the USA but had no immediate influence on British developments. Howell Evans, the inventor of the cubicle, was awarded the MBE for this service to agriculture and so became the first man officially honoured for developing a new type of farm building. (Atkinson, R. 'A private bedroom for every cow', *Farmers Weekly*, vol 59, no 11, 16 March 1962, p vii; Livingston, H. R. *Cow cubicles*, 1965, p 7; Evans, H. *Cow cubicles*, 1964, passim.)

33. Morris, W. L. and Boyd, L. 'Time and effort to milk cows', *Agricultural Engineering*, vol 36, no 8, August 1955, pp 532–5

34. Easton, P. H. and Harvey, C. N. *The development of performance of the herring-bone parlour*, 1964, pp 7–9

35. The first pilot scheme for the bulk collection of milk began in 1955. By 1962 there were some thirty schemes in operation. (*Bulk milk collection, the producer's guide to bulk collection*, Milk Marketing Board, 1962, p 3)

36. Macintosh, J. 'Dairy farming and dairy work', *Journal of the Royal Agricultural Society of England*, vol 99, 1938, p 259; Brighten, C. W. 'How to keep a bull till proven', *Agriculture*, vol 51, no 7, October 1944, pp 301–3. The first official pamphlet on the housing of the bull was published in 1951. (*The bull pen*, HMSO.)

37. Wellesley, R. 'Labour-aiding in practice', *Journal of the Farmers Club*, 1958, pt 6, pp 82–3; Jones, J. L. 'The case for zero-grazing', *Country Life*, vol 130, no 3376, 16 November 1961, pp 1188–9

38. *Barn hay drying*, National Agricultural Advisory Service Technical Report 10, Ministry of Agriculture, 1957, pp 1–2;

Greencrop drying, Electricity Council (EDA Division), 1967, pp 11–12

39. Raymond, W. F. 'Grassdrying', *Agriculture*, vol 75, no 4, April 1968, p 156

40. Turner, C. 'Self-feeding of silage', *Agriculture*, vol 60, no 8, November 1953, pp 358–9; Beynon, V. H. and Langley, J. A. *Self-feeding of silage in Devon*, 1958, pp 1–2; Powell, R. 'The self-feeding of silage', *Agricultural Merchant*, vol 38, no 4, April 1958, p 53. A variation of this system, called 'bed and breakfast' because cows were bedded on the silage pack which they later ate, was introduced to this country from Northern Ireland in 1956. (Long, D. 'Bed and breakfast', *Farmers Weekly*, vol 54, no 14, 7 April 1961, p 91.)

41. See note 35, Chapter 8.

42. Farmer, P. 'Haylage', *Agriculture*, vol 69, no 9, December 1962, pp 435–6. For a detailed account of the development and production of these silos in the USA see Suter, R. C. *The courage to change*, Interstate Printers and Publishers Inc, 1964.

43. Hebblethwaite, P., Phillipson, A. and Hepherd, R. Q. 'Forage harvester performance in field tests', *Journal of the British Grassland Society*, vol 14, no 2, 1959, p 140

44. *Post-war building studies, no 17, Farm buildings*, HMSO, 1945, p 123

45. *Post-war building studies, no 17, Farm buildings*, HMSO, 1945, pp 113–23

46. Ministry of Agriculture and Fisheries Bulletin 160, *Housing the pig*, 1953 and 1962 editions.

47. Sainsbury, D. W. B. *Pig housing*, 1963, pp 39–40

48. Ministry of Agriculture and Fisheries Bulletin 160, *Housing the pig*, 1953 edition, p 32; 1962 edition, p 20

49. Easton, P. H. and Harvey, C. N. *Slatted floor systems for pigs*, 1965, pp 7, 22–4

50. This expansion was encouraged by the development of small, hybrid birds which needed less floor space per head than the old breeds. Further, the older system required one bird per cage so that the farmer could identify and cull poor yielders. But the evenness of performance of the new hybrids rendered such culling unnecessary. Consequently more than one bird could be housed per cage with a further reduction in floor space. All these factors reduced the capital cost per head of the cage system, and also provided a classic illustration of the effects of technical change on housing systems.

51. Coles, R. 'Current developments in the poultry industry', *Journal of the Royal Agricultural Society of England*, vol 122, 1961, pp 40, 43. The favourable report on the deep litter system by an official mission to North America was the main cause of its adoption in Great

The Last Age: 1939–60 255

Britain. (*Development of the poultry industry in North America*, HMSO,
1947, pp 7, 13, 26.) Two of the farmers on this mission had, however, already pioneered it in Great Britain. (Coles, R. *Development of
the poultry industry of England and Wales, 1945–1959*, 1960, p 24.) The
continuing influence of its country of origin was illustrated by the
production in England of a wide span house on American lines
and the inclusion of American designed equipment in a prefabricated house. (Soutar, D. 'Deep litter poultry houses', *Agricultural
Review*, vol 3, no 4, September 1957, pp 36–7.) A Wiltshire farmer
developed an indigenous system, the less intensive, less efficient but
also less expensive henyard. (Sykes, J. *The henyard system*, 1952, p 30.)
But this failed to survive the competition of the more intensive
systems and fell into disuse.

52. Benoy, W. G. 'Recent developments in farm buildings',
Journal of the Farmers Club, pt 6, 1959, p 73, regarded poultry housing
as a matter for specialist firms.

53. It also created as a by-product a new and more intensive
form of egg-production house. The first deep litter house with ther-
mostatically-controlled ventilation as well as automatic feeding,
watering and cleaning equipment was built about 1956 to produce
hatching eggs from specially selected stock for the broiler industry.
(Rogers, R. E. 'Some aspects of West Country farming', *Journal of
the Royal Agricultural Society of England*, vol 118, 1956, p 21.)

54. Sykes, G. *Poultry. A modern agribusiness*, 1963

55. Golden, E. F. *Broilers*, 1955, pp 22–3; Feltwell, R. *Broiler
farming*, 1960, pp 13–40; James, B. J. F. *Economics of broiler production*,
1960, pp 8–10; Law, E. M. *Broiler production in Berkshire*, 1960, pp
7–9

56. Williams, L. J. 'Lambwintering sheds', *Agriculture*, vol 66,
no 2, May 1959, pp 65–70. Young breeding stock had been housed
in certain Pennine areas 'for generations', but this practice was
highly exceptional (Clifton, E. 'Wintering housing of ewes',
Agriculture, vol 71, no 1, January 1964, p 13). General interest in the
inwintering of in-lamb ewes dates from about 1960. (Roberts, L.
'Inwintering ewes in-lamb', *Farmbuildings*, no 7, Summer 1965,
p 37.)

57. Weller, J. B. *Farm buildings*, 1965, pp 89–93

58. 'Regrettably, tiles and slates must be considered things of the
past.' (Dominy, J. N. 'Progress towards economic farm buildings',
Agricultural Review, vol 3, no 7, December 1957, p 37.)

59. Grigson, G. *An English farmhouse*, 1948, p 64

60. The do-it-yourself habits developed partly by the long years
of the depression and the sudden and acute scarcities of wartime and

partly by the increase of owner-occupation, continued throughout this period, particularly on the smaller farms. In England, about a quarter of the labour used on farm buildings erected between 1945 and 1961 was provided by farm staff, a third by contractors, including estate labour on tenanted farms, and the remainder by a combination of farm and contractor's staff. In Wales, the land of small farms, the figures were half, a quarter and a quarter respectively. (Charlick, R. H. *Farm buildings surveys, England,* 1967, p 10; Charlick, R. H. *Farm buildings surveys, Wales,* 1965, p 10.) No systematic information on the use of second-hand buildings or building materials is available, but the farming press and the farming landscape alike bore witness to the strength of the farmer's interest in cheap improvisation. One of the most successful farmers of this period, for example, mentioned with pride his grain store built 'mainly by farm labour with scrap steel'. (Paterson, R. *Milk from grass,* 1965, p 19.) A textbook of the 1950s, written by a farmer for farmers, typified this tradition. It was entitled *Build your own farm buildings* and contained advice on the use of strawbales, Nissen huts and materials salvaged from demolished buildings. (Henderson, F., 1955, pp 15, 40, 70, 174–7, 202.) Ten years later, another textbook which sought to 'show the farmer what is available by way of new methods of construction . . . and to present the architect, surveyor, or engineer or contractor with the farmer's problems', described ways of using railway sleepers for the walls of yards and horizontal silos. (Pasfield, D. H. *Farm building design and construction,* 1965, p 131.)

61. Benoy, W. G. 'Recent developments in farm buildings', *Journal of the Farmers Club,* pt 6, 1959, p 74

62. See p 211

63. 'It is essential that new farm buildings should be capable of adaptation to other used without unreasonable difficulty or expense'. (*Post-war building studies, no 17, Farm buildings,* HMSO, 1945, p 6. See also pp 6, 10.)

Chapter Ten

POST-WAR FARMSTEADS:
SOME EXAMPLES

NEW WINE IN OLD BOTTLES

The Hanoverians were primarily concerned with planning new
farmsteads for new farms, the Victorians with planning new
farmsteads for old farms. But their successors in the last generation were preoccupied with the improvement of old farmsteads
on old farms. So the main theme of case-studies in this period
was the remodelling of particular sets of buildings for particular
needs, and such plans of new farmsteads as were prepared
illustrated the desirable rather than the immediately practical.

PRINCIPLE AND PRACTICE IN OXFORDSHIRE

The discrepancy between technical possibilities and economic
realities was strikingly shown by the work of the Henderson
Brothers. In the 1920s this remarkable couple bought a run-
down farm of 85 acres in Oxfordshire and by the sustained
application of the traditional agricultural virtues gradually
made it one of the most successful and famous farms in the
country. As the farm improved, so did the farm buildings, and
by the outbreak of war a series of adaptations and additions had
converted the original farmstead, which probably dated from
enclosure-time and consisted of a barn, a range of livestock
buildings and a yard, into a set of buildings capable of meeting
the needs of an intensive farm carrying pigs, poultry and a
milking herd.[1]

The farmstead thus developed, shown in Fig 22, was markedly

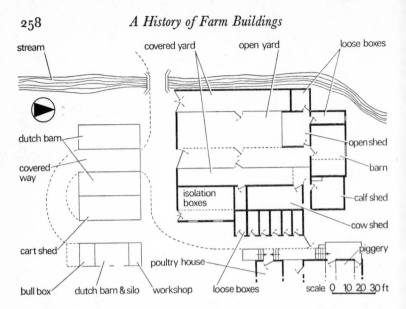

stream · covered yard · open yard · loose boxes
dutch barn · covered way · isolation boxes · open shed · barn · calf shed · cow shed
cart shed · poultry house · piggery
bull box · dutch barn & silo · workshop · loose boxes · scale 0 10 20 30 ft

22   Plan of steading on an Oxfordshire farm of 85 acres in the early 1950s. The barn and some of the livestock buildings forming the yard probably date from the late eighteenth century when the parish was enclosed (see p 257)

above average. But the Hendersons were well aware of the weaknesses inherent in such piecemeal improvement. So the design of a steading for a farm of 100 acres with which Frank Henderson won first prize in a national competition in 1947 illustrated by contrast the consequences of a more radical and less restricted application of contemporary resources to contemporary problems.[2]

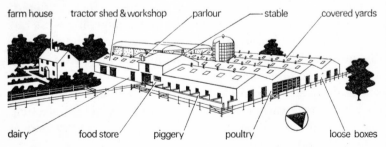

farm house · tractor shed & workshop · parlour · stable · covered yards
dairy · food store · piggery · poultry · loose boxes

23   Model farmstead for a farm of 100 acres designed by the farming brothers who developed the steading shown above (see p 259)

The proposed farmstead is shown in Fig 23. Its advantages over the real one were numerous and obvious. It was more compact and therefore wasted no space and minimised travelling and haulage distances; it provided easier access to the road from which came the lorries to collect milk and livestock and deliver feedstuffs, fertilisers and tractor fuel; and it gave better protection to men, animals and manure, for roofing covered everything except the pigsty runs. Many of these benefits were secured simply by better planning and better design. But there was one significant change of method, the abandonment of the cowhouse system for the loose-housing system. For the combination of milking-parlour and yards, the former allowing more thorough mechanisation of the milking process, the latter the removal of manure by tractor, illustrated the growing use of machinery in the farmstead which was so conspicuous a feature of this period. Nevertheless, the days of general mechanisation in field or buildings were still in the future. The plan included stables as well as a tractor shed and assumed human prime movers for most of the farmstead chores.

MODERNISATION OF A DORSET FARMSTEAD

Fig 24 shows a typical example of remodelling, which was undertaken in the early 1950s on a large Dorset farm whose buildings had already seen considerable adaptation to changing needs. The original steading, built in traditional fashion around a yard, dated from the earlier nineteenth century and implied a corn-and-meat system of farming in which yarded bullocks trod straw from the barn into manure for the light and hungry fields of the area. A lifetime later, when this system was overthrown by imports from the new lands overseas and the British farmer turned increasingly to the production of milk which faced no such competition, a dairy unit of cowhouse, yards and loose-boxes was added. But the present modernisation was less drastic. It sought not to introduce a substantial new enterprise but to improve the efficiency of existing ones.[3]

The main change was the replacement of milking in the

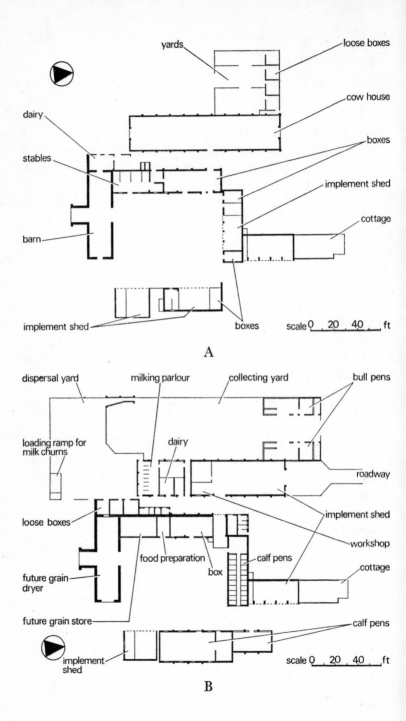

yards

loose boxes

cow house

dairy

boxes

stables

implement shed

cottage

barn

implement shed

boxes

scale 0 20 40 ft

A

dispersal yard

milking parlour

collecting yard

bull pens

loading ramp for
milk churns

dairy

roadway

loose boxes

implement shed

workshop

future grain
dryer

food preparation

box

calf pens

cottage

future grain store

calf pens

implement
shed

scale 0 20 40 ft

B

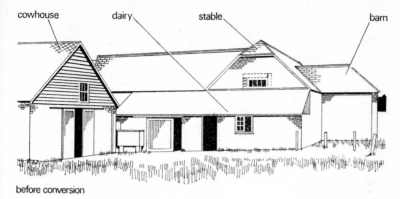

cowhouse dairy   stable   barn

before conversion

C

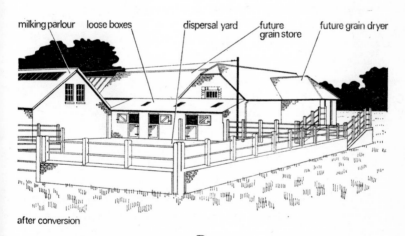

milking parlour loose boxes dispersal yard future future grain dryer
                grain store

after conversion

D

24 A Dorset farmstead before and after modernisation in the 1950s:
(A) plan before modernisation;
(B) plan after modernisation;
(C) view from the south-west before modernisation;
(D) view from the south-west after modernisation (see pp 259, 262)

cowhouse by milking in the parlour. This necessitated new yards to control the cows as they entered and left the parlour but, since local soil and climate allowed the herd to lie out in the fields all the year round, released the cowhouse for other uses. Part of it was converted, appropriately, to the milking-parlour, the remainder to an implement shed and workshop. At the same time, the barn was made ready for a grain dryer to condition the corn received from the new combine-harvester, the stable for the silos in which this grain would be stored. Minor improvements included the adaptation of two existing ranges of buildings to calfsheds for the increased head of young stock and the housing of the farm's two bulls in special-purpose pens which were safer and healthier than the dark, constricted loose-boxes of the old order.

Externally, the modernisation showed itself in a series of comparatively minor structural improvements and additions whose factory-produced concrete, tubular steel, asbestos-cement sheeting and plastic glazing contrasted technically as well as physically with the older materials from brickyard, quarry and woodland. But the refurbished buildings of the pre-mechanical age now housed the new mechanised processes of parlour-milking and bulk-grain handling and the routines of the farmstead were rearranged around them.

NEW WORK ON A DEVONSHIRE FARM

As the years passed, it became increasingly difficult to fit the growing mass of new techniques and equipment into the old farmstead framework. This last example, therefore, illustrates the tendency to house new systems in new ranges of buildings instead of adapting existing ones to them. (See Fig 25.) The particular unit shown was completed in 1964 and represents advanced practice as known at the very end of our period.[4] (See illustration p 176, right.)

The general problem of this 177-acre Devon farm, the modernisation of an old farmstead to meet new needs—in this case the housing of a sixty-head dairy herd—was familiar. But

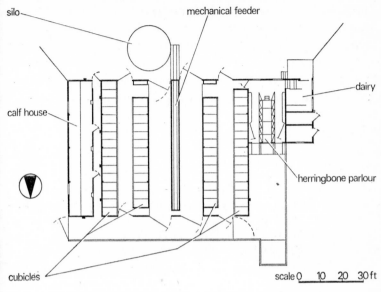

silo

mechanical feeder

dairy

calf house

herringbone parlour

cubicles

scale 0   10   20   30 ft

25   Plan of dairy unit built in 1964 (See page 262)

its solution used a combination of new techniques, notably
cubicles for housing the cows, a herringbone parlour system for
milking them and mechanical conveying equipment for feeding
them with bulk fodder from the silo, at once too large and too
complex to be incorporated into the existing buildings. So a
new dairy unit, designed around a series of industrially-
equipped mechanical processes and constructed of industrially-
produced or industrially-treated components and materials,
was built on the opposite side of the road and the old farmstead
relegated to such subsidiary jobs as housing dry cows.

The physical change on this farm was greater than in either
of the previous examples. Indeed, it came near to fulfilling the
dream of Henderson when he had planned his model farmstead
over fifteen years earlier. But it fulfilled it with substantial
technical differences. Henderson assumed the mechanisation of
the milking and mucking-out. This new design included a more
comprehensive mechanical milking system, a simplified because
strawless form of mechanised muck-removal which pumped the

liquid wastes on to the fields, mechanical refrigeration in the dairy and the even more recent innovation of machinery for transporting silage from store to trough. But this comparison offers more than technical lessons. It also illustrates the speed of change in the modern agricultural economy. By 1964 the prize-winning proposal of 1947 was already part of history.

NOTES

1. Henderson, G. *The farming ladder*, 1956, pp 18, 168–71
2. *New ideas for farm buildings*, published by *Farmer and Stockbreeder*, 1947, pp 3–6
3. Benoy, W. G. *Farm buildings*, 1956, pp 74–5
4. *Farmbuildings*, no 8, Autumn 1965, p 104

EPILOGUE

By 1960, the major innovations of the previous thirty years had substantially and successfully established themselves in general practice. The loose-housing system and the milking-parlour, grain-drying and storage plant, silage installations, environmentally-controlled piggeries and poultry houses, and concrete and asbestos construction had between them transformed the farmstead in a generation. Yet the dominant feature of this period was not any particular change. It was the general increase in the speed of change. The continuing and accelerating technological revolution of which these developments formed part had now become the basic fact of agricultural life. Even as these developments were taking structural form in the farmsteads of the post-war years, new problems were arising to influence the design and construction of farm buildings in the years ahead.

Some of these, of course, are merely new forms of old problems. For example, the importance of minimising capital outlay and maintenance costs is inherent in any type of investment in the fixed equipment of the farm. Again, there is nothing unfamiliar in principle in the demand for more and better mechanical aids to economise labour, for more efficient systems of housing and storage, and for designs which allow greater adaptability to possible future changes. A more direct legacy from the previous age is the need for an improved information system, so crucial in a form of development which depends increasingly on the findings of research stations. But some reflect more immediately contemporary pressures.

Thus, economics today favours the larger unit. So the number of farms is falling and the average size of farms is rising, which

R   265

means, of course, bigger steadings for bigger acreages. At the same time, the growing concentration of livestock enterprises, and the increasing intensification of livestock systems, has raised general problems of husbandry and specific problems of manure disposal. In particular, many farms can no longer satisfactorily dispose of the waste products of the farmstead by traditional means, while the frequent replacement of solid farmyard manure by liquid slurry from litterless animal houses makes necessary new methods of manure handling. More generally, the farmer is now being integrated into the industrial society of the internal-combustion age, even as his grandfather was integrated into the industrial economy of the steam age. The modern townsman expects recreation as well as food from the countryside and is empowered as voter to make felt in legislation his resentment of the cruder structural reminders that the farms he sees are merely the rural equivalents of the factories he has left behind him in the city.

The farming community strives to meet these problems in a variety of ways. Nearly all their improvements, however, depend upon the increasing use of the increasing volume of new knowledge, new equipment and new materials which come to them from the scientific economy that lies beyond the farm gate. Such innovations as the preservation of undried grain by chilling, the appearance of automation in certain farmstead processes, unfamiliar systems of manure disposal and the growing use of plastics bear conspicuous witness to this inevitable trend. Less obviously, even the revival of the ancient practice of in-wintering sheep, which requires only the simplest of structures, owes much to the findings of the research centres on ways and means of housing the flock.

Nevertheless, in all this change there is no break with tradition. On the contrary, the landowners and farmers of today are continuing the oldest and wisest of all the traditions that guide those who equip farmland with buildings. Like their professional ancestors down the centuries, they are using the resources of the time to meet the needs of the time.

A NOTE ON SOURCES

As is clear from the references quoted in the preceding chapters, most of the material on the history of farm buildings comes from more general agricultural and architectural sources which deal only incidentally with farm buildings. Such sources are given in the appropriate general bibliographies, notably the 'Lists of books and articles on agrarian history' published annually in the *Agricultural History Review* since its first appearance in 1953.

This note, therefore, lists only the more specialised sources concerned with the subject.

Bibliographical sources

The *List of books and articles on vernacular architecture* issued periodically by the Vernacular Architecture Group contains a section on barns and other farm buildings. The first such list appeared in 1956.

Sources on archaeological work

Excavations on Saxon and medieval sites can be followed in the appropriate sections of *Mediaeval Archaeology*. This first appeared in 1957. For excavations on later sites see *Post-mediaeval Archaeology*. This first appeared in 1967.

Modern books

These include:
Peate, I. C. *The Welsh house*, 1940
Grigson, G. *An English farmhouse*, 1948

Briggs, M. S. *The English farmhouse*, 1953
Harvey, N. *The story of farm buildings*, 1953
Cook, O. and Smith, E. *English cottages and farmhouses*, 1954
Barley, M. W. *The English farmhouse and cottage*, 1961
Horn, W. and Born, E. *The barns of the Abbey of Beaulieu and its granges of Great Coxwell and Beaulieu-St Leonards*, 1965

Local studies

General or minor area studies include:
Sheldon, L. 'Devon barns', *Transactions of the Devonshire Association*, vol 64, 1932, pp 389–95
Crump, W. B. 'The little hill farm', *Proceedings of the Halifax Antiquarian Society*, vol 35, 1938, pp 139–52
Walton, J., 'South Pennine barn buildings', *Architectural Review*, vol 90, October 1941, pp 122–4
Weller, J. B. *Farm buildings of Shropshire before 1837*, 1952. In typescript. Kindly lent by the author.
West, G. T. *Farm buildings in south-east Surrey before 1837*. Royal Institute of British Architects Bannister Fletcher Silver Medal Essay, 1952. In typescript.
Pilkington, P. *Sussex downland farms*. Thesis submitted to the Architectural Association School of Architecture, 1962. In typescript. Kindly lent by the author.

More detailed area studies include:
Walton, J. *Homesteads of the Yorkshire Dales*, 1947
Fox, Sir Cyril, and Raglan, Lord. *Monmouthshire houses*; pt 1, *Mediaeval houses*, 1951; pt 2, *Sub-mediaeval houses*, 1953; pt 3, *Renaissance houses*, 1954
Davies, D. C. G. *Historic farmstead and farmhouse types of the Shropshire region*, MA thesis, Manchester University, 1952. In typescript.
Brunskill, R. W. *Design and layout of farmsteads in parts of Cumberland and Westmorland*. Royal Institute of British Architects Neale Bursary 1963. Manchester, 1965. In typescript.
Alcock, N. W. 'Devonshire linhays, a vernacular tradition',

Transactions of the Devonshire Association, 1963, vol 95, pp 117–30

Case-studies of the historical development of particular farmsteads include:
Bonham-Carter, V. *Farming the land,* 1959, pp 49–57
Alcock, N. W. 'A Devonshire farm; Bury Barton, Lapford', *Transactions of the Devonshire Association,* vol 98, 1966, pp 122–9

The following national surveys include information of historical value:
National farm survey of England and Wales 1941–3, HMSO, 1946, pp 39–41, 59–69
Charlick, R. H. *Farm buildings survey of Wales,* 1965, and *Farm buildings survey of England,* 1967

Textbooks

These provide information on contemporary principles and practice and therefore rank among the most valuable sources of farm building history. They include:
Board of Agriculture. *Communications to the Board of Agriculture on farm buildings,* 1796
Waistell, C. *Designs for agricultural buildings,* 1827
Loudon, C. J. *An encyclopedia of cottage, farm, and village architecture,* 1833
Ewart, J. *A treatise on the arrangement and construction of agricultural buildings,* 1851
Andrews, G. H. *A rudimentary treatise on agricultural engineering;* vol 1, *Buildings;* vol 2, *Motive power and machinery of the steading,* 1852
Starforth, J. *The architecture of the farm,* 1853
Stephens, H. and Burn, R. S. *The book of farm buildings,* 1861
Denton, J. B. *Farm homesteads of England,* 1863
Scott, J. *Farm buildings,* 1884
Clarke, A. D. *Modern farm buildings,* 1891

Malden, W. J. *Farm buildings*, 1896
Henderson, R. *The modern farmstead*, 1902
Taylor, S. *Modern homesteads*, 1905
Winder, T. *Handbook of farm buildings*, 1908
Lawrence, C. P. *Economic farm buildings*, 1919
McHardy, D. N. *Modern farm buildings*, 1932
Gunn, E. *Farm buildings*, 1935
Post-war building studies No 17, Farm buildings, HMSO, 1945
'New ideas for farm buildings', *Farmer and Stockbreeder*, 1947
Henderson, F. *Build your own buildings*, 1955
Benoy, W. G. *Farm buildings, conversions and improvements*, 1956
Pasfield, D. H. *Farm building design and construction*, 1965
Weller, J. B. *Farm buildings*, 1965
Sayce, R. B. *Farm buildings*, 1966

All dates given are those of first publication.

ACKNOWLEDGEMENTS

The writer wishes to thank all those who have given him permission to use their illustrations, as formally acknowledged elsewhere, and also all those who have so generously helped in other ways, namely: Mr P. D. Anderson of the Milk Marketing Board; Mr G. A. Barley of the Milk Marketing Board; Mr M. M. Barnes of the Cement and Concrete Association; Professor Maurice Beresford; Mr R. H. Charlick; Mr John Clayton; Dr R. Coles; Mr Philip Easton; Mr G. G. English of Messrs Gabriel Wade and English; the Librarian of the Forestry Commission; the Librarian of the Forest Products Research Laboratory; Mr Peter Girdlestone, editor of the *Farm Buildings Association Journal*; Mr J. R. Gray; the Controller of Her Majesty's Stationery Office; the Librarian of the Institution of Civil Engineers; Commander H. R. Kidston, RN; Mr David Lee of Turners Asbestos Cement Co Ltd; Mr David Long, editor of *Farmbuildings*; Mrs N. R. Lloyd; Mr C. L. Matthews of the Manshead Archaeological Society of Dunstable; Mr John Moffitt; the National Buildings Record; the Librarian of the National Institute of Agricultural Engineering; the Librarian of the National Maritime Museum; Mr R. P. de B. Nicholson; Mr L. M. Parsons; Mr K. O. Pawley of Unigate Ltd; Mr Peter Pilkington; Mr S. E. Rigold; the Librarian of the Royal Institute of British Architects; the Librarian of the Royal Institute of Chartered Surveyors; the Librarian of the Royal Society of Arts; the late Mr A. R. Sarsons, editor of the *Journal of the Chartered Land Agents Society*; Mr T. R. F. Skemp; the Librarian of the Society of Antiquaries; the Librarian of the Timber Research and Development Association; Mr J. L.

Vosper of Express Dairy Group Services Ltd; Mr H. J. Vaughan; and Mr John B. Weller.

It is with particular pleasure that the writer thanks Professor Duckham for interrupting his retirement to write a foreword; Mr Keith Huggett for the care and skill with which he has prepared simplified and standardised drawings from such a variety of originals; the Librarian of the Ministry of Agriculture, Fisheries and Food and his staff for their unfailing helpfulness over a long period of steady demands on their time and knowledge; and his wife, Barbara, for so patiently and cheerfully checking text, proofs and index.

INDEX

Illustrations are indicated by italic type

Milking parlours, 181–3, 204, 229–30, 259, 263, *140, 176, 231*

Milk production, regulations concerning, 134, 177–9, 227

Ministry of Agriculture and Fisheries, later Ministry of Agriculture, Fisheries and Food, 202, 218–19, 227

Moss, 42

Oasthouses, 58, 97, 142, 196, 226–7

Offices, farm, 200, 211, 244

Oilcake, *see* Concentrate feedstuffs, purchased

Open Field system, 22–3, 28–9, 31, 67–8, *33, 74*

Outlying buildings, 82–3, 103, 146, 172

Overseas technical influences: general, 184–5, 217, 249; Danish, 190–1; Dutch, 105–6; Flemish, 58; French, 225; German, 89, 253; New Zealand, 217, 230; Northern Ireland, 254; Norwegian, 238, 241, 252, 253, 255

Owner-occupying farmers, *see* Designers of farm buildings

Pig housing, pastoral system, 24, 37, 39, 46, 55, 76, 100, 190; in farmstead, 37, 39, 55–6, 79, 83, 100, 113–14, 136, 189–91, 206, 222, 236–9, *161, 239*; urban, 85–6; Danish-type houses, 190–1, 206, 237

Plastic building materials, 245–6, 262, 266

Polygonal designs for farmsteads, 89, 105

Population, growth of, 49, 66, 118

Potato stores, 226, 252

Potato cellars, possible ancient construction of, 26

Poultry housing, 39, 46, 79, 113 136, 192–3, 222, 239–41, 254–5; battery system, 193, 207, 241, 254–5; broiler houses, 241–3

Prefabrication, 199–200, 224, 245–8, *176*

Railways, effects of, on used building materials, 142, 163–4, 197; on liquid milk industry, 133–5, 177

Railways for transport in farmsteads, 89, 94, 130–1, 145, 151, 159, 162–3, *162*

Reclamation, 22, 30, 44, 49–50, 66–7, 119, 167

Remodelling, *see* Adaptation

Research affecting farm building development, 132, 150, 153, 186–8, 193, 216–18, 219–20, 225–6, 229, 235, 237–8, 249, 250, 251, 252, 265–6

Road transport, effects of, on liquid milk industry, 177

Sheep housing, 24, 38–9, 43–4, 56–7, 63, 79, 80, 83, 136, 151, 202, 243, 255, 266

Shelter for farmstead sites, 22, 28, 31, 37, 75, 249

Silage, buildings and equipment for, 184–7, 199, 205, 235–6, 254, 258, 263, *122, 176*

Slates, 61, 99, 109, 143, 154, 164, 197, 244, 255

Slatted-floor systems, 151–2; for fattening cattle, 86, 104, 152, 233; for dairy cattle, 229, 253; for calves, 83, 89; for pigs, 238; for sheep, 151, 243

Smallholdings, farmsteads for, 167, 202

Soilage, *see* Zero-grazing

Stables, 46, 56, 81; for oxen, 37, 39, 55, 79; for horses, 37, 39, 55, 79, 90, 106, 135, 194, 254, *88*

Steel, 244–5, 262; *see also* Dutch barns

Stone, 31, 37, 42, 43, 47, 60, 98–9, 109, 110, 143, 164, 197, 208

Tallet, *see* Two-storey buildings

Tar, 98